CONDÉ NAST TRAVELER
WHERE ARE YOU?

© 2011 Condé Nast Traveler
Assouline Publishing
601 West 26th Street, 18th floor
New York, NY 10001 USA
Tel.: 212 989 6810 Fax: 212 647 0005
www.assouline.com

ISBN: 978 2 75940 515 2

Color separation: Luc Alexis Chasleries.
Printed in China.
Graphic design by Camille Dubois.
All rights reserved.
No part of this publication may be reproduced, stored in a retrieval system,
or transmitted in any form or by any means, electronic, mechanical,
photocopying, recording, or otherwise, without prior consent from the publisher.

Foreword by Klara Glowczewska

CONDÉ NAST TRAVELER
WHERE ARE YOU?

ASSOULINE

FOREWORD

Klara Glowczewska
Editor in Chief, *Condé Nast Traveler*

Our goal at *Condé Nast Traveler* has always been to give our readers trustworthy guidance to the world. We want not only to inspire your travel dreams but also to give you the information you need to make them come true. Each month, we publish independent, authoritative, detailed answers to travel's what, when, how, why, and, of course, where. Okay, not exactly…

There is one exception: our "Where Are You?" contest. Since March 1993, every issue of the magazine has contained a mystery: a spread photograph of a spectacular geographic enigma, the answer to which we provide two issues later. It may be a structure or a landscape; it may be man-made or natural. It is invariably arresting. Where is that sprawling, tentacled boulder set between an improbably blue sea and blindingly white sand? That red horn, fit for giants to play, embedded in an idyllic green hillside? And what about that string of futuristic igloos set amid a snowy vastness? Sorry, we're not telling…. But we do provide clues, tips, and intriguing details. It's up to you, dear reader, to tell us where you are. Call it role reversal.

From the contest's debut until the press date of this book, we will have published 216 "Where Are You?" images, culled from the work of the world's greatest photographers. More than 1,200,000 *Condé Nast Traveler* readers have submitted answers—at first via mail and then, since 2003, online. Avid travelers are clearly excellent researchers—an impressive 787,000 answers have been correct, and all those have been entered in an annual drawing for travel prizes.

In this volume, we have collected one hundred of our favorite "Where Are You?" images. The answer to each puzzle has, of course, previously been published. But you can, in this case, assume that it remains a mystery and solve the riddle yourself. (If you get stuck, turn to the Answers section in the back. And for a fresh challenge, pick up the latest issue of *Condé Nast Traveler*.)

We live in the age of the Global Positioning System. Getting lost, feeling disoriented—the sine qua non of all travel, until now—is virtually a thing of the past. That's mostly all to the good, but it is a bit of a shame. Not having your bearings can be revelatory and exciting. The world, as the images in this book attest, is grand and full of wonders. At *Condé Nast Traveler*, we hope to always help you find your way but also to help you, if only momentarily, lose it. Here's to a touch of mystery—which every good trip, armchair or real, deserves.

So, where are you, anyhow?

> "The real voyage of discovery consists not in seeing new landscapes but in having new eyes."
> — MARCEL PROUST

> "One's destination is never a place, but a new way of seeing things."
> — HENRY MILLER

> "The world is a book, and those who do not travel read only a page."
> — SAINT AUGUSTINE

> "Who lives sees much. Who travels sees more."
> ARAB PROVERB

> "All journeys have secret destinations of which the traveler is unaware."
> MARTIN BUBER

> "Don't listen to what they say. Go see."
> CHINESE PROVERB

> "I see my path, but I don't know where it leads. Not knowing where I'm going is what inspires me to travel it."
> ROSALIA DE CASTRO

Congratulations. Few people make it this far. This remote tree house may look like some schoolboy fantasy, but in fact the nomads in this area (for now) call it home. Enter this cozy cabin built of willow, rattan, bark, and leaves via its supporting trees—the ability to shinny is an important part of the local lifestyle. Attenuated foundations such as this one protect the inhabitants not only from the voracious insects and marshy conditions below but also from intruders. And the spectacular view gives homeowners advance warning of invasions by neighboring tribes. Local folks started receiving visitors from the considerably more modern outside world just a few decades ago. (After all, though you did manage to get here, it wasn't exactly easy.) Their land is part of a province on the eastern boundary of their nominal country. The province stretches over more than a

fifth of the nation's land and echoes with over 250 languages—although it houses only one-hundredth of the nation's people. And what land it is! White sand beaches, impenetrable rain forests, and mountains capped year-round with snow. But the modern world has brought new invaders—covetous copper-mining and logging companies aggressively plunder this natural splendor. Traditional land rights are ignored, and the local people, ethnically and culturally different from the majority of the nation's citizens, suffer military persecution. Persistent pleas for independence fall on deaf ears in the capital of the motherland, thousands of miles to the west—the country's presidents have vowed that it will never be free. Would that a house in the sky could keep this world and its people out of harm's way.

You are standing before the most biodiverse spot in the world. Really. That may be hard to believe given the fact that there are tens of thousands of twenty-five-foot fiber-optic rods swaying in the breeze in front of you, but enter the structure and you'll find embedded at the tip of each shaft an embryo from a different plant species. In other words, this is a bank of sorts. Straddling a river, the enormous fairgrounds you are touring have taken over two valuable square miles of a densely populated municipality. Some consider events such as this, which showcase cultural traditions and stroke national egos, outdated—even kitschy—in this age of instant communications. Yet more than seventy million people, most of them curious locals, will have explored the two hundred corporate- and government-sponsored attractions here before their six-month lease is up. The year's theme is sustainable development—ergo, the emphasis on botanic promulgation.

The designer of these "hairs," as he calls the poles, is known for having built a hoity-toity boutique in Manhattan and, in his hometown, a fantastical bridge that curls up. In his conception of the opus before you, the building is the exhibit. The interior, resembling a space-age movie set, is suffused with sunlight by day and glows from within by night. While some have nicknamed the structure after the common aster that you pull out of your lawn, creative bloggers have dubbed it everything from a pincushion to a hedgehog to a Chia pet. Whatever the heck it is, just be glad it's not your job to clean it.

How ecological can the thing really be, you wonder, if it's made of acrylic? Well, at least the bulk of the raw materials were sourced from within a 180-mile radius and will be reused or recycled later. And the embryos will be distributed in this country and in the designer's home nation after October 2010.

For all the exposition's perspective on nurturing the planet, the pavilion was also dreamed up as a great place to unwind and contemplate after a day spent wandering this huge campus. No doubt your own brilliant visions will be germinating in no time.

You're not exactly standing on high-end lakefront property. The scruffy, scraggly shore beneath your feet seems to be located in a proverbial no-man's-land. Looks are deceiving, however. The entire seventy-thousand-square-mile region you are visiting is extremely rich in minerals. Considering that a large chunk of this country's revenue is extracted from the ground, you might want to stake a claim in the coppery hills surrounding you. Some years ago, a style director traveled seven hundred miles from the capital to conduct a fashion spread in terrain much like this. His work appeared in a renowned travel magazine (okay, the one associated with these pages). "It was the hardest shoot I've ever been on, but it was worth it," he says. "I was surprised by the natural beauty and by how incredibly diverse the landscape is." It's so varied that you'll wonder at times if you're touring one of the lowest points on earth or a windswept plateau (looks can be deceiving, as we said).

The brackish lagoon before you is hardly the only body of water you'll see on your trip. A famous alkali flat spreads over a thousand square miles,

amplifying the sense of emptiness. Are you thinking of a desolate land of yaks and yurts? Again, things may not be as they seem. In fact, this region is crawling with people. One town in an oasis north of the lagoon is packed with visitors as well as expats. You may want to join them for a popular two-week bike trip on which you'll pedal as many as fifty miles a day past volcanoes and a geyser and spot gregarious rosy creatures strutting around the waters, combing the mud for dinner.

The terrain you are exploring is situated more or less on the knob of a walking stick–shaped country, in an area called the Grand North, or, officially, the Second Region. To this day, a nineteenth-century war that lasted four years defines this nation's relationship with a neighbor (you go annex someone's coastal access and see if he likes it).

The lagoon is often described as emerald green—although it's anything but in this light. More proof that things are not what they seem. . . .

When this shot was taken, you were standing at the southern tip of a lake, the nation's third largest, contemplating this skinny pavilion of 151 bright wood columns, an impermanent edifice of affirmation. We hope you weren't alone, since the experience awaiting you was constructed specifically for couples. The concept proposed a journey through the creation (or re-creation) of a relationship. Chances are you were roaming the country, traveling from lake to lake, in search of just such ineffable confections and architectural fantasies, the work of artists in multiple media who conspired to transform your social and artistic consciousness. Perhaps you had already seen a four-thousand-ton floating monument or visited a structure that was just like a cloud. If not, too bad, because within twelve or so months—poof!—all these experiments had vanished. This country went to some trouble to entertain you in this fashion, spending more than $900 million to lure and enlighten you and millions of your

culture-vulture friends. Among the exhibition's five locations was this western industrial market town, named for its natural thermal baths. Such extravagance may seem surprising in a nation that makes an art of measurement and discretion. With a refined sense of chronology and economy, not to mention a sweet tooth, and a vertiginous geography (at its lowest, it is still 640 feet above sea level), this enduring democracy—one-fifth of its population is foreign—is loath to be provoked by the passions of cultures and countries below. Such phlegm has been known, on occasion, to antagonize outsiders: for instance, a flamboyant nineteenth-century playwright, who wrote that the nation "has produced nothing but theologians and waiters . . . their cattle have more expression." Ah, that the wit could have witnessed, like you, such whimsy living large.

It seems you have reached an impasse. You are standing thousands of feet above sea level, in front of a wall of diorite that is one of three which once formed the ramparts of a fortress . . . or temple? Construction of this complex began in the 1400s and took about a century to complete—little surprise, since some of the boulders tower thirty feet high and weigh in excess of three hundred tons. The compound was shaped to represent the head of a feline animal, and its walls, which zigzag, signify jagged teeth. Such organic architecture was the work of a technologically advanced and rigidly hierarchical tribe whose control extended thousands of miles. This fortress was the site of a struggle that heralded the end of an empire: After killing millions of indigenes, invaders stamped out the civilization, even crowning native buildings with churches and houses of their own.

The creature's body is a city that lies a couple of miles south of here and which served as the capital and spiritual center of this people. A British writer ambivalently described it as "one of the most beautiful monuments to bigotry and sheer stupid brutality in the whole world." Nonetheless, it remains a magnetic location, especially for enthusiastic hikers and seekers. The city is no longer the capital—that rests about 360 miles to the northwest, on the coast of a country just smaller than Alaska.

A s you stroll along, admiring this glittering city, you and your co-revelers have just forged a pact à la Vegas. You may be shocked to find that there's no gambling going on, but never mind, sybaritic indulgences are legion.

You may think you know the source of the prosperity enjoyed by this kingdom, the second-largest in a federation, but a slick answer would prove off the mark. Its wealth comes courtesy of those who, like you, appreciate its sundry cuisines, fine film festival, and world-class horse racing. Where else would more than three million people participate in an annual monthlong event dedicated to the pursuit of premium duty-free booty.

Since more than eighty percent of the population is foreign born, this just might be the expat capital of the world. Perhaps the absence of personal and

property taxes will induce you too to put down roots. Should you find the harsh environment overwhelming, you can escape to a state-of-the-art water park or schuss down an indoor ski slope.

The metropolis has just started to tap its potential, according to its leaders, who intend its tech industry to rival Bangalore's, its media to blossom, and its bourse to boom (a Dow of sorts should already ring a bell). Glitz notwithstanding, this town—like that other urban oasis—has an underbelly, and for the expats who toil hardest, the bijous that sparkle in mega-mall vitrines are a mirage. Still, you can't help but marvel at a creekside trading village that was transformed in less than thirty years into a skyscraping colossus. As you amble, tip your hat to the visionaries who conjured these sand castles in the sky.

You are at the northern tip of a shape-shifting world: As the water ebbs, the contours of the sand emerge. More than two centuries ago, when a British naval captain—after whom this island group was named—spotted these shores, this isle was undoubtedly just as mutable. When the ocean flows, this skinny coral atoll becomes a sequence of fragments that look like the vertebrae of a fragile, curled spine.

The ocean soon beckoned sailing ships hunting a giant toothed mammal; and decades later, more blood was shed on a dot of an islet at the other end of the atoll. Evidence of this territorial battle, which robbed scores of soldiers of their lives, lingers still: rusting tanks, shore batteries, and bayonets.

Such violence is today unimaginable in this placid country that comprises more than thirty islands—their total landmass four times that of Washington, D.C.—spread thousands of square miles across the sea. Independence came in July but last century, and with it a new state name. As that century waned, the nation's leader sought to reallocate time and a regional tiff ensued. Yet here in the play of coral, air, and water, how could time even be relevant?

In the mid sixteenth century, a missionary and future saint called the island-nation you are visiting "the delight of my soul." More than four centuries after he carried out his evangelical work, the Western spiritual presence he established here can still be felt—although these days it is more often seen in its Protestant forms, such as this church whose glowing nave invites you.

Completed in 2005 by an architectural firm whose name means red sky, the church has received raves from those who worship at the altar of urban design. Natural light fills the ten-thousand-square-foot space; its wavy interior is clinically clean, all white save for random pews dashed with purple, orange, and yellow. The acoustics are excellent—for the best tonal experience during a concert, sit in any of the loges that have been built into the six arches.

A recent book on contemporary church architecture places this chamber in the company of other recent celebrated ecclesiastical structures, including Steven Holl's Chapel of St. Ignatius in Seattle, José Rafael Moneo's Cathedral of Our Lady of the Angels in downtown L.A., and Richard Meier's Jubilee Church in Rome. Given the meetinghouse's whimsical facade (was that looping cutout inspired by a toddler's shape-sorting toy?), it might not come as a surprise to learn that the chief architect has also designed a nearby kindergarten. For big kids, he went on to build—on another island to the south—a spa hotel owned by a native cosmetics mogul.

The capital city you are in, whose erstwhile name derived from its estuarine position, came into its own in the 1980s, when a booming economy fueled ubiquitous displays of haute couture and high-tech goodies. The neon-and-flash buzz has now subsided.

Stationed in the capital, an early-seventeenth-century British trader wrote in his diary that "there hapned an exceeding earthquake in this city . . . it was soe extreame that I thought the howse would have falne down on our heads . . . the tymbers . . . making such a nois and cracking that it was fearfull to heare." Be not afraid. The city has adapted, and you're in for an exalting experience.

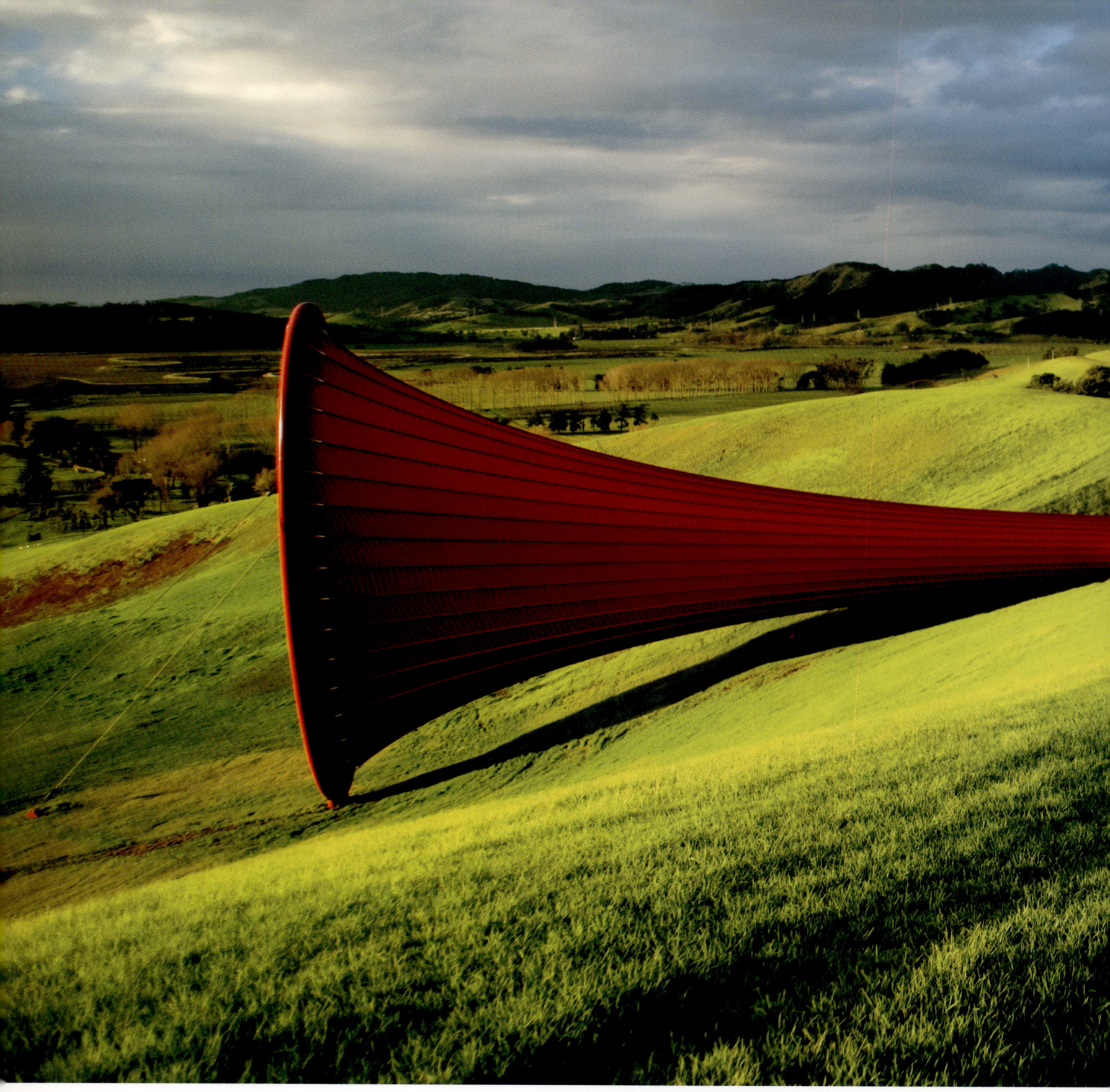

You are looking at the Ferrari of sculptures—literally. This sleek, sexy red form before you is wrapped in sixteen thousand pounds of PVC fabric that was made by a company named Ferrari. The elliptical steel ends—one horizontal, the other vertical—weigh 95,000 pounds each, yet the work was designed to move with the strong winds that blow off the sea. At nearly three hundred feet long, it's clearly visible on satellite images. You know the Indian-born artist's oeuvre if not his name; think of a silver cloud in Chicago and trumpets in London. His patron, a septuagenarian with an outsized personality, made billions in telecommunications, autos, and banking (that in a country more famous for fleece than finance). When he's not contemplating art commissions for his thousand-acre sculpture park, he's busy tinkering with an amphibious car (if you book a ride on it, you'll be dodging the zebras, giraffes, water buffalo, and yaks he keeps). Elsewhere in these hills he has placed site-specific works like an

undulating Serra steel wall and a series of Goldsworthy arches that seem to march into the coastal shallows, as well as a Stonehenge-like pile of slabs and a tesla coil. A grave there belongs to a nineteenth-century native chief.

The park lies to the east of a huge bay on the northern of this country's two main islands. The first settlers (invaders, some would say) in this district were Scottish timber millers. Today, their historic towns lure visitors to hot springs and to wineries founded by Dalmatians (the people, not the canines).

But don't think you can just waltz into this park any old time. Though it opens on occasion for benefits, it is private. So check the calendar and plan ahead—there's no way to put this Ferrari on the fast track.

Wow, is that a hydrothermally altered granitoid before you? Maybe you see a Botticelli Venus rising from her scallop shell. Hey, you did just knock back some robust shots of local coconut cream liqueur. . . . Either way, the rock, you'll learn, is iconic.

This nation of more than a hundred granite and coral islands has fewer than a hundred thousand inhabitants. Two thousand people—most of them clumped in west-side villages—call the small reef-protected isle you are on home. A thousand-foot-high peak spreading out from the interior (see if you can spot the rare "widow" bird species) leaves little room for a runway, so you arrived by boat. You could get around by helicopter—but really? Be eco-correct and hoof it, bike it, or bullock it (you always wanted to test-drive an oxcart). Recently, this republic was pledged big bucks by a

federation to build up its coast guard, and it signed an agreement with the United States to protect against buccaneers. Since voyagers account for a huge chunk of the nation's revenue, it opened a new tourism office in Europe, while a faraway country launched a direct air route here just for honeymooners. Long ago, two foreign powers competed for dominion over this archipelago and imported a mix of peoples from several continents to exploit its rich cinnamon and vanilla plantations (which accounts for the Creole tongue you hear today). The colonial state that ultimately gained the upper hand used to dump prisoners here, but guess what: A lot of the detainees found it a happy banishment. Your friend on the rock is in exile—a self-imposed paradisiacal exile, complete with SPF 50, chilled coconut water, and an iPod. We should all be so lucky as to languish on rock piles such as this.

Mom warned you about playing on the roof, didn't she? Well, Mom probably never set eyes on a vast karstic world like this. Nor has she ever witnessed fifty thousand acres of cruciferous plants exploding in a riot of Van Goghian chartreuse. So take it all in—we won't tell.

As it turns out, your perch is hardly the tranquil place you had anticipated on the climb up. All over these hills, hordes of pixel-possessed visitors jostle for space, and with so many people snapping away, tickets are required for some lookouts. The celebrated cover crop below belongs to the mustard family, and while storms can severely damage the spring's harvest, this country remains the world's top producer. Historically, the plant's oil was extracted to fuel lamps. Today, it's used as a biofuel and in the kitchen: You'll probably dine on a spicy local mushroom delicacy that was braised in it. (Perhaps the stuff you use in your salad at home comes from a Canadian cultivar, rebranded by growers to mask the plant's rather unfortunate English name.)

From the six-thousand-foot-high provincial capital to the west, both a road and a railway will take you to these hills in three hours. With forty-four million inhabitants, the province you are in is larger than many a nation and so geomorphically rich—plateaus and gorges abound—that these vivid tracts don't even rank among its tourist highlights. Neither does a nearby series of tiered waterfalls, even though one four-hundred-foot-wide cascade tumbles two hundred feet.

Every year, members of an ethnic minority celebrate the harvest here in embroidered costumes. Look closely and you'll notice that the crops, which support a honey bee industry, also grow on terraces. Climb down, jump on a Flying Pigeon bike or the back of a Brahma bull, and start exploring. Just wear a helmet—for Mom.

You are out with crimson- and saffron-robed monks in the noonday sun, climbing to a remote, obscure temple that's more than four hundred years old. Your companions descend from a nomadic people, most of whom live in this area, but whose present-day populace would barely fill the seats in Yankee Stadium. The temple carved into a mountain face above hides a complex of caves and places of prayer connected by cramped passages and winding stairs. It is named after the hoof of a warrior's horse, which, according to legend, left a mark when it landed on the impressionable sandstone cliff.

These pious journeymen, along with Bactrian camels and a rare species of monkey, live in a mountainous region populated by numerous ethnic groups, followers of at least two major religions. A determined explorer is believed to have resided here for one year—not surprising, really, since this north-central province is bisected by a mercantile route that famously supplied goods in all directions. This is a poor area, despite deep reserves of oil, coal, and iron, in part because nature keeps all those riches in a tectonic cauldron, the center of the nation's earthquake activity.

This country has an extraordinary, diverse, and intricate political and cultural history—one that has long had more interest in artistic expression than in free speech. (As far back as the seventeenth century, an English traveler wrote, "for Arts and manner off governmentt I thinck noe Kingdome in the world Comparable to it." From an Englishman, this is high praise indeed.) In October, the country observes its national holiday, hosting celebrations for the enjoyment of millions. How might these pilgrims be spending the day? Perhaps with a walk under a parasol up the sunny side of a mountain.

T his is your brain on fire. While it might appear that you've stumbled upon a giant interactive exhibit at a science center, you are actually poised to enter a forty-four-foot-wide labyrinth, or, more precisely, a unicursal maze. With no false paths to negotiate, you'll have no need to call on Ariadne.

So who built this elegant turf twister? Don't dust off your copy of *Chariots of the Gods* in search of ancient astronauts; it was likely created in the Middle Ages and resembles a pattern found in the nave of an Île-de-France cathedral. Whereas monks may once have walked this circle to do penance, a gayer purpose evolved as villagers played games here during fairs.

You are at the edge of a hamlet of 450 inhabitants, in a county described by an early naturalist as a place "where hogs shite sope, and cows shite fire." The region is indeed fertile, having contributed a king, a poet laureate, a scientist known for his gravitas, and a tough P.M. who engendered an ism. Today, visitors come to hike and bike and to boat in the estuary in the distance, where a plan is under way to revive the intertidal habitat for the resident harriers, tits, and terns. Movie companies, too, have come to shoot the habitats preserved in the area's rugged national parks and ornate manor houses.

In the interest of preservation, perhaps it's best if you sit back and admire the artistry behind this transient illumination. Meander the concentric path in your mind, unraveling the spiral's sacred and mathematical properties, or ponder Borgesian literary concepts of the labyrinth or the story of Theseus. You just might leave a wee bit smarter for your efforts.

L et's be clear: This stainless steel Santiago Calatrava–esque structure may look like a newfangled can opener, but it's really a whale tail. More specifically, it's one of three such twenty-six-foot-tall vanes that function as windbreaks on the blustery boardwalk of this nation's Coney Island. At its base, a swiveling baffle shelters a bench—just the place to sit back while you gather your courage for a roll on that coaster.

You are in a city thought to be the first on the continent to have installed electric lighting and trams. (The latter are still in operation, and the double-deckers are things of real beauty.) And still standing is a graceful tower, modeled after Gustave Eiffel's, which has dominated the skyline since the 1890s. In the 1910s, a novelist looked around and wrote that "[it] is an ugly town, mean in its vastness, but its dancing-halls present a beautiful spectacle.... This is the huge flower that springs from the horrid bed of the factory system." Indeed, in this seaside resort's long-gone heyday, mill workers flocked here for R and R, and Bernhardt and Bankhead performed in its grand theaters. In the thirties, Dietrich was invited to visit and lost a piece of jewelry; incredibly, workmen happened to dredge it up in the construction of a new high-tech coaster.

A giant rotating ball covered with 47,000 mirrors—an homage to the resort's ballroom past—is part of an ambitious arts display, like the stainless steel sculpture before you. If art truly inspires, this whale tail of a windbreak could help revitalize the city. Talk about a lucky fluke....

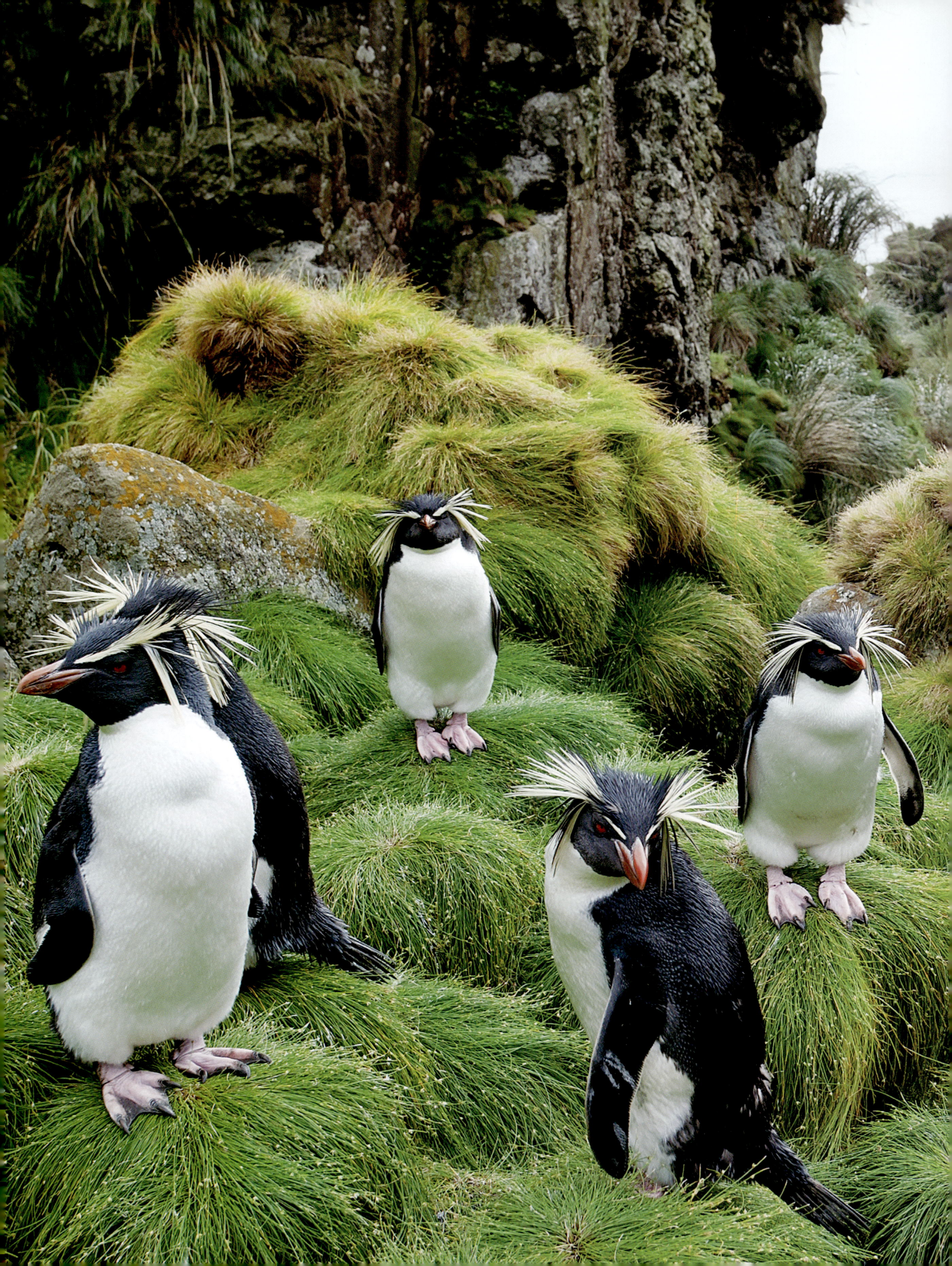

Talk about a supercilious reception. This phalanx of natty islanders seems a little ruffled by your presence as you disembark after a marathon sea journey. The fellow on the left assesses you with a crimson eye that says, "Watch your step, landlubber." "If looks could krill," you mutter. Alright smarty, you might avoid any *March of the Penguins* allusions to break the, er, ice—they get that all the time. Besides, for all their attitude these guys aren't even emperors. Just ask Robin Williams.

You are in the middle of nowhere—no kidding—on a volcanic isle that lies some two thousand miles south of the island which administers it (both are a long way away from their parent nation). A few decades ago, this outcrop, which rises three thousand feet above sea level, was declared a wildlife reserve, together with a distant extinct volcano whose stark name affirms its insurmountability. Maybe your plumed greeters will deign to guide you up the cliffs....

Sixteenth-century Portuguese explorers are credited with finding this thirty-some-square-mile peat-covered rock, but it was ultimately christened after a non-Lusophone captain whose name rhymes with the common word for tussive activity. Over the centuries, this part of the ocean was sailed by clipper ships that sought the winds which thunder across southern latitudinal belts. The island wasn't thoroughly explored until the mid-1950s, however, when a nearby—a relative notion in these parts—country built a weather station here that it still operates. (You might ask why: The climate can pretty much be summed up as a hundred inches of rain a year.)

Until recently, the reserve was considered a fowl haven. Lamentably, it was reported in 2008 that common rodents, which arrived with whalers back in the day, are now enormous and make a habit of devouring some small endangered species. These flippered avians struggle as well: Millions once made up the world's colonies, but now the numbers are only in the tens of thousands. Maybe these tough guys aren't sizing you up. Maybe they're imploring you for help.

A building squashed ignominiously under a corrugated metal tube and jammed between unadorned train trestles—you wonder if you've landed on the wrong side of the tracks. Relax. You've stumbled upon a new student center belonging to an institute of higher learning. That postindustrial look didn't come cheap, either; that's the cool tune of $48 million you're hearing the trains whistle.

In 2000, the designer—an international "starchitect" whose odd name literally means "cabbage rabbit"—nabbed his discipline's equivalent of the Nobel Prize. You may find yourself as turned on by this commission as the critics are: According to one reviewer, trains plunging into the tube conjure "certain erotic associations." The interior is—take your pick—"a sexy . . . high-tech dance floor," "an oversized pinball machine," or, as a particularly influential arbiter wrote, "a bazaar of a building, a souk of sensations, spatially exploded, rather like a Cubist painting." Once inside, just follow the map embedded in the floor to navigate the 110,000 square feet of workstations, auditorium, minimarket, and café/bar/movie theater, all laid out on a grid of diagonals.

Regardless of whether this bold scheme lives up to the accolades in the long term, how apropos that it was realized in the very city that perhaps most enriched twentieth-century architecture in this nation and on the very campus where, in the 1930s and '40s, a giant of modernism erected some twenty buildings. How fitting, too, that the innovative construction also hints at the city's raucous past—this is not the first time fighting the racket has made headlines. The architect most closely associated with this metropolis was frankly right when he described it long ago as an "immense gridiron of dirty, noisy streets." In the last decade of the last century, trustees even considered moving the institution elsewhere. But urban and academic fortunes have changed dramatically in this city where political nepotism is still a daily affair: Its famous stadium was given a startling makeover in 2003 while yet another renowned architect designed an elegant, futuristic dormitory to complement this center. Perhaps you'll decide to stay and enroll in the revival.

Classic Ming, you think as you gaze at the craggy landscape before you. Two Poets on a Mountaintop would be the evocative title on a scroll depiction. Just maybe, though, you've come upon a pair of latter-day cowpokes perched on the spire to the left, on the lookout for the steam engine Calico chugging through the valley below.

Let's split the geographic difference: The truth is you're hiking in a nation that is roughly equidistant from the two countries you might be thinking of. A famous Romantic artist, whose first name suggests that of a cartoon ghost, was inspired enough by the bizarre peaks in this range to paint them many times. Tales of the Old West fired the imagination of a local nineteenth-century writer (though he never ventured beyond Niagara Falls, his sagas are best sellers to this day). And a prominent composer passed through too—did an exploration of the mysterious caves here fuel his mythological fantasies?

You are trekking in a Cretaceous seabed, chunks of whose sandstone cliffs were carted 20 miles to the state capital to be transformed into Baroque churches and to the federal capital where they form a celebrated arch. A noble river courses through this rugged 270-square-mile region, which goes by a name that refers to a mountainous land located to the southwest. In 1990, a national park was carved out of a small section, as was a sister park in yet another country in 2000.

A million visitors a year cross an iconic footbridge built in the 1850s of—what else?—sandstone. Some of them slink across precipitous catwalks that link many of the peaks. A good many choose to grapple with the thousand-some towers that make this area a free climber's mecca. Beware as you hike along the 250 miles of trails that crisscross the bosky terrain: The temperature in this microclimate fluctuates so dramatically that within a mere 150 vertical feet, the difference can be as great as that between Baghdad and Stockholm.

A sixteenth-century composer wrote in his autobiography that the people in this nation are "geven to delyt in their dayly drink to much, yet thoz fawts be not so hurtfull to otherz, neyther do giyv kaws of offens." After you've sated your sense of adventure, head to an inn to knock back a few with the locals. And if you giyv in too much to the delyts, no worries. It's not your fawt.

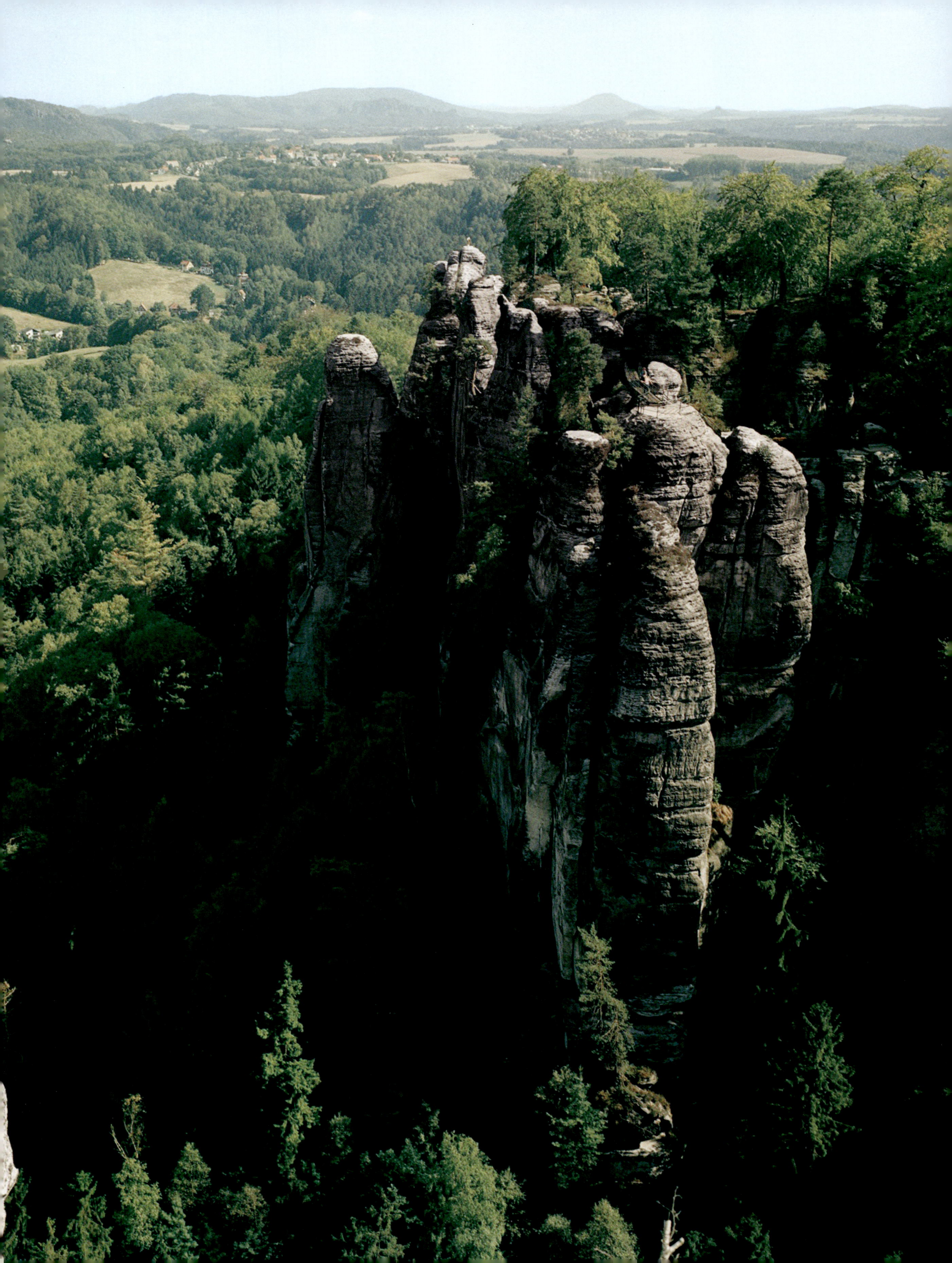

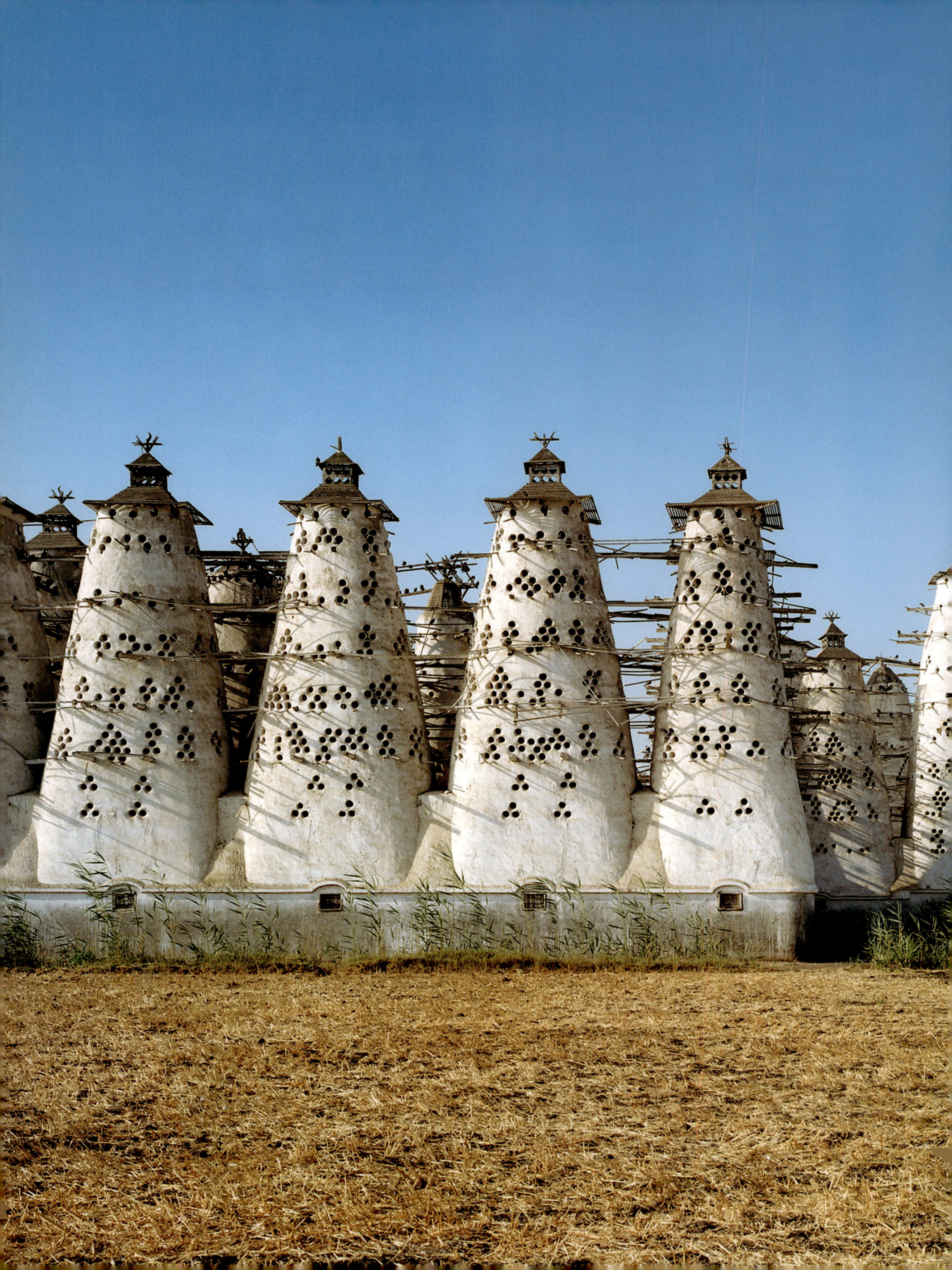

A crack team of architects spent years designing the innovative new high-rise hotel complex before you, its dimensions calibrated to mitigate the effects of this searing climate, its portholes intended to afford maximum shade. Whimsical touches include widow's walks with a samurai kabuto helmet motif. Soon the scaffolding will be removed, and photos of the environmentally sensitive adobe structures will be splashed across the pages of the world's glossy design magazines.

Okay, so you caught us in a fib. In truth, these towers are crappy—literally. Enter and you'll step into guano—lots and lots of it—since the only guests to flock to this gated community are doves by the tens of thousands. You are looking at so-called pigeon castles, the largest of their kind in a dovecote-crazy country. While the ubiquitous fowl are grilled, stuffed with rice and wheat, or plopped into casseroles—a finger-licking-good delicacy in a land where digital dining is perfectly polite—the bird droppings themselves make for superb fertilizer (some fifteen tons a year get hauled out).

Indeed, the agriculturally rich fields around you have been cultivated for thousands of years. Date palms and indolent donkeys suggest that you are visiting a postcard-quaint oasis when in fact you're touring a lotus-shaped sediment bed the size of a small nation. To get here, you traveled north by road or rail from the capital, which Melville called a "contiguity of desert and verdure, splendor & squalor, gloom & gayety . . . too much light and no defence against it." If you continue north another two hours, you'll reach an ancient port city where you can find your muse in the mother of all libraries.

It's worth noting that pigeon breeders are assumed, according to local tradition, to be lying thieves who poach one another's birds, and as such they are not allowed to testify in court. So don't depend on them to come to your defense if you have trouble with the authorities. And might we suggest you bring a parasol. . . ?

Unimpressed these bovine visitors may be, but a more curious traveler can't help but ruminate on these fifty-eight monoliths. Why are they here? Perhaps they chart the seasons, since the endpoints are arranged along a northwest-southeast axis, marking the sun's progress in the sky. Or possibly they were part of a burial ritual: Together the stones form the shape of a ship, which may have symbolized the deceased's passage to the next world. Or was this simply a meeting place? The rock slabs are up to ten feet high and are spread over more than a hundred feet, so the site must have been even more attention-grabbing when it was created, between A.D. 800 and 1050. Should you develop a notion about how it was assembled, think again: The rocks are not local, and no one knows how they got here. Such a conundrum may seem paradoxical in a country known for finding solutions to problems. After all, this is a culture that prizes safe automobiles and excellence in thought. But even here, mysteries abound: When a political leader was unexpectedly murdered, the nation was thrown into turmoil; more than two decades later, his killer remains at large. And still the greatest uncertainty is how this realm will maintain a comprehensive welfare system in tough economic times.

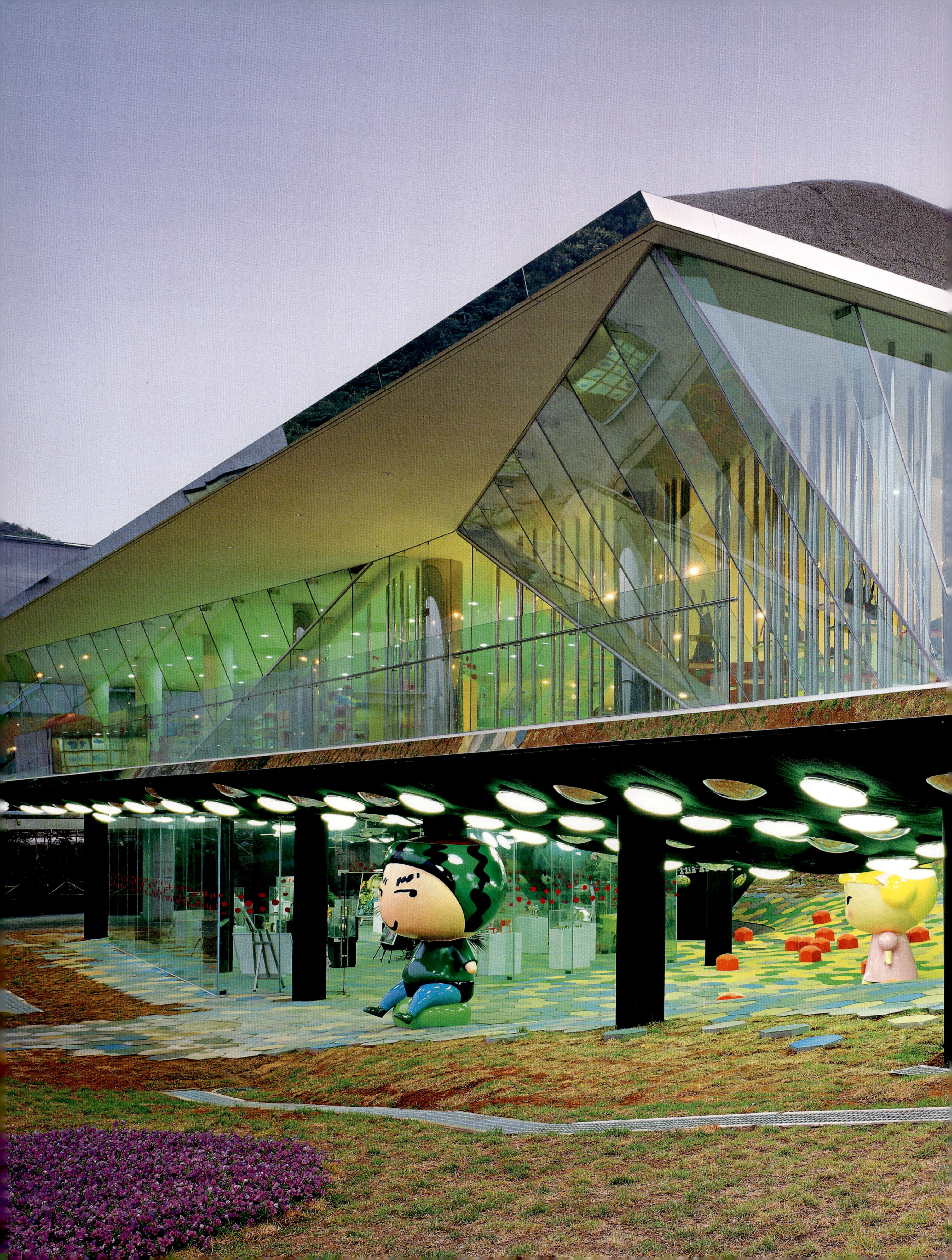

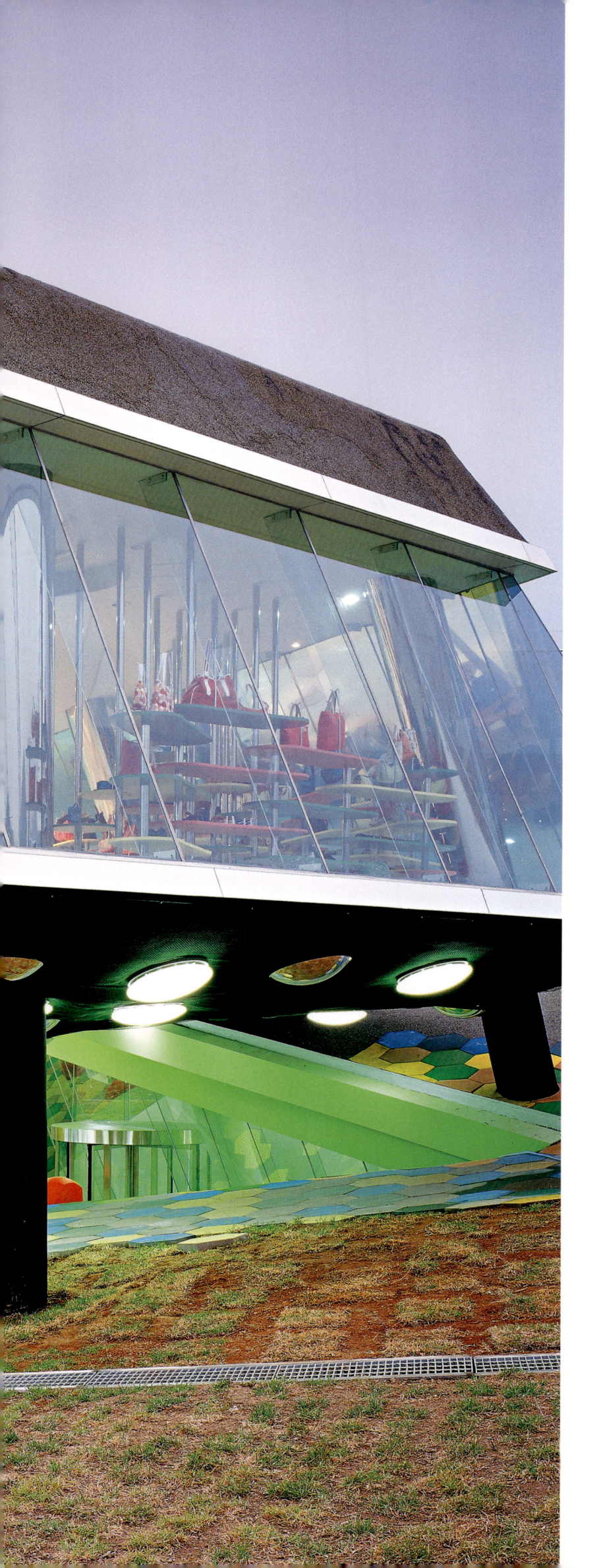

Teletubbies redux? Close enough. You're about to enter a spacey theme park dedicated to a popular cutesy character and her coterie of fruity pals, all of whom live in a strawberry patch (that's Watermelon on the left, pulling column-support duty).

You're just a few miles from a six-hundred-year-old capital whose name means "place where the ruler lives." Although the population is becoming "super-aged," this is nevertheless a culturally youthful and economically dynamic society: Its pop music is the continent's hottest; its film industry is gaining recognition, with a cinematic thriller that won a coveted international grand jury prize; the passion for online gaming has spurred capitalwide broadband saturation (and has Las Vegas casinos itching to break ground here); the leading car company is busy developing hybrids; and a famous religious figure is promoting the feasibility of an undersea tunnel to another country (some think he's a lunatic).

Nearly a quarter of the population shares a single surname in this land that lies at a crossroads of civilizations, one where the past weighs heavily. Officials have held diplomatic talks in recent years to establish the boundaries of a kingdom which disappeared more than thirteen hundred years ago, the prime minister having declared that "history should not change even though territory can change."

Given the retail space inside this building, it is in effect a giant commercial for a clothing-accessories company. It was also entered in a major architectural competition and adds a dose of levity to a tense border area. If it draws more visitors than the exhibition halls and observatories at this global hot spot with a hip-hop–sounding moniker, chalk one up for Watermelon.

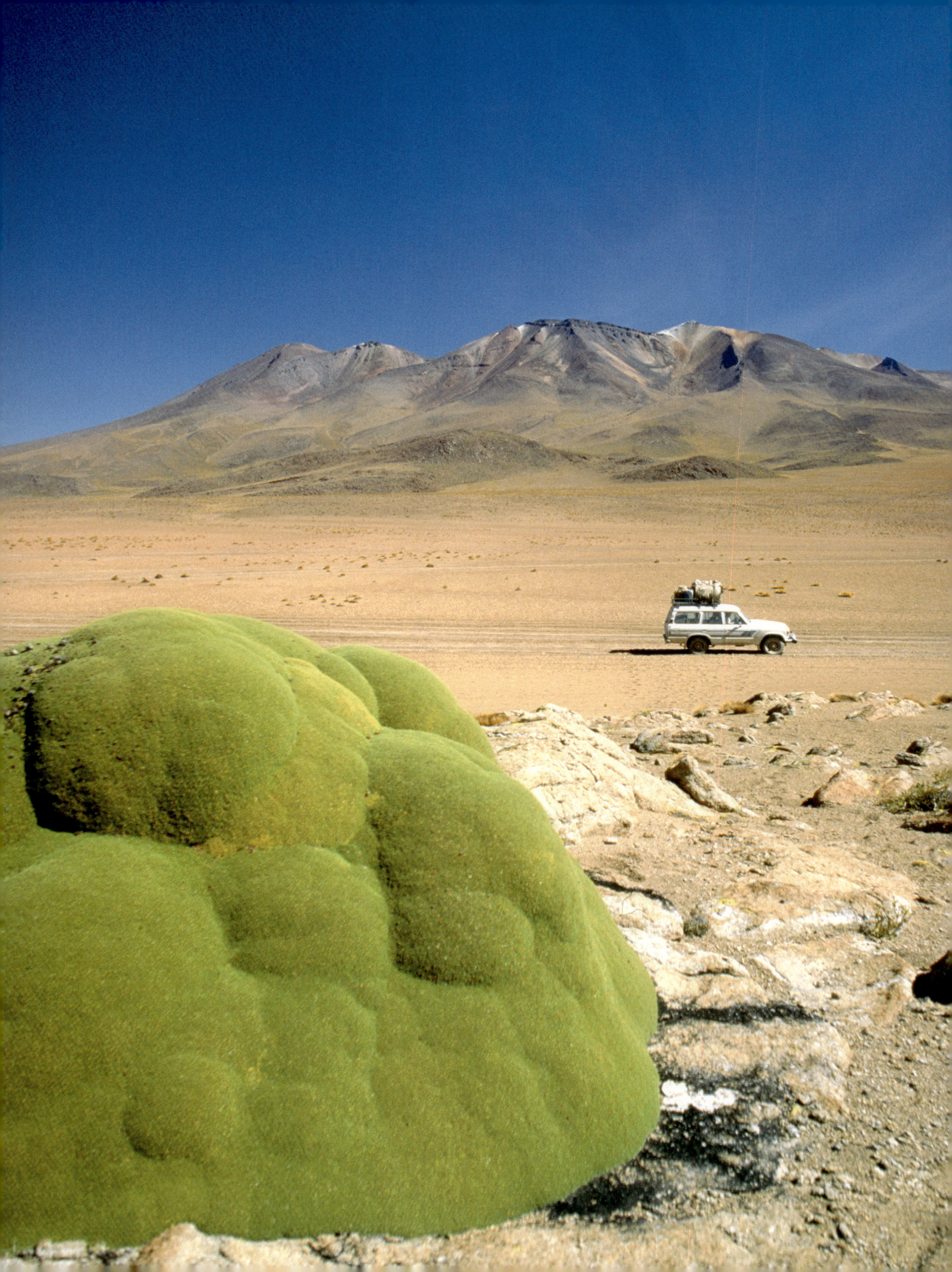

More than ten thousand years ago, this land was hidden by lakes—massive, brackish water holes that have since evaporated and forsaken the turf. Reminiscent of the moon, the parched landscape was once ruled by a people who worshipped the sun. They in turn were conquered by colonists who landed in the sixteenth century with determined iron fists and a thirst for silver. Three centuries later the land won independence, inspired by the two men for whom the country and its legal capital are named. Yet subsequent wars have not been so successful: The country has seen its borders eaten away by hungry neighbors, and it surrendered its only claim to the coast about a hundred years ago. To arrive at this very spot, you pass a military checkpoint, an active volcano, and simmering fumaroles. But you're only on the outskirts of your destination, still some miles south—a bloodred lake inhabited by rare pale flamingos once thought extinct and recently rediscovered. That plant in the foreground is a clue that you're close: Indigenous to this saline terrain, it's a perfumed perennial burned for fuel and used medicinally. The locals, who rely on its bounties, are not known for their hospitality, however: Said one visitor, "You can live here three months without ever seeing a person smile."

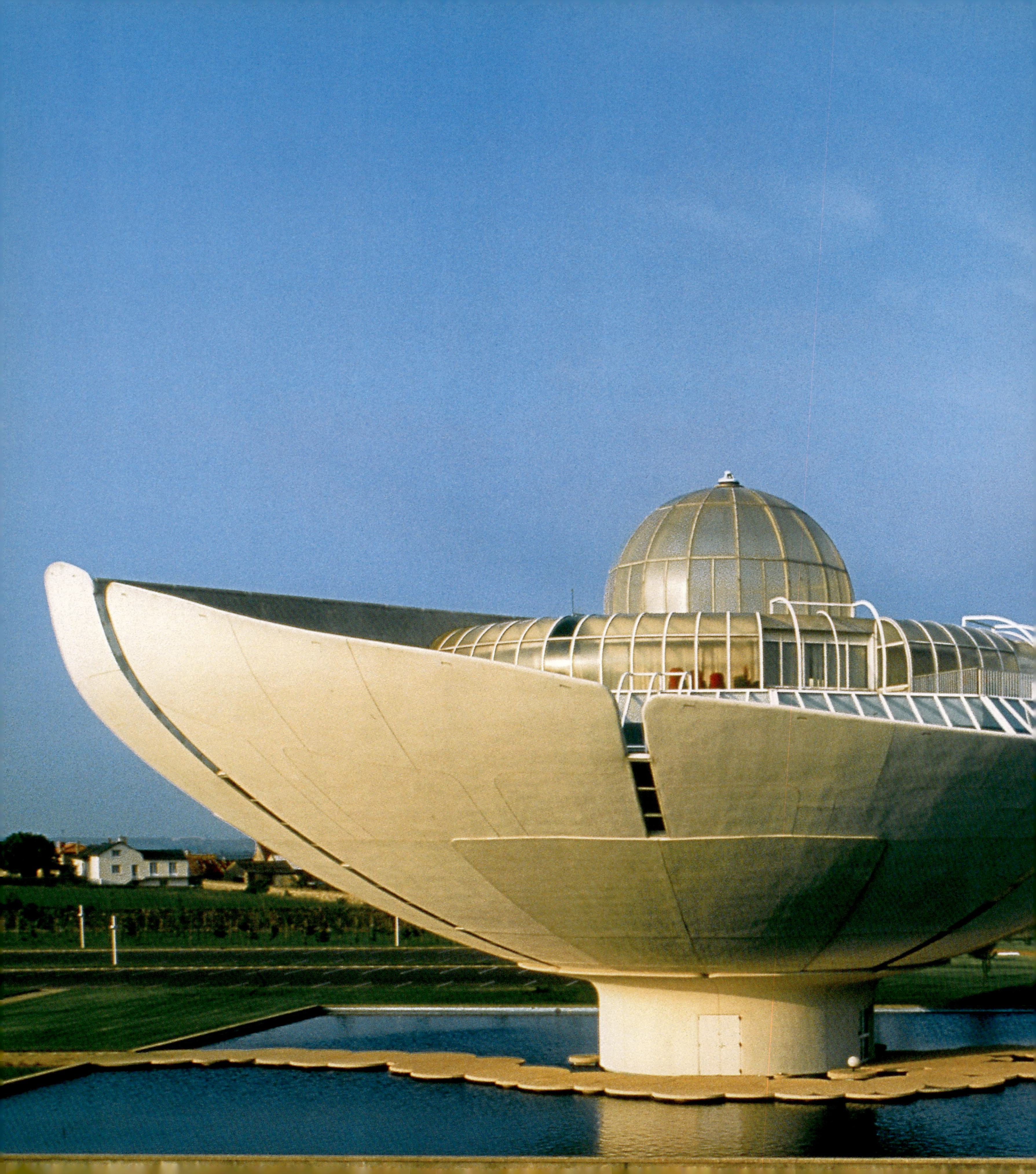

Y ou are staring into the future, a version of it anyway. This pavilion—that's a conference center floating in the bowl—is one of many on a lake-filled campus. Collectively, they form a science complex and theme park whose space-age, virtual-reality movies and rides suggest that the emphasis is more on play. In fact, an IMAX visit to the International Space Station was recently added.

If you find the future too nebulous to ponder, simply shift your focus to the rich past that surrounds you. The perfect antidote to a day of hyperstimulation in the land of high tech might be to retire to one of the still-inhabited troglodyte dwellings in the nearby villages or to take a languid boat trip on labyrinthine canals through primeval marshlands.

The park itself is a few miles outside a regional capital known both as the City of a Hundred Bell Towers and as the Smallest of the Big Cities. Named for an ancient tribe, the burg features a UNESCO-protected church and one of the oldest universities in this land. It lies between a famous river and a massive plateau that have historically marked the country's north-south divide.

How apropos that the park's buildings come in a variety of geometric shapes—parabolas, globes, prismatic cubes—since the great polymath to whom we owe the requisite knowledge did a lot of his cogitating at this university. Others with a local link include a gargantuan literary figure and two women of stature—one a celebrated consort, the other a maiden who was interrogated here and passed muster (it was she, not the former, who said, "Send me men in such numbers as may seem good").

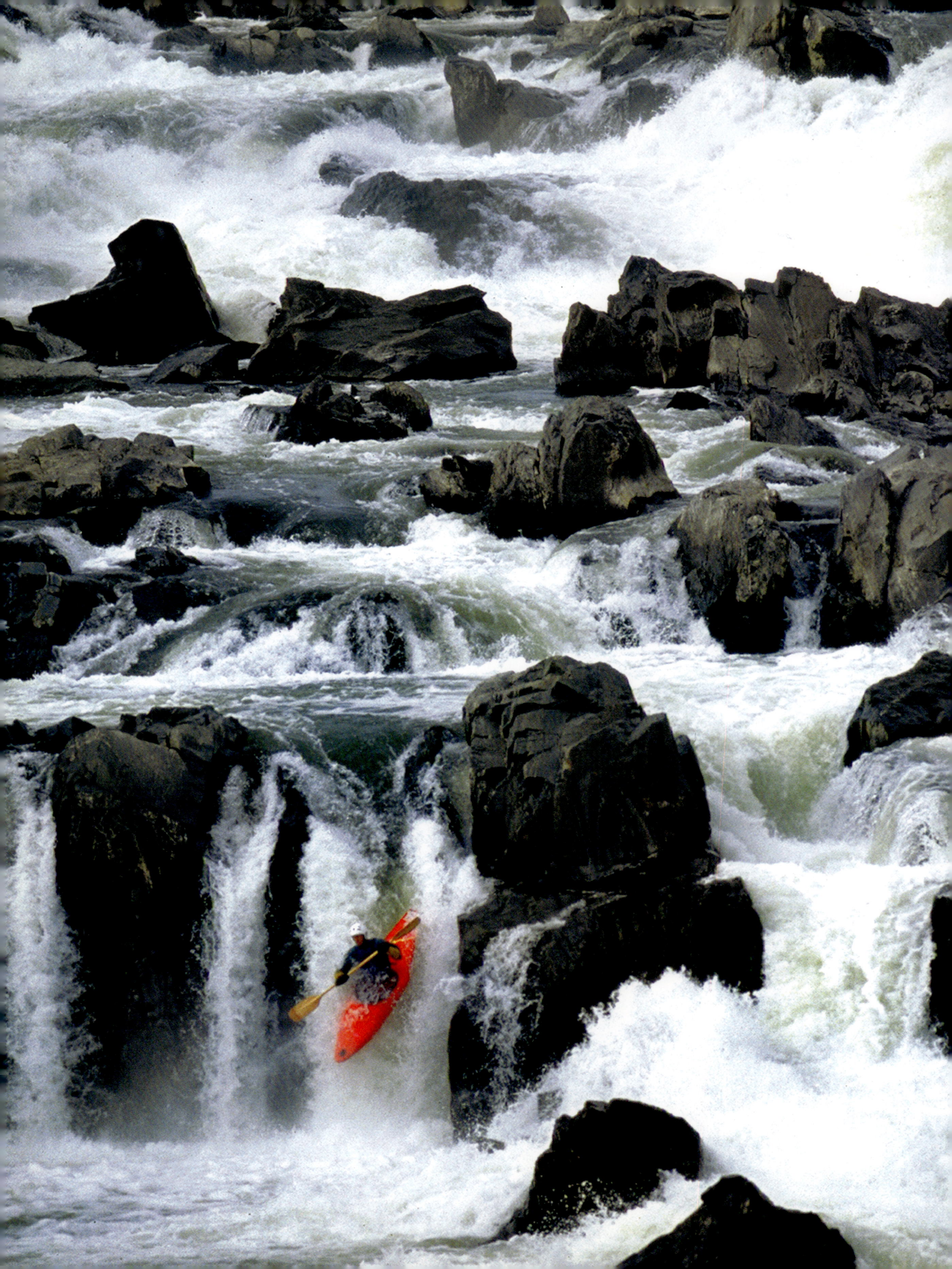

You are in the middle of the river, balancing on a rock slick with spray from the torrents raging around you. As you catch your breath, you watch a fellow paddler brave one of the last in a series of jostling Class V white-water drops. The river carved its bed when the sea level fell during the last ice age, forming these spectacular falls, exposing the metamorphic and igneous boulders around you, and cutting a gorge downstream. Because it drops nearly seventy-six feet in less than a mile, the river was considered unnavigable. Yet the country's first leader dreamed of a waterway to transport goods, so a canal was built—one of the most significant feats of engineering in the eighteenth century. Trade declined, however, and a few decades later, the canal company went bankrupt.

A six-foot dam was constructed in the 1850s, and "flying horses" enlivened the banks of the river in the early 1900s; thirty-four years before century's end, eight hundred acres along the river became a park named for the falls you've just come over. To the west is an area dubbed the Internet Capital of the World, while to the east lies one of the world's greatest estuaries. Beavers, birds, and bunnies make this wilderness corridor their home, but twenty minutes away, in the monument-laden city to the southeast, you'll find an entirely different breed of animal.

You are standing on one of these astonishing basalt rocks, the product of volcanic lava flows, strewn by nature along this shore. Before you stretch voluptuous sand dunes sculpted by constantly pounding winds blowing in from a chilly ocean. It's these thirty-knot winds that draw those who love to ride the surf, like the wave sailor before you: Throughout the summer they congregate to catch the waves as well as big air. This contoured beach and the neighboring town (with a population of only a few hundred) have the same name—that of a nearby waterway where a firearm was found in the 1800s. Twelve miles to the north is a river that's been called "an angler's heaven"; twenty-seven miles to the south grow ninety percent of the country's lilies. The region has been described by one of the nation's eminent historians as "pleasant, homogeneous, self-contained . . . full of pleasant, homogeneous, self-contained people." It makes up part of the country's 12,380 miles of coastline and has impressive geographic diversity, from rain forests to mountains to deserts. Such extraordinary natural beauty has been noticed not only by the free-spirited aquatic athletes but also by the world of big business—commercials for one of the largest domestic industries have long been shot right here, right before your eyes.

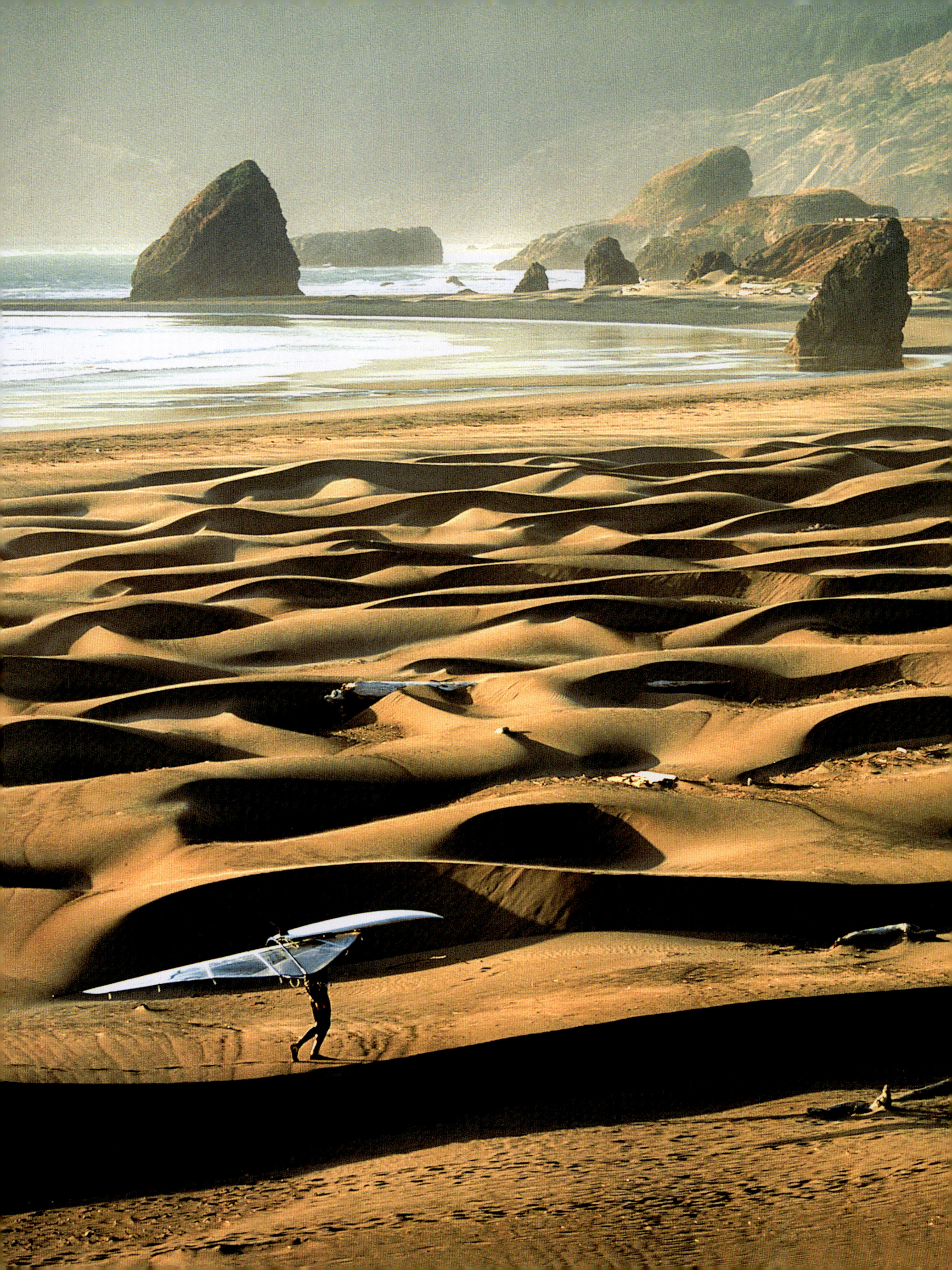

Y ou are looking at the ruins of a powerful Hindu empire. Its monarchs chose this site because it basked in the sacred shadows of a 4,600-foot mountain that resembled a lingam, the phallic form of the god Shiva. By the thirteenth century, the empire lost its grip on this "Land of a Million Elephants," and Buddhism infiltrated these pavilions, scattering giant sandstone heads in its wake. Christianity didn't get its first glimpse of the site until 1866, through the eyes of French explorer Francis Garnier.

The French were not the last to turn up: Another nation, despite its capital being 8,500 miles distant, attempted to correct the region's Communist bent by dumping dishwashing detergent, beer, and more bombs than were dropped in World War II onto a trail 140 miles north of here.

Dense jungle and mountains have isolated this country from modernity, if not incursion. In February, if you journey along its main highway, a 2,600-mile river that flows a couple of miles from here, you will witness worshippers as they rattle the reverent peace with water buffalo fights while celebrating the full-moon festival. Roam around monks meditating on rocks as they capitalize on the purificatory powers of the nearby spring.

In this nation, one of the most sparsely populated on its continent, many of the people practice their own form of meditation by drugging themselves into an opiate stupor. The size of Great Britain, it is the world's third-largest producer of opium. Even so, frangipani ("temple tree") eclipses the poppy in popular regard, having earned the moniker National Flower. Inhale its heady scent as you enter these gates—remember, you're treading on hallowed ground.

It's the kind of fairy tale that gives one nightmares: In order to impress a princess, a smitten ogre tried to carve out a giant crater with a coconut shell in a single night. His valiant, if fatal, effort gave birth to this six-mile depression—though what you're really after is one of three volcanoes within it. Regularly sputtering cinder and ash, this puzzle's answer rises from a black sea of sand. Against this unearthly backdrop, you won't bat an eye at the sight of flying squirrels, barking deer, and abundant crops grown on impossibly steep slopes. If you travel here in January or February—in truth, the worst time of year to visit—you might witness the annual midnight pilgrimage to the crater's rim, where residents blithely toss in everything from money to live animals (a vestige of another not-fit-for-bedtime story and a marked improvement over earlier, human sacrifices). The local lore may be far-out, but the location is anything but: This archipelago nation is smack in the middle of the globe. Spanning the distance between London and Moscow—twice—it is home to more than four hundred volcanoes. Still lost? Two more clues: The mountain shares its name with a bubbly sedative; the island, with a pick-me-up.

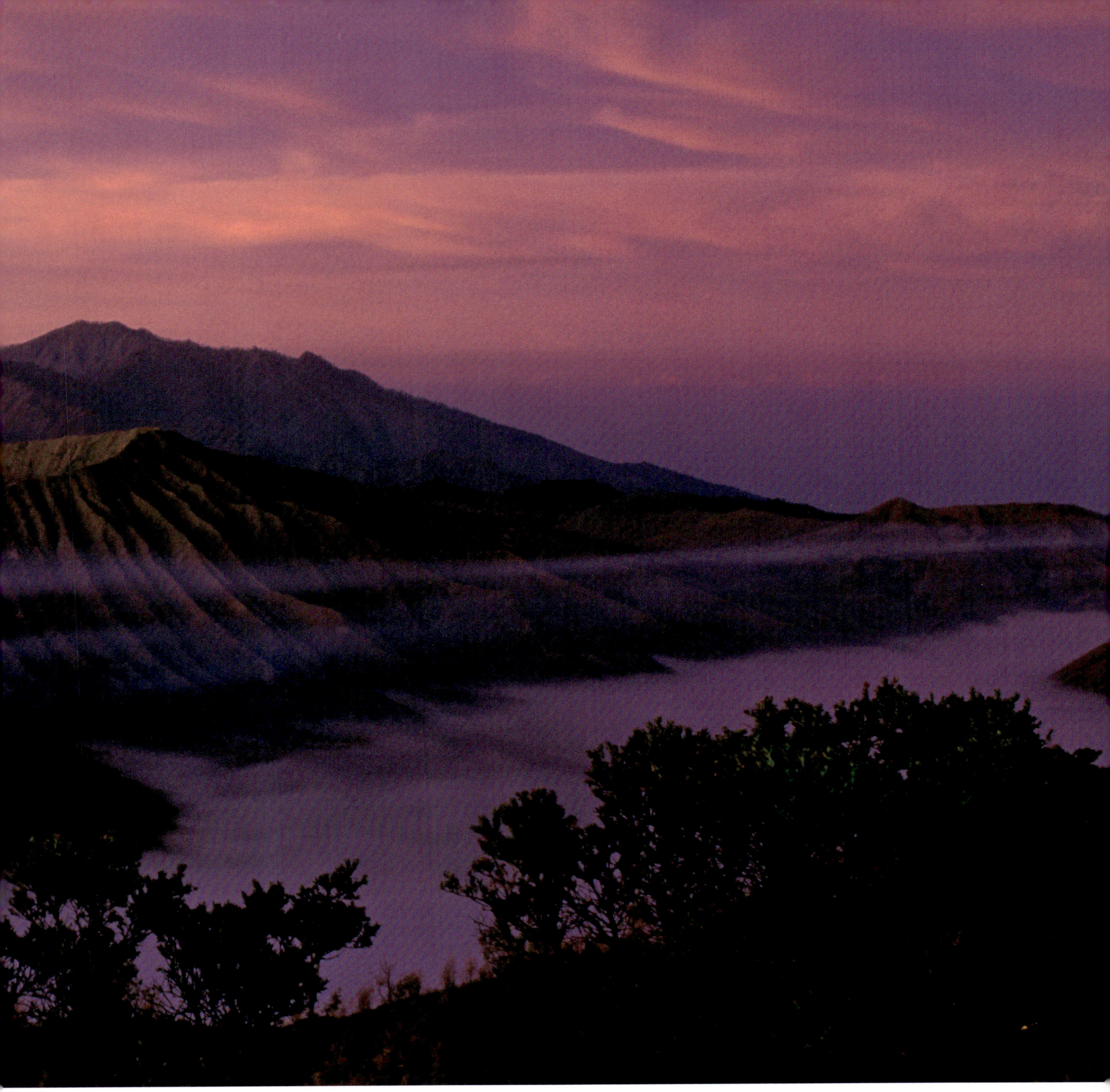

Beauty is such a twisted thing. Hauntingly elegant trees like the one before you spread their gnarled trunks all over the western tip of this triangular island, which itself lies at the western end of an archipelago. You're not about to drop off the face of the earth in this gothic terrain, but in the Ptolemaic world you might have.

The Hellenic astronomer described this island chain with a synonym for *providential*. Perhaps you'll find its contemporary name a little birdbrained, but look closer: It refers to dogs in an ancient vernacular. Yet why, you might ask, if the chain lies just sixty miles off the coast of one continent, does it belong to another?

Fifty thousand years ago, half of Little Island (its nickname) slid into the sea in a cataclysmic volcanic eruption that displaced one hundred times more earth than Mount St. Helens did in 1980. With its ten thousand inhabitants clustered in several towns, the isle is today the most remote and undeveloped of the seven in its chain. With luck, it will remain so, UNESCO having recently granted sixty percent of it Biosphere Reserve status, protecting the vast number of endemic plant species as well as a giant lizard once thought to be extinct.

Book a stay in a traditional country house and you can hike the hundreds of volcanic cones that dot the landscape or soak in the medicinal waters that abound. Come back for the grand quadrennial July festival and you can help musicians and dancers carry a statue of their patron saint from a chapel in the west to the mist-shrouded capital in the east.

Buffeted by trade winds into sweeping Fred and Ginger poses, thousand-year-old junipers such as this are the symbol of the island. Their wood long gathered to carve into utilitarian objects, they are also somewhat endangered. Yet, thankfully, efforts are now being made to preserve them. Like all survivors, they bend but do not break.

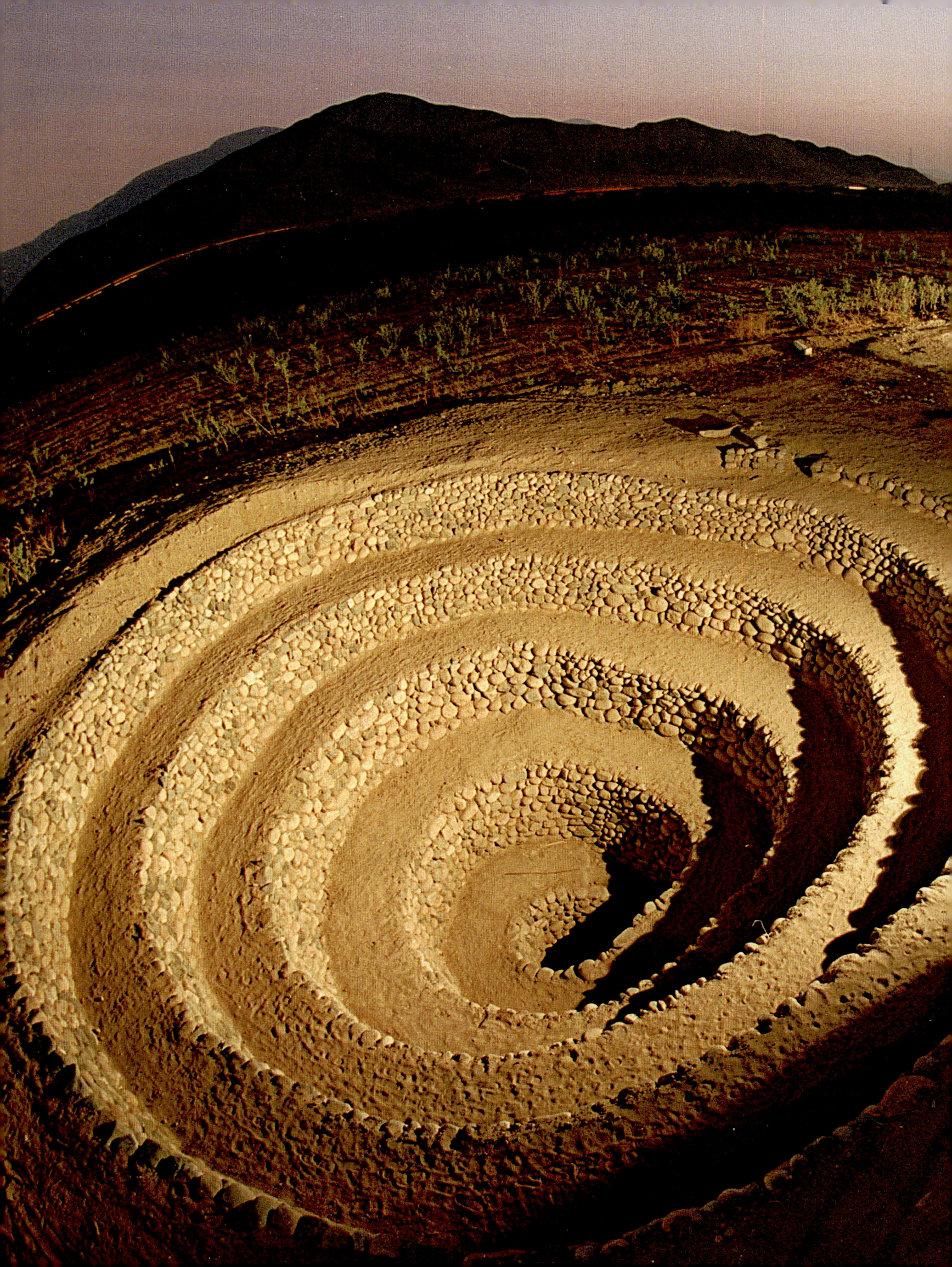

You are looking into a spiral pit, one of a series dug into the arid ground by a pre-Christian civilization. No doubt you are wondering what these descending paths signify. Some believe them to be routes for a ritualistic procession. More likely they collected valuable additional water for aqueducts—at times forty feet underground—running from fabled mountains to the east for crop irrigation. Others, including you and perhaps the couple before you, admire the sites as just plain art. Indeed, this culture, organized as a federation of villages sharing a common faith, is famed for its pottery and land art. Thanks to the climate—the region receives an inch of rain each year—numerous huge etchings of animals and geometric shapes, which the people carved into the earth throughout the region, remain in existence. The outside world learned of these glyphs in 1927, when a native archaeologist discovered them.

The spirals are just outside a town that shares the name of this long-gone, highly developed society, which is 275 miles from the capital of its country. Somewhat disdainfully, a Chicago-bred journalist wrote in 1967 that this is "the only nation in the world which lived basically for a long period on bird manure." Husbanding natural resources has a lengthy history here, and a future as well. The country may be the only one in the world to have a hotel that offers oxygen-enriched rooms—to smooth the transition to the property's lofty location. This is, after all, a place where cooperating with Mother Nature leads to successful invention.

Y ou are standing at the edge of a Neolithic lunar observatory 1,800 miles from the North Pole. Or perhaps, as legend suggests, you are amid a family of giants turned, Medusa-like, to stone. (Washington Irving, whose father hailed from these parts, based "Rip Van Winkle" on another local legend.) Whatever their origin, the slabs before you have stood sentry here for 3,500 years. They saw a king named Christian sign away this land as partial payment on his daughter's dowry. And each September they greet pods of gray seals, which come to breed and molt. You have unquestionably arrived here by boat, having traversed the same waterways that now conceal the German Imperial Navy. Edwin Muir referred to this locale in 1935 when he described it as "just outside the circumference of the industrial world—near enough to know about it, but too far off to be drawn into it." It is sixty-three degrees Fahrenheit at lunchtime in June and fifty-one degrees at midnight, when golfers can still be found prowling the links. The water temperature that month is the same as it is on December 25: damn cold. If you spot a purple primrose with a pale yellow eye, you'll know you're nearby. But if you spot a tree—any tree—you're not even close.

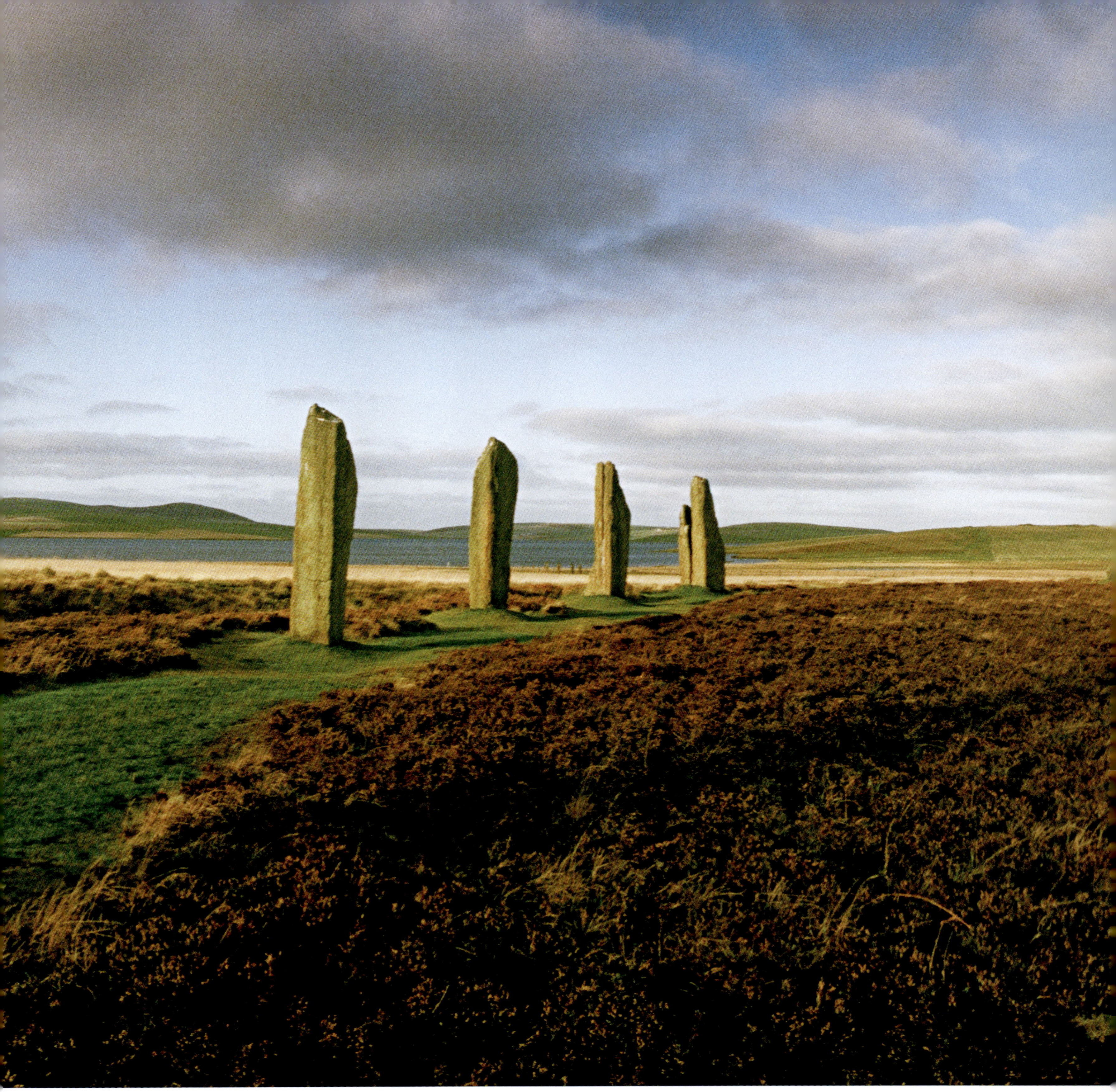

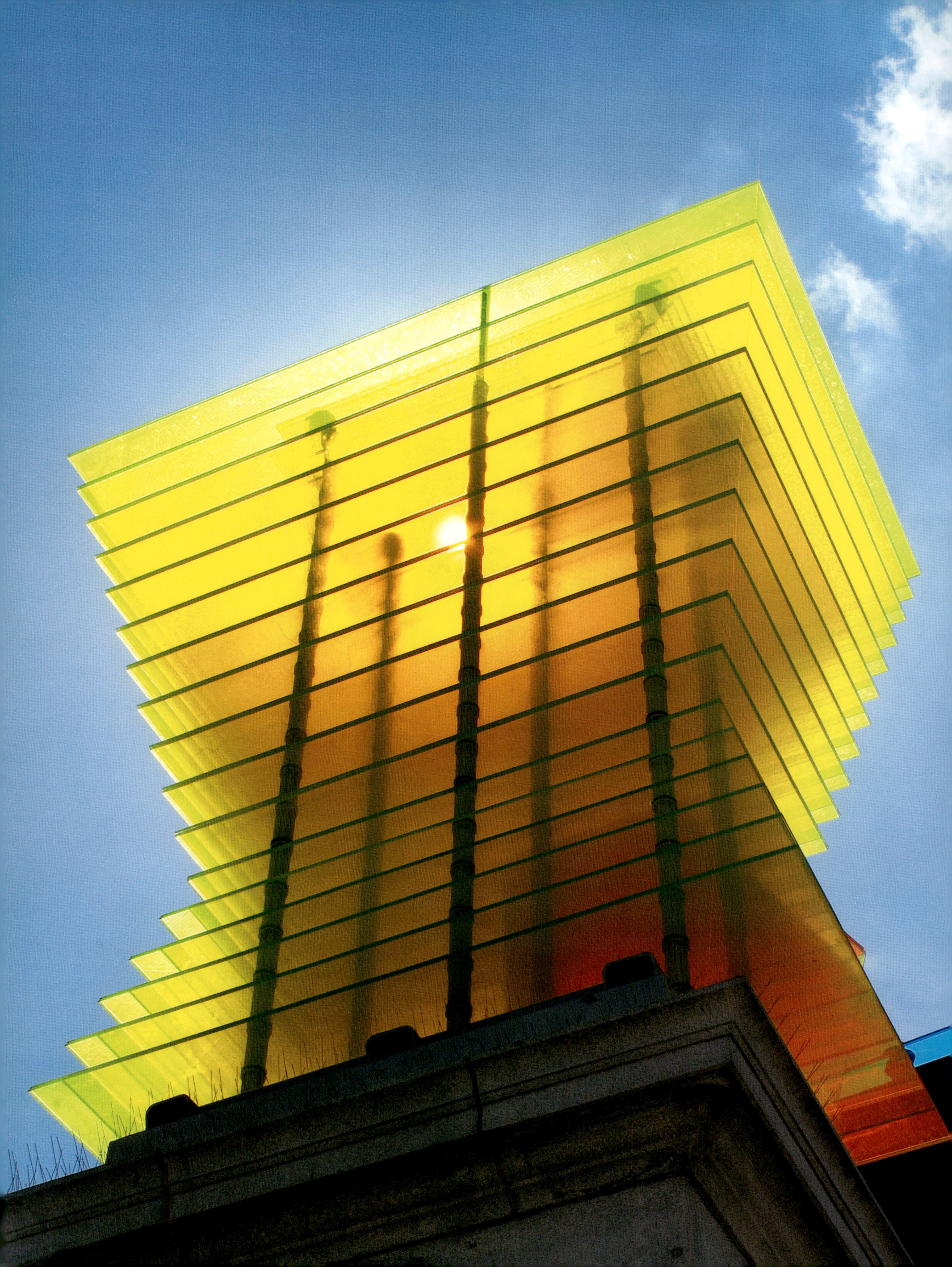

Look, it's a stack of those acrylic shelves you tricked out your den with in the '70s. Have you stumbled upon a yard sale? Maybe you can pick up a lava lamp and a beanbag chair on your prowl for vintage wares? Not likely. The luminous sheets you're looking at weigh in at a grand total of eight tons and represent $400,000 worth of laminated glass set atop a granite base, one of four such foundations in the public space you're visiting. This base was intended to support an equestrian statue of a monarch, but—wait for it—the funding dried up.

For the past decade, contemporary artists have been mounting their works here on a rotating basis. This light-refracting piece was designed by a German as a maquette for a high-rise. Earlier occupants included a marble-resin Christ as well as another anointed one: a football star who made a brief, unauthorized appearance as a wax figure.

Since it was first laid out at a crossroads in the mid-nineteenth century, the space you are in has seen its share of riots and continues to attract every nut job in the city who wants to grind his ax. It also hosts sports victory celebrations and peace rallies. Of late, it's become a full-service pedestrian zone with loos, lifts, and a café, thanks in no small part to the release of hawks that helped cause swarms of feral birds to hightail it out of here. A prominent column and two fountains have been restored. The plaza is now so user-friendly that should you wish to make a movie in it—stage a huge Bollywood dance number, say—the application process can be done online. If this urban hive of activity ever overwhelms you, remember that you can always seek refuge in the corner church, where a renowned chamber orchestra just might be playing.

This radiant display will vanish very soon. Next up is a work by a sculptor whose angel with airplane wings you discovered a few years ago; after that, a ship in a bottle with sails stitched from ethnic textiles. Which means that these days, the only riots you are likely to see here will be purely aesthetic.

"Can you hear me now?... Good!" The lone figure calling you from the top of this steep slope isn't actually touting cell phones, but he is in the middle of nowhere and he does live in a part of the world where that technology is all the rage. To get here, you have endured not only a six-hour bus ride from a former provincial capital but also a six-hour hike through rice terraces whose graceful snakeskin patterns lace the hillsides for miles. You are exploring a remote district where the ethnic minorities have retained the old ways and still live in traditional wooden dwellings. Their ancestors took it on the chin when an early imperial dynasty swept down from the north and founded the former capital you set out from, a city that is today among the most touristed in the whole country. If you are adept at deciphering the national written language, you might recognize more than one suggestion of wood in the former capital's name, referring as it does to a species of tree. And once you've caught a whiff of the divine scent given off by these ubiquitous arboreal treasures (perhaps you've even spritzed on the fragrance back home), you'll surely want to relax by the river that flows through town, sipping one of the wines or teas made from the blossoms and bark. Should the local fishermen languorously plying the river's waters in their flat-bottom boats inspire you to cast off, you'll be transported into a landscape right out of a classical painting, with massive, craggy outcrops looming over you from both shores.

Some fifty miles downstream, you might choose to dock at another of the region's gems, a village set in such a paradise that backpackers the world over have long flocked there seeking bliss (or whatever it is that backpackers seek). It was not always so: In 1979, the province was the staging ground for a brief war that broke out between this country and its southern neighbor, one which had the two antagonists crossing what was, it seems, a thin red line.

All is calm now, however. So turn off your phone and join the man on the hill to silently reflect on the human ingenuity—and brawn—that went into constructing this geoponic marvel. Locals like him know, after all, that this awesome scene speaks for itself.

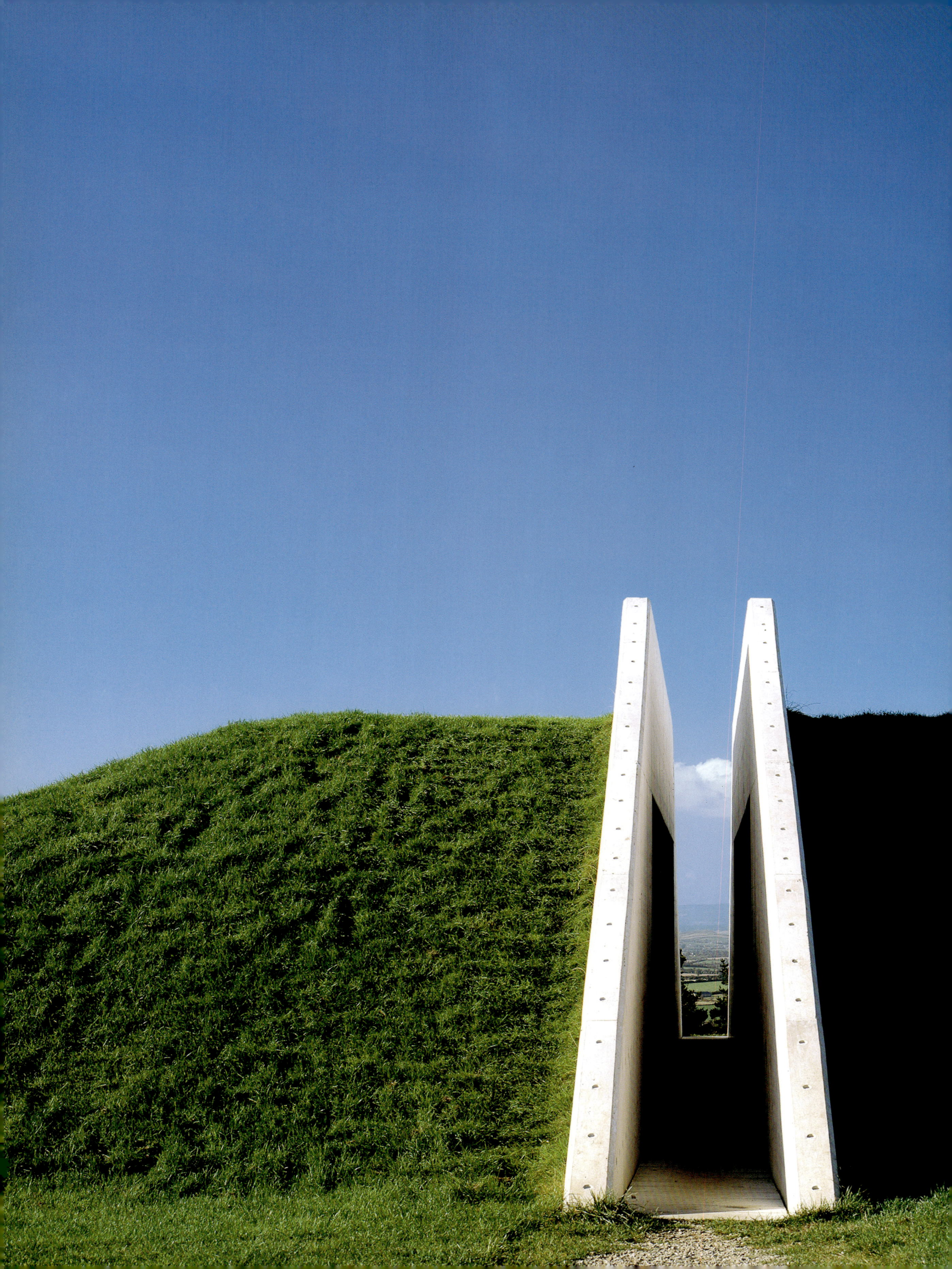

You've come upon what locals call a luminous mound. Despite its appearance, the pathway ahead leads not to the Elysian Fields but to a chamber in which reside two massive oak sculptures—saplings at the time of the legendary battle, a little more than two hundred years ago, that this monument commemorates. Disaffected with local rule and armed with pitchforks, the region's spirited inhabitants rose up against their much stronger foes. For a time, the rebels succeeded against the odds: Despite a lack of central support and organization, they fended off their tormentors for six weeks, before some thirty thousand gave up their souls. Just as the monument's split suggests the break between serfdom and enlightened revolutionary ideals, so it echoes the bifurcated politics that has determined much about life in this land.

The Vikings gave the region its name, which derives from the Norse for "estuary of the mud flats." Foreign and local sovereignties alike coveted this thriving port for its strategic location. It was here, in 1169, that another group of powerful conquerors first landed, bringing with them a new form of social organization—and centuries of strife.

In a country of word spinners, locals still sing boisterously of their ancestors' exploits and the rebels' zeal. Although the nation's most famous writer—born in the capital city about sixty miles north—described his country as "the old sow that eats her farrow," visitors in search of sandy beaches and soft green hills, stately mansions and living history, come in droves. Should they stop here on the summer solstice, the day that the battle was finally lost, they will see the sun illuminate the heart of this memorial, a reminder that past losses are the source of future gains.

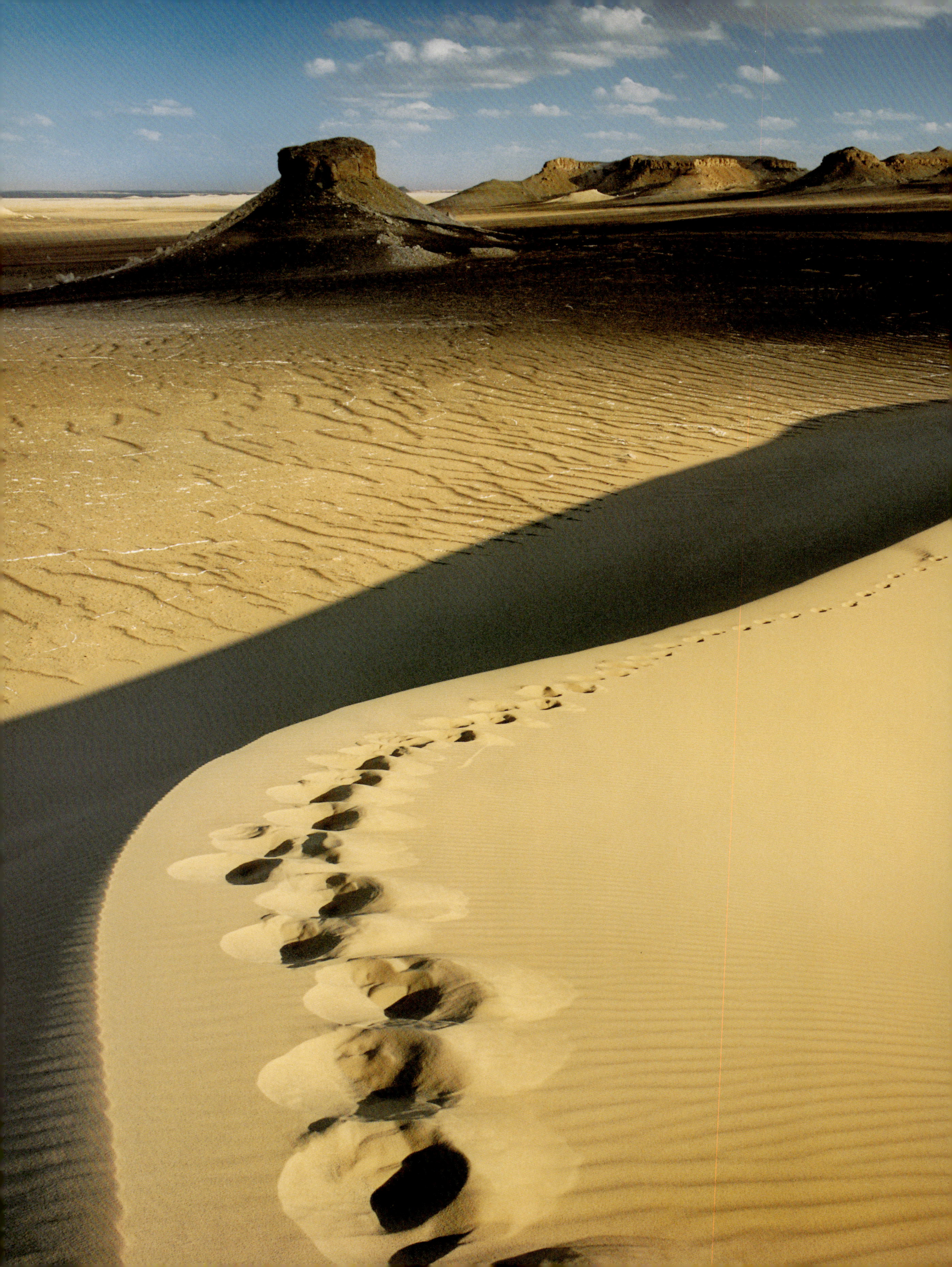

You are walking through one of the world's hottest and driest patches of terrain, 262,800 square miles of sand punctuated only by five far-flung oases. In ancient times, the murderous brother of a god was said to dwell here, providing explanation enough for the desert's inhospitable nature. Yet countless nomads roamed this land, as did a famed historian in 450 B.C. and, some 119 years later, a 25-year-old conqueror who came seeking confirmation of his divinity. But there have also been more antagonistic visits, from the numerous invasions of an aggressive western neighbor in the second millennium B.C. to those of forces farther afield in the twentieth century.

This palimpsest of a country has produced multiple empires and nurtured diverse and influential cultures, evidenced especially by prized architectural relics that stand to this day. The nation has survived plagues, colonization from abroad, and, in the last fifty years, a series of wars. And it has weathered this long history of political and religious turmoil well enough, producing a Nobel laureate and welcoming a surge of visitors in the past decade. Recently, a prize-winning story brought international fame, with the arid landscape before you taking as much a major role as the ill-fated protagonists.

You are near a towering plateau, a gathering point for this country's political right, eighteen hundred miles from the Arctic Circle. Seven hundred years before the sixties gave us love-ins, the fortified town in the distance prompted paeans to courtly love, though the mood would not last: The following century, the most cold-blooded member of its ruling class took to shoving convicts off the surrounding precipice, laughing diabolically as they plunged to their death. Considered today to be one of the loveliest spots on earth, it nevertheless retains something of its unfavorable reputation. "This is where Dante got his idea of Hell," wrote Virginia Woolf in 1928. To which a visitor a quarter-century later added: "Of the present inhabitants... it were better not to speak." Depending on whom you ask, this former marquessate draws its moniker from either the word for "high place" in a now-dead language or a bastardization of the name Balthazar, one of the three Wise Men. The evidence on-site suggests the latter: One enters the now-ruined castle through the Magi Gate, and you'll find the Christmas star on the founding clan's coat of arms. What you won't find are overhead wires or TV antennas (it's a classified historic monument) or cars on the streets of the plateau (at 2,600 by 650 feet, it's simply too small).

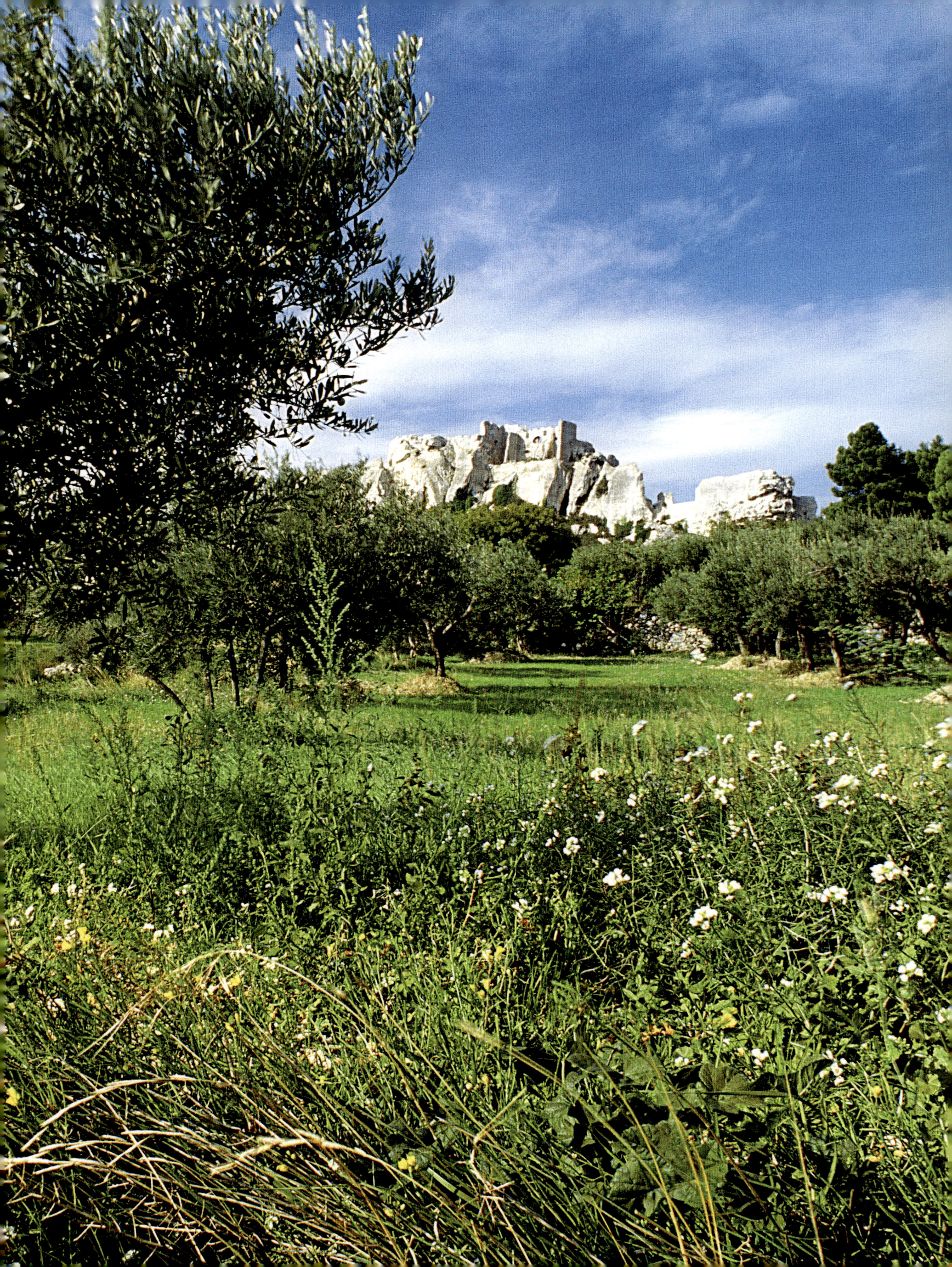

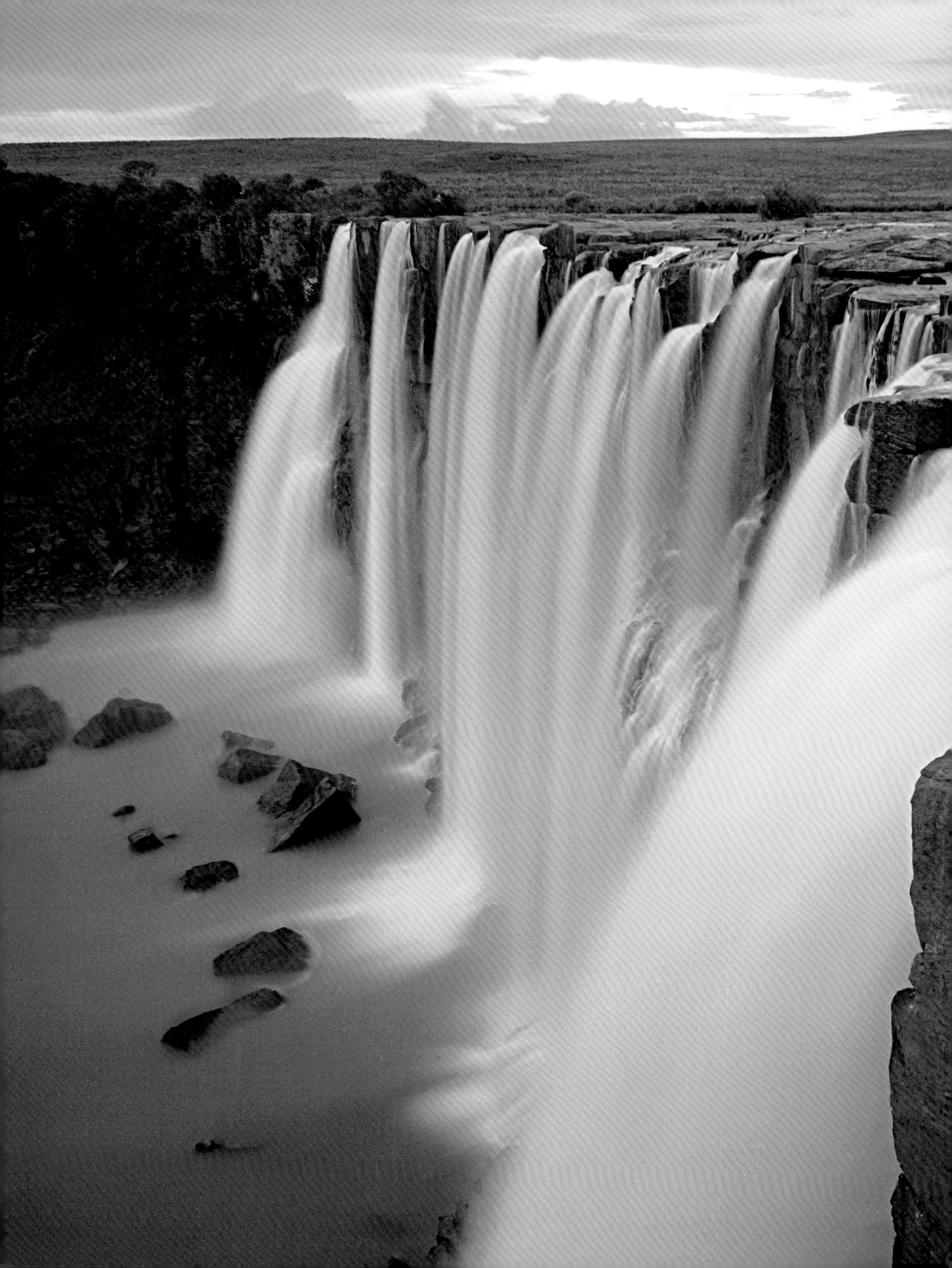

"This Countrie is somewhat melancholicke, overflowne with many waters, as wel of maine Rivers, as from the Skie." Like the sixteenth-century diarist who made this observation, you are in awe of the many rivers from the Skie, for this region is called the Land of Giant Waterfalls. Indeed, the landscape is punctuated with nearly three hundred of them, and had you tried navigating its waterways, you too would have found the Countrie melancholicke. But you flew here from the coast, and your encounter with this gossamer cascade has brought you bliss.

As soon as you hear a distinctive birdcall, you realize that the name of the cataract before you is not scatological, as you first thought, but onomatopoeic, borrowed from a long-billed wader (the head of an ancient god, a patron of scribes, recalls a bird of the same family). Although you don't enter a different country if you cross this river, it was baptized for another river where you do. Follow these waters far enough and you'll reach the confluence of three international borders, a territory where smugglers have roamed free. More happily, you'll also arrive at a magnificent series of saults that recently won UNESCO status; they were discovered 450 years ago by an adventurer whose matrilineal surname means "cow head."

The bovine motif lives on: Today, cattle farming dominates this, the third most southerly of the nation's twenty-six states. You can gorge on all-you-can-eat barbecue, in a style that originated here and is now trendy abroad, but you'll probably struggle if you try to down a bitter tea drunk through a straw.

You might wonder if this country's president during the aughts is a supporter of the nearby reserve dedicated to a rare species of pine tree—after all, his cognomen suggests woods (though you know him by his affectionate nickname, which means "squid"). While you would expect this left-leaning leader to be sympathetic to the environment, there is cause for concern: A hydroelectric plant now stands just below these falls, and a larger dam is planned downstream (already, one of the world's largest operates in these parts). So take it all in slowly, for this view—as magnificent as Ansel Adams' iconic *Bridal Veil Falls*—could become a memory.

The gilded orb before you may look like a massive, slightly malformed confection, but don't expect to see a bake-off world record set today. The reality is almost as quirky: You're looking at a twenty-four-foot-high pagoda that sits atop a precariously balanced granite boulder. As legend has it, a mere hair of the Buddha is all that keeps the stone from tumbling off its perch.

You've arrived, along with hundreds of worshippers, at the beginning of the four-month pilgrimage season. Now's your chance to practice your appliqué skills—go ahead, add gold leaf to the boulder to prove you're a man (literally, since only males are allowed to do so). This is one of several magnificent pagodas in the country. Upon seeing the largest one of all, a renowned poet wrote that "a golden mystery upheaved itself on the horizon—a beautiful winking wonder that blazed in the sun." He could just as well have been talking about this one; indeed, most devotees time their trip so they can behold the splash of colors at sunset.

You traveled a few hours from the former national capital to reach the base of this 3,600-foot mountain. While many visitors get to the summit in forty-five minutes by jumping on a truck, you slogged your way here on foot in five humid hours (or did you make like a grand pooh-bah and hire a sedan?). Though several modest inns looked tempting on the trail, you were content to plop down in a plastic chair at some of the outdoor snack bars for a quick pick-me-up.

You are at the northern tip of a 150-mile-long sliver of a coastal state that belongs to the tail of this country (the lower half is off-limits to foreigners). The provincial capital was once famous for its teak export. When policeman George Orwell lived in town and ventured beyond the area called Little England, he wrote, "I was hated by large numbers of people—the only time in my life that I have been important enough for this to happen." Clearly, the locals under his charge hadn't forgotten the nineteenth-century wars the British waged here.

Speaking of things Orwellian, the name of the nation's brutal military cabal (whose former acronym had a James Bond–villainous ring to it) includes the word *peace*. So light candles and ring the pagoda's bells to protest the regime's fictions. Amazingly, you can even rock this big rock. If only it were that easy to make the junta teeter. . . .

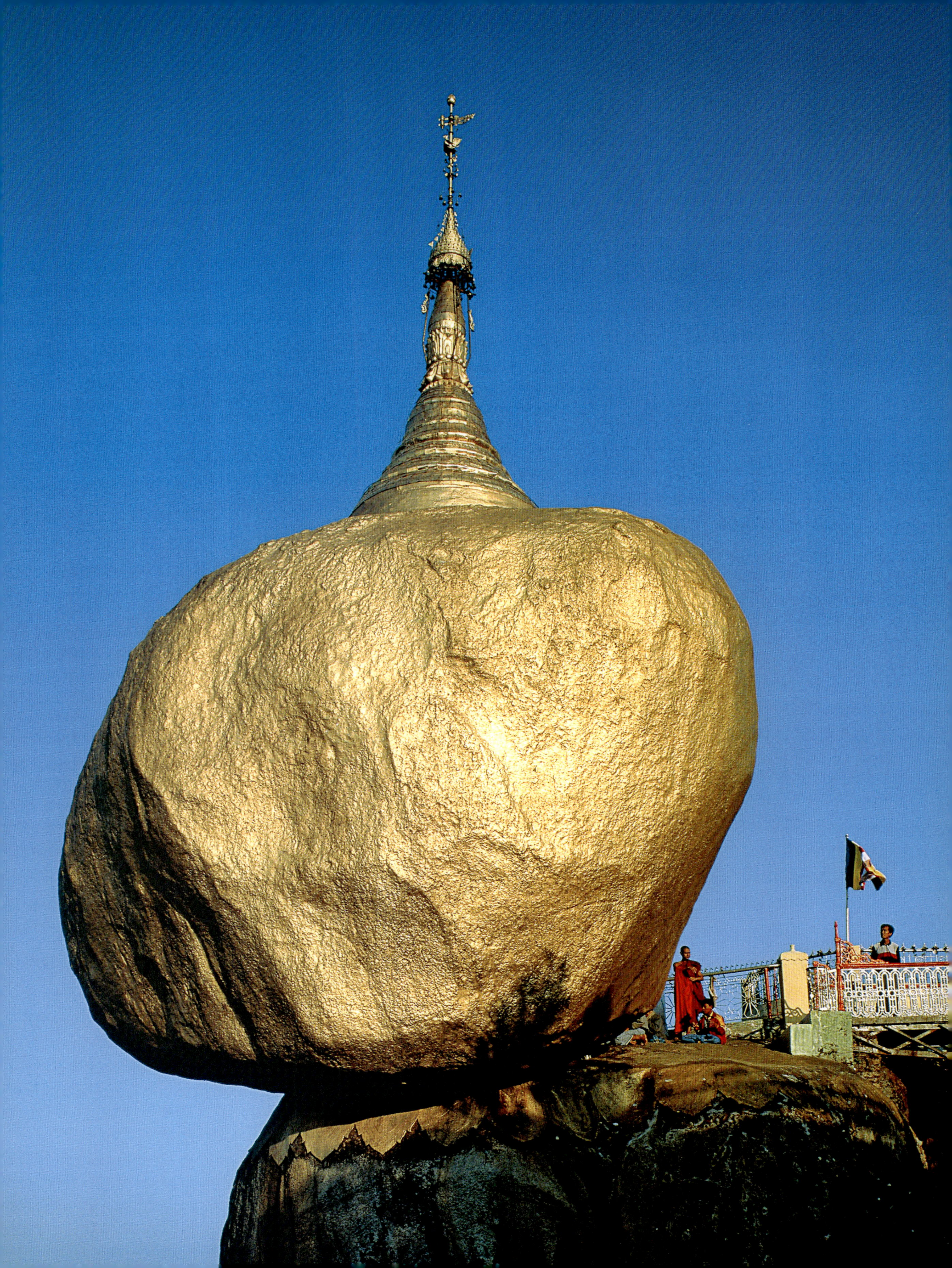

You are standing on what was once farmland, and the crumbling structure before you is the most recent sign of life—a landowner's house from the 1600s. One of the country's most famous writers coined a name for this place in a novel penned two centuries later—a name by which it is still known today. Wild storms in the late 1800s unearthed glimpses of past treasures long hidden below. Archaeologists mining the layers have found five civilizations, each literally built atop the other, an impressive record of 4,500 years of continuous settlement. As you wander the site, three acres spread across a promontory, its complex excavations reveal the shells of buildings constructed throughout the ages—as far back as the Bronze Age.

The island, rich in moldered booty—a mile from here is perhaps the largest ongoing dig on the continent—is one of a group of about a hundred, fewer than twenty of which are inhabited. Perhaps this fact, along with the security of rugged, indented coasts and steep hills, makes the area very popular with avifauna. The relatively few humans who do live here identify with their heritage of isolation rather than with the proud country to which this island chain belongs. Historically, local industries have capitalized on residents' survival skills—farming and fishing—but more recently, buried treasure of another sort has brought riches that earlier cultures could never have foreseen.

Your encounter with this handsome tower crowns a day spent traipsing through a corner of a venerable realm. As you pause to admire the skyscraper's features—how its proportions elegantly diminish as it rises—you might also ponder the purpose and precepts that inspired the design. But even if you know that such archetypal structures represent the cosmos fixed in architecture (and that they often served as reliquaries), you might still be surprised to learn that you are standing some two thousand miles from the country of their derivation.

It is no mystery why the tower was erected in this area, for it stands an hour's drive from an ancient city known as one of the most crowded crossroads in antiquity (X marks the spot, you might say). Long home to a multitude of religions, the city was most famous as the starting point—or, depending on your perspective, the terminus—of a very smooth shipping operation that lasted for the better part of a millennium. Today, this provincial capital is one of the country's most popular attractions, a bustling place where visitors still walk atop the six-hundred-year-old, nine-mile wall that encloses the city center. A massive army garrisoned just outside town actually welcomes civilian inspections—especially by foreigners, who admire the well-accoutered troops for their precision and dedication but know that their lack of mobility renders them impotent. Should the tower in front of you inspire spiritual yearnings, you will no doubt repair to the more famous—and imposing—one that looms just beyond the gates. And if you choose to tackle the steep ascent of a nearby peak that is one of the country's five sacred mountains, reward yourself afterward with a soak in the local hot springs.

Even though the country has embarked on a mad rush to modernize, the outside world clings to an antiquated image of this land, one as sepia-toned as this scene. Indeed, most of us would be hard-pressed to name its leader. But never mind. Why not make this tranquil moment last? By the time our notions catch up to the reality, many relics such as this will have vanished, a reminder that nothing—no matter how astounding—is set in stone.

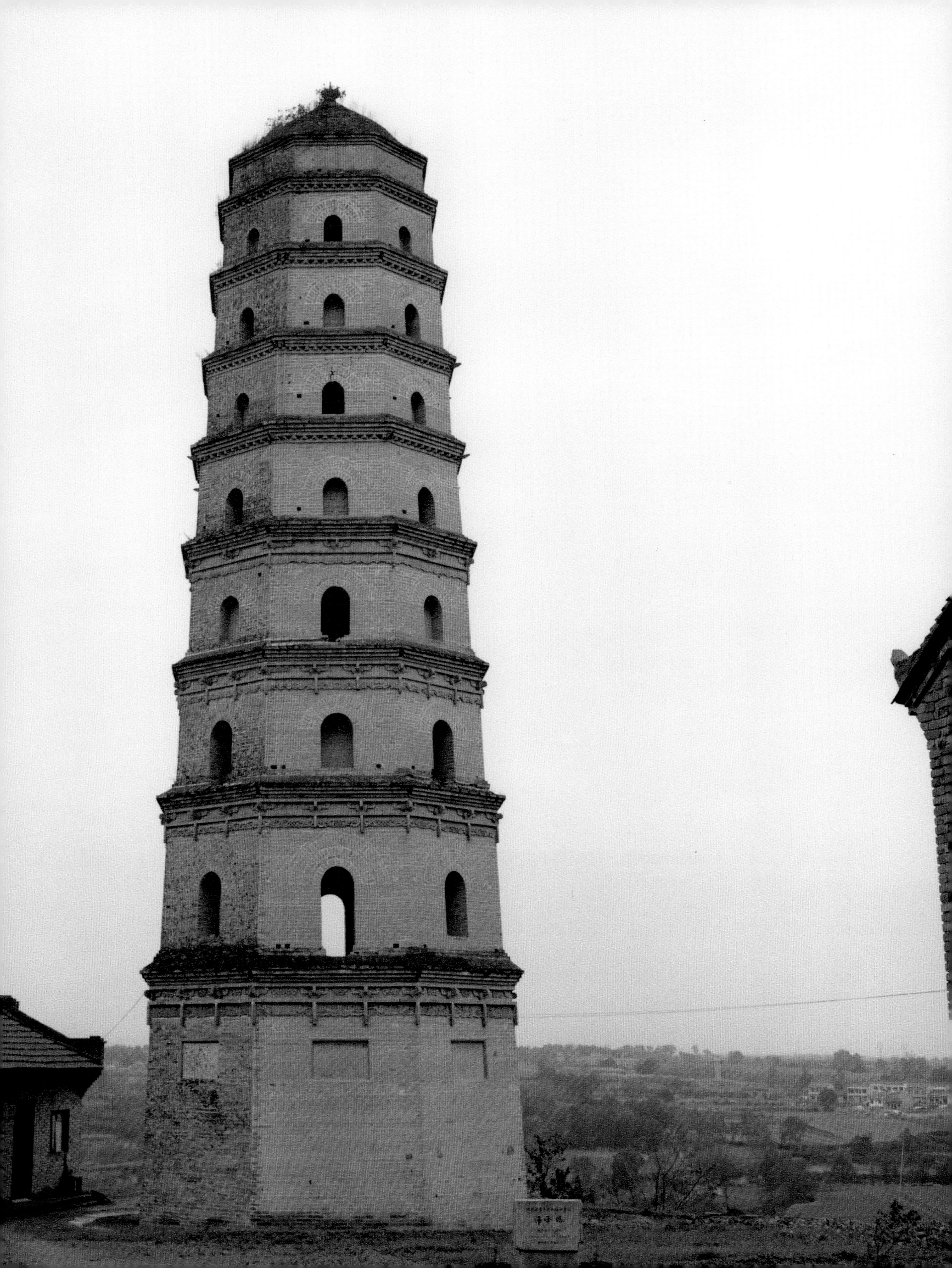

Attention ladies and gentlemen: You are not approaching Fantasy Island (Mr. Roarke and Tattoo are not down there with leis and daiquiris). No, these tiny isles are in the northeast of a country whose history has been anything but a dream: aggressive sixteenth-century colonists (who invaded in search of gold), numerous natural disasters (including earthquakes that twice in the twentieth century more or less razed the capital), and a notorious dictator (about whom our thirty-second president reputedly conceded, "He may be a son of a bitch, but at least he's ours"). And that's just the beginning. In recent decades, its citizens have fought a civil war, watched inflation rates soar, and endured widespread unemployment.

Yet these eighty or so lush keys are far removed from the turbulence of the mainland, just thirty-five miles away. Largely uninhabited and difficult to get to, they are in the territory of an English-speaking indigenous tribe, after whom they are named and whose name, in turn, is a homophone of an all-too-familiar pest. Paul Theroux fans might recognize the shoreline nearby: It inspired him to write a best-selling novel. If you think you're prepared for a mad adventure, just remember: Once you step off the plane (ze plane!), even the coolest among you will undoubtedly sweat. "The heat is devastating," wrote one novelist. "It's [like] a hot liquid clinging to you, encasing you, through which you have to move."

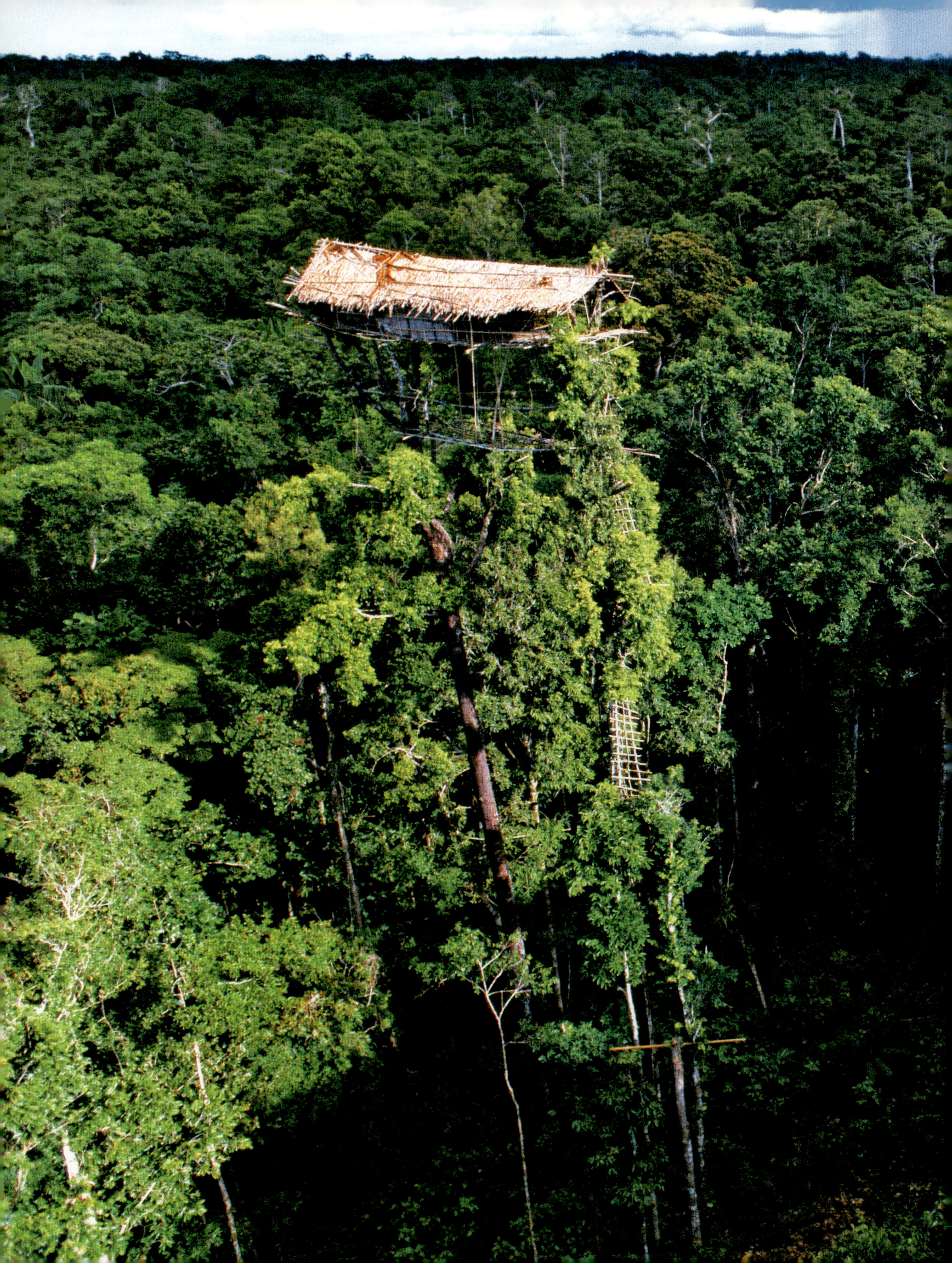

Cowabunga! You've got your bungee cord with you, right? The residents of this arboreal abode may want to send you hurtling through the forest canopy—your fate depends on whether they've pegged you as friend or foe. If you were shopping for a home here, your real estate agent's gambit would be to point out that you'd be living well above the swarms of mosquitoes and other hostiles. Tree houses like this one were constructed not for the soaring views but for defensive purposes. Some of these sky condos, built to accommodate a family of 8, with women and men in separate quarters, are set 150 feet up. (You thought your current daily commute was a drag?) Don't worry about the isolation; in recent decades the government began to clump many clans together in villages. Can't speak the language? Neither can your neighbors on this polyglot island.

The indigenous people in this forest number in the low thousands, and are led, as all local clans are, by strongmen who favor ornamental pig's teeth—don't let the gourd or leaf coverings that the males wear elicit adolescent titters. If you're hungry, you may wonder if the caloric benefit of the community's starchy palm diet is worth its exhaustive preparation: First you slit the tree trunk, then you mash, knead, wash, and strain the pith.

In a sense, east meets west here: You are in the easternmost and largest province of a country, but in the western part of a bird-shaped land. A few years ago the provincial name was changed from the one you learned, and the bird's head was chopped off and given its own administration. Either way, a Tibet-like state of affairs reigns in this region, many would argue. If you want to chill, you can always head up the cordillera to marvel at the astonishing glaciers in a famous national park.

Your best chance of getting to this hood is by a Cessna flight and a trek through the marshy jungle that lies between two rivers. You may want to bring along an architectural award to break the ice since the tree-house dwellers are clearly pioneers in ecolodge design. Be on guard, though, since these suspicious people do turn on outsiders occasionally. But isn't it time to make that leap of faith?

Y ou are gazing upon a remote piece of earth that was once a coastal swamp overrun by vegetation and ruled by dinosaurs. Seventy million years later, receding oceans and epochs of erosion have left a Martian landscape of nearly four thousand barren acres. Sandstone spires and hoodoos dominate, surrounded by billowing shale hills, their distinctive red hue the result of baking temperatures. The only evidence that life ever touched this land is the petrified wood and fossils underfoot.

Fittingly, this spot is found in a region where Henry Miller insisted that "Nature has gone Gaga and Dada. Man is just an irruption, like a wart or pimple." But that "irruption" has been significant. Control of the territory—christened with its current name in the 1560s—has been passed back and forth for centuries, first between competing indigenous groups, then from one colonial power to another. The result is a thriving tricultural society in which diverse groups have both mixed and retained strong identities. And during the past fifty years, the population has more than doubled as new settlers have arrived: industrialists lured by the vast natural resources, and artists drawn by the sunlight of unrivaled clarity and the views—like the one before you—found only here, in the land of enchantment.

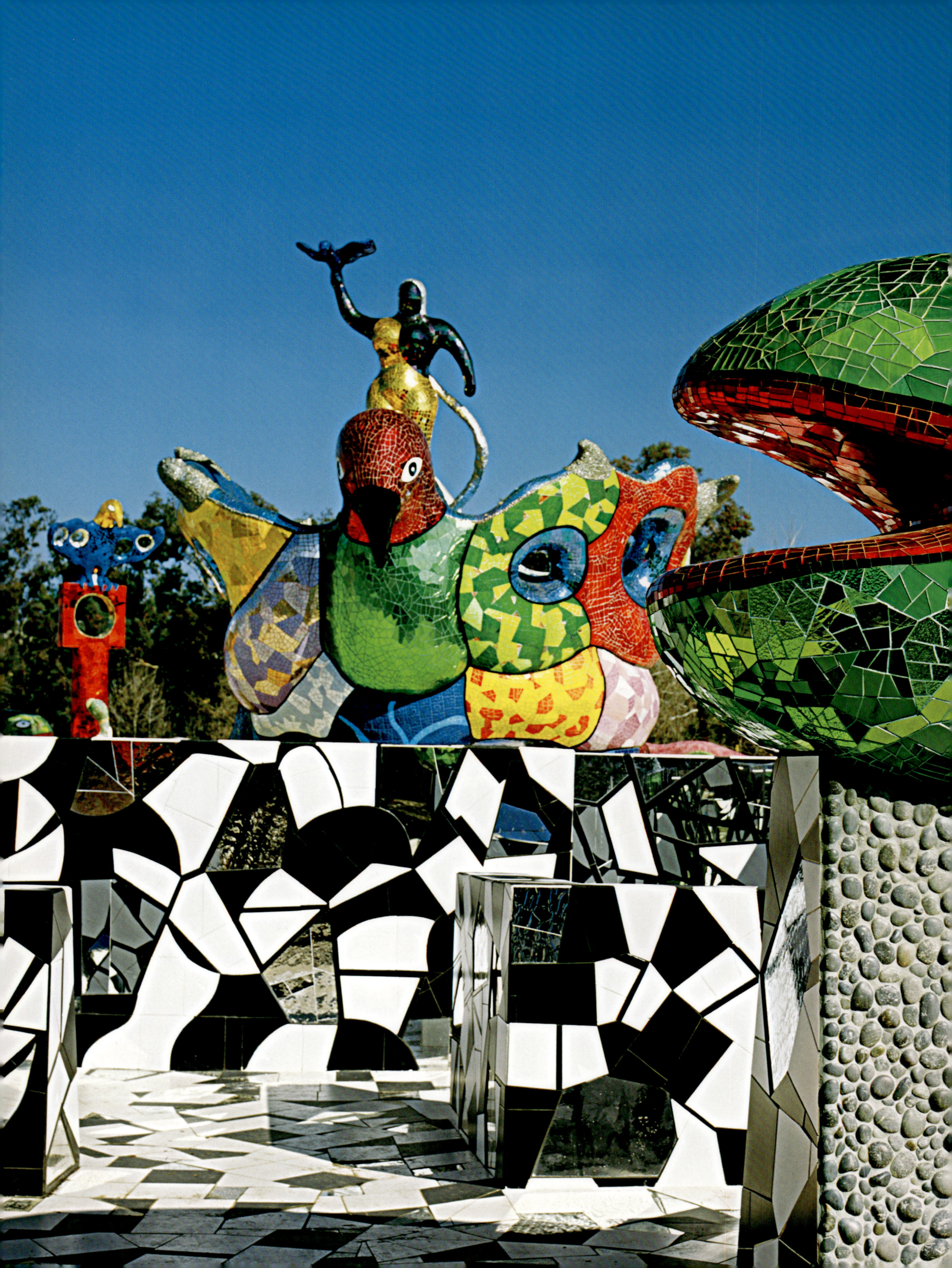

You've talked your way past viperous praetorian guards and are about to genuflect to a golden warrior queen mounted on a five-legged eagle, surrounded by deities and monsters, birds, reptiles, and animals endowed with sacred powers. Sounds like you're on a chemically induced trip, but no, you've taken this one to check out a whimsical twelve-acre sculpture garden. Nine totemic statues are scattered here behind a four-hundred-foot "snake wall"; covered in mosaics of quartz, agate, travertine, turquoise, and mirrored tiles, they reflect the myths and the mixed cultural roots of the region.

The sculptor, who died in 2002, was not an iconic art-world figure, and yet her life—along with her name—was as chromatic as her work. A neighbor of Brancusi's in 1950s France, she shot her way into a new art movement there in the early '60s—only to launch, two decades later, a perfume line and to create festive figures that still sit in a fountain next to a pompous Paris museum.

The city that hosts the garden, her final project, basks in the sun a hundred miles south of one major metropolis and thirty miles north of another. Its name means "hidden" in a local language, a reminder that this shallow valley eighteen miles inland was once a remote spot. Considering the natural disasters that strike these parts, the original name of this erstwhile cattle farm—it meant "Devil's Corner"—might have better described the place. The city is hardly incognito anymore, with a population of 140,000 crowding out Pomona's fruitful bounty (holy moly, the main crop is green gold!). An observatory and a major zoo also draw plenty of visitors, as do a museum dedicated to a bandleader and a winery that displays a collection of vintage convertibles with its premium varietals.

The queen who inspired the phantasmagoria before you was the heroine of a sixteenth-century adventure, a tale from which colonizers borrowed her name for the territory. Of the present society, one critic wrote, "a sense of history is continually sacrificed to a dream of the future." Like, yeah! But trip amid this plein air pastiche and you'll be one with the ur-mother of this land.

Y ou are in the land of the reborn—2,500 miles from the site of Jesus Christ's resurrection and more than three times that distance from Shirley MacLaine's birthplace (her most recent one, anyway). "The arts of littleness are tragically lacking [here]," wrote E. M. Forster, and how right he was: This is a nation big on languages (eighteen major and some sixteen hundred minor tongues), deities (hundreds of gods and goddesses), and festivals (a celebration nearly every day). One of the world's most extravagant monuments is about a two-hour drive from here, but if you're considering a road trip, consider this: Drivers are notorious for ignoring lane makers and for honking their horns with annoying frequency—about twelve times per mile. Amid these sandstone columns looms a lone ferrous one, of a metal so pure that it has remained rust-free since its fourth-century construction. They say that if you can encircle it with your arms extended behind your back, your wish will be fulfilled. Before you try, however, stretching out with the local guru might be wise.

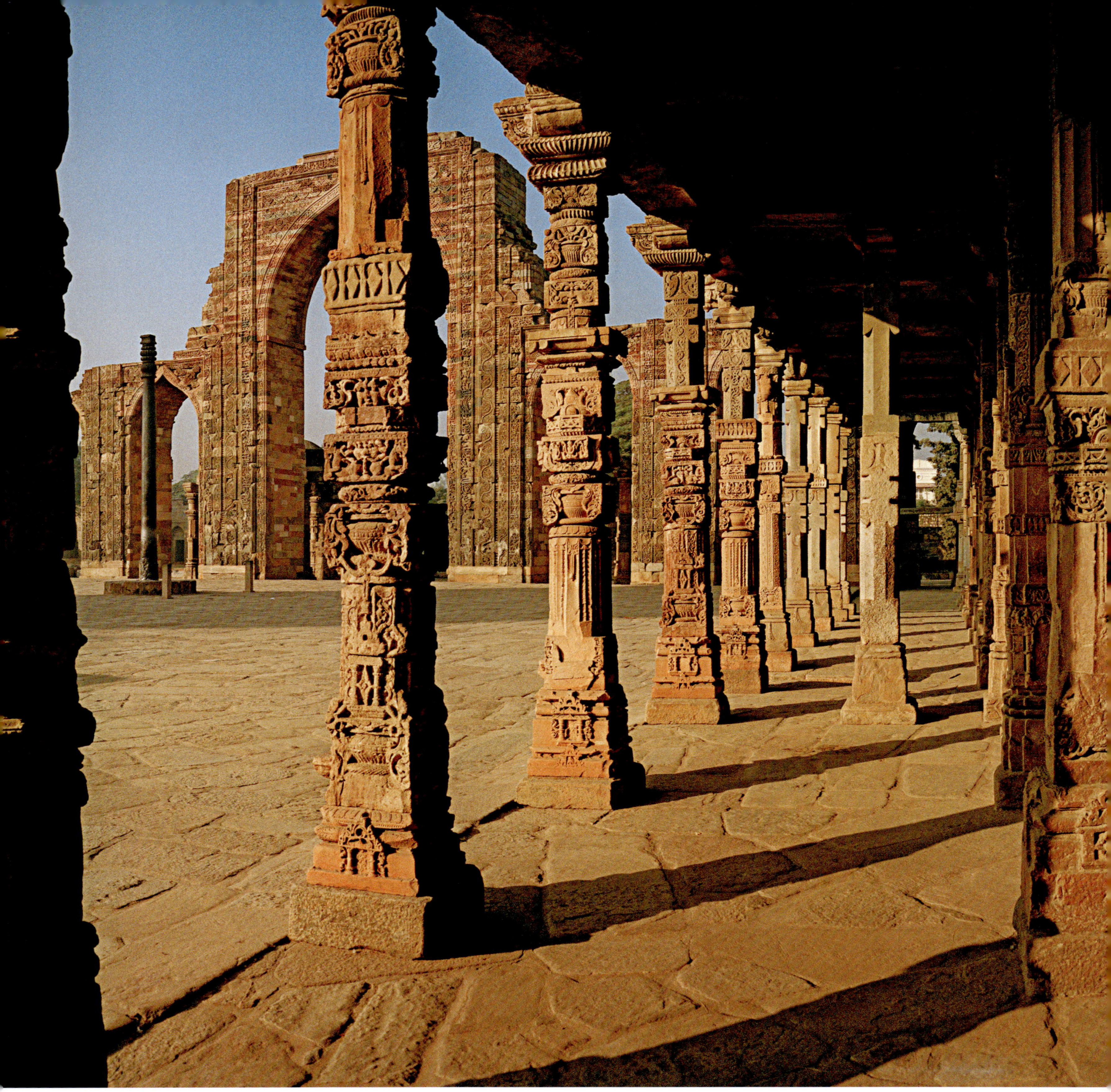

Y ou are contemplating a concrete structure, conjuring up, perhaps, the shell of a hulking, hungry oyster or the brutal end of a highway going suddenly nowhere. But that's not it at all—in fact, this is a memorial, built in 2002, to commemorate a historic catastrophe and to pay tribute to the hundreds of thousands who perished because of it. More than a century ago, the calamity befell a distant island to the east and caused many of the surviving inhabitants to flee.

As you approach, you'll see that the glimmering lines between the bands of imported limestone are text—quotations, letters, government reports, recipes, song lyrics, and statistics—that trace the story of the horror left behind. The site tries to evoke the fatherland's rural landscape: Should you walk around the back, you'll find a seemingly abandoned stone cottage, stone walls, and wetland flora. The project cost about five million dollars to assemble and was built not just to remember those who died but also to remind us that the world's people continue to suffer from this scourge.

The monument is located in a cynosure of a city with a reputation for its dynamism as well as for dirt and danger. Concern about perils, in fact, for years hampered (and eventually halted) redevelopment of a multi-lane road a stone's throw to the east, despite that route's resemblance at times to the unexpected highway terminus suggested by this architecture. Many Americans have vacationed in the country where you are currently standing, a place once described as "useful in proving things before held impossible." Known for its political stability and natural resources such as copper and coal, it is home to millions of cell phone users. But then, as many of the folk driven to this land by the machinations of nature and history well know, home is a mobile concept.

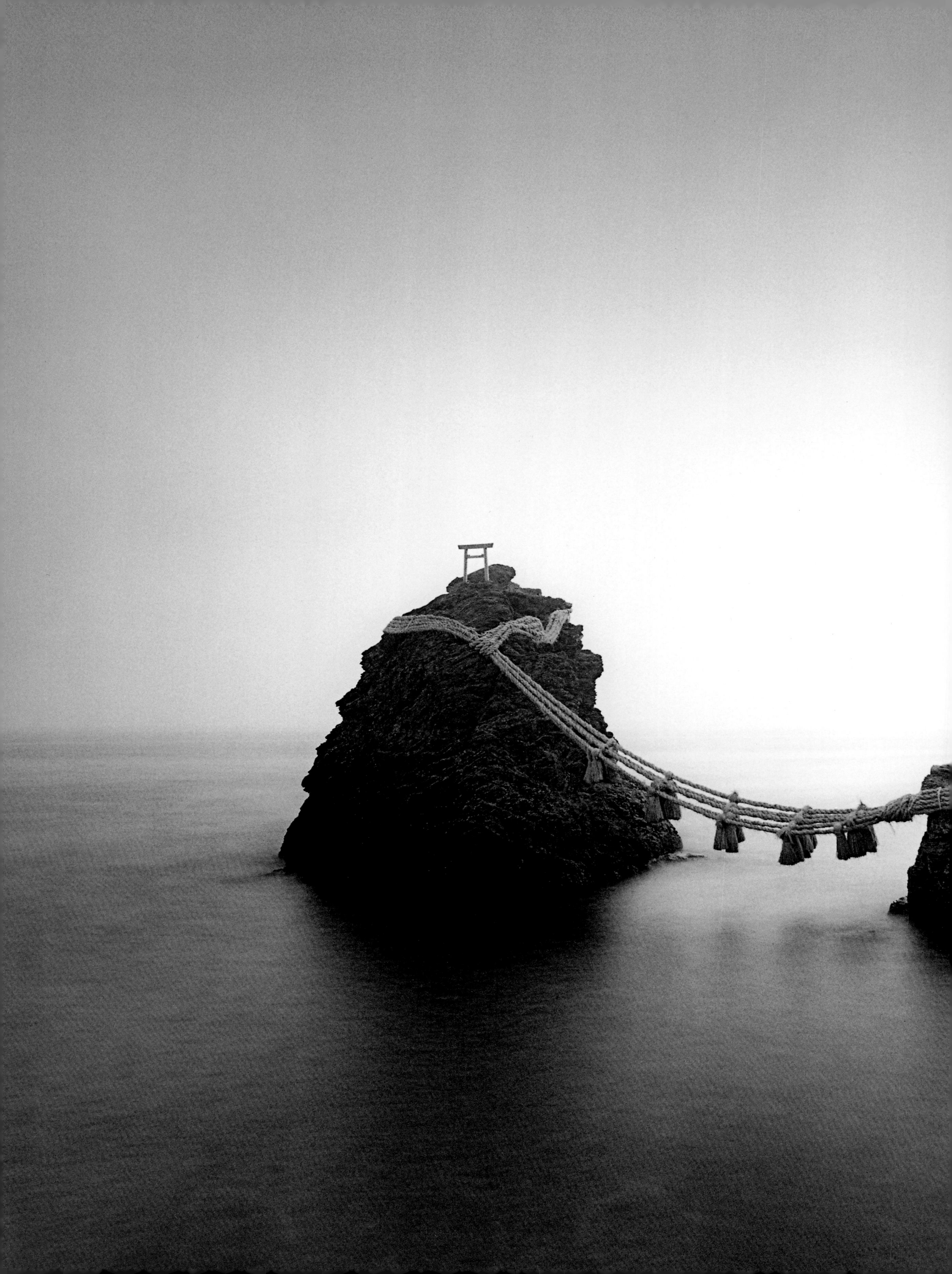

Someone left quite a mark here. You may be wondering if the rope draped in front of you is the beginnings of another Christo wrap job. Or if Jack Sparrow is about to swoop by (perhaps the cord is a Hollywood prop upon which a mascaraed Johnny Depp will be performing acrobatic feats of rescue?). Just what kind of twisted tale lies behind this thing, anyway?

Made from the braided straw of a cereal, the one-ton rope does in fact have an unlikely function: It unites the two rocks in matrimonial bliss. The pair represent a deific couple who figure prominently in this nation's creation story. Thrice annually a ceremony is performed to renew the entire strand, thus keeping divorce lawyers at bay.

It is said that happiness is ensured to couples who see the sun rise between the mini peaks. If you're lucky, you might catch a glimpse of the silhouette of a legendary volcano behind you. You are in a national park in which a famous shrine is divided into two compounds that lie a few miles apart. Every two decades, the wooden structures are rebuilt to great fanfare—at a cost of billions in the local currency. Had he witnessed all the hoopla, a seminal American architect might never have exclaimed, "At last I . . . found one country on earth where simplicity . . . is supreme."

If you're looking for culture along this ria coastline, pay a visit to the huge bivalve harvesting operations. Some guidebooks call the small local city drab. Yet where else in this part of the world will you find a St. Patrick's Day parade—one with jig-dancing, baton-twirling natives? Though not within lassoing range, you're close to several of the nation's most historically significant cities (got a beef with that?).

A small shrine onshore, across from the godly stone couple, is devoted to a tail-less amphibian. In the surrounding shops you may find yourself stocking up on irresistible goofy trinkets. And just this once, you won't mind getting roped in.

Y ou are straddling a fiery rift between two tectonic plates, amidst a mad geological laboratory brimming with black lava fields, aquamarine thermal springs, crystal glaciers, and emerald knolls. Publisher of more books per capita than any other country in the world, this cataclysmic terrain—the gateway to a Jules Verne sci-fi journey—is one hundred percent literate. Such erudition probably comes naturally to a people whose language has survived largely unaltered since the Middle Ages (while we struggle with Chaucer, they read their ancient historical sagas as readily as they do popular magazines). Inhabiting less than twenty percent of their homeland, these tightly knit residents are arranged in the phone book by their first names, and they grew closer still when in 1944 they separated from a kingdom whose crown is located more than a thousand miles to the east.

The sod-roofed farmhouses pictured here are on display at a popular folk museum that also features live demonstrations of traditional farm tools and musical instruments. A word to the unadventurous: Don't expect a cozy train trip to these verdant foothills. This is a nation without railroads. And travel with lunch in hand, or be prepared to savor such native delicacies as putrefied shark meat, ram's testicles, and singed sheep's head, occasionally chased down with a brew nicknamed Black Death. As one visitor observed, "If the Italian landscape is like Mozart . . . then we may take [this region to resemble] the music of the moderns—say Schumann, at his oddest and wildest."

You are at the same latitude as Richmond, Virginia, in a climate Shakespeare called "delicate, the air most sweet." Churchill relaxed nearby in 1955. In February, almond blossoms blanket the surrounding fields, and the temperature at lunch is fifty-five degrees Fahrenheit. Pindar called this ancient metropolis "the fairest of all mortal cities." Two Allied military egos collided down the coast from here. Diane Keaton worked with a former lover fifty-five miles north. Arabic, Greek, and Latin were once the official languages, even though they're seldom spoken here today. Local tradition says that this temple should be visited by a husband and wife on their wedding day. Scylla and Charybdis might once have barred your path to this place. Lawrence Durrell described it as "not just an island, [but] a sub-continent whose... variety of landscapes simply overwhelms the traveler who has not set aside at least three months to deal with it." But which three months? April, May, and June—before the sirocco blows in from the south. Cole Porter, who had honeymooned here in 1919, returned as a widower in 1956 and declared it still a "breathtaking sight."

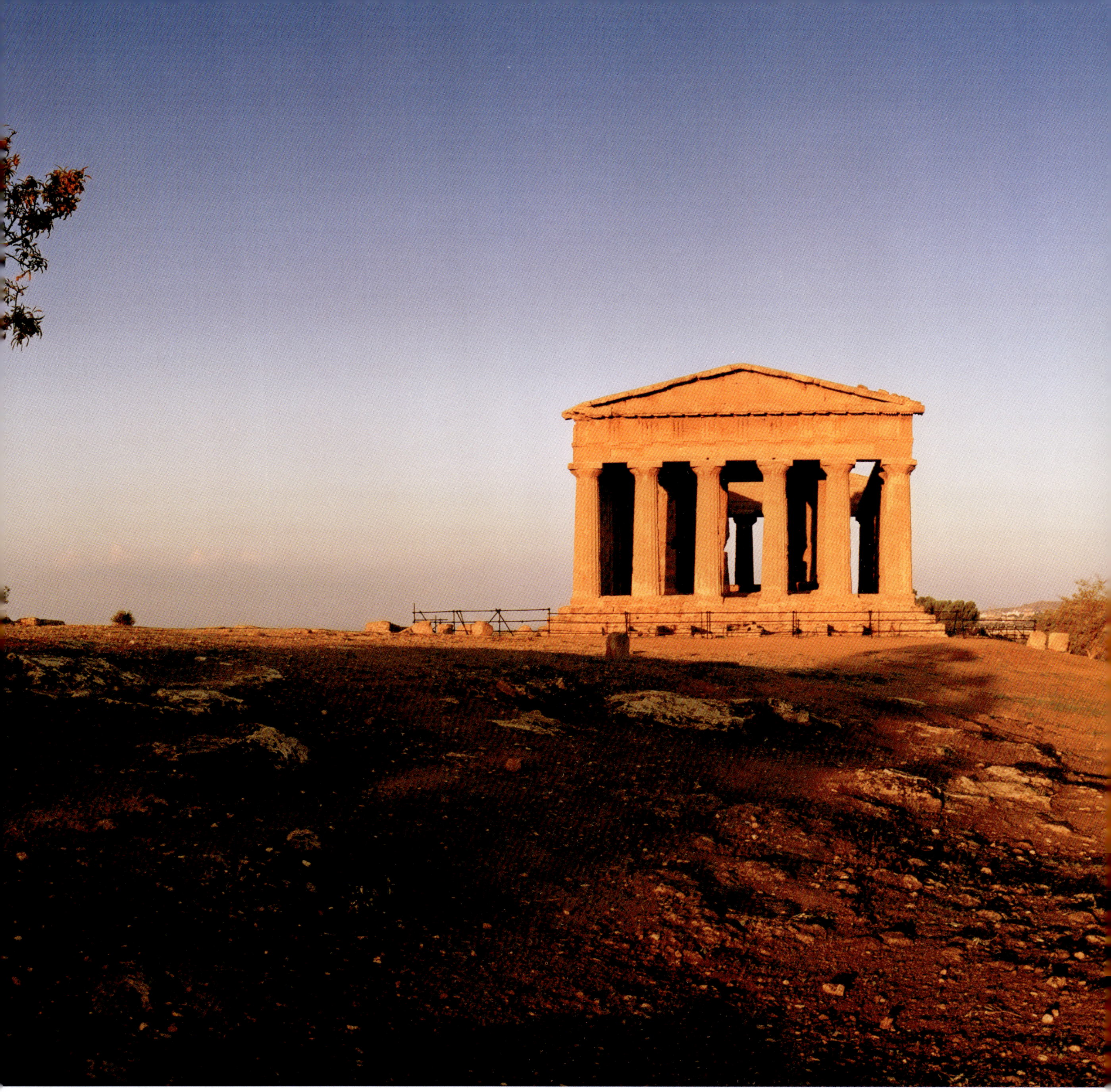

W ith soiree after soiree filling your evenings, life has been so exhausting. You were in town for the—what was it, $20 million? $40 million?—grand-opening party in fall '08 for a resort whose construction costs were well over a billion dollars. You were gobsmacked by the fireworks, which made the Summer Olympics ceremony look like a backyard barbecue. Not to mention the nearly four thousand pounds of lobster served by five hundred chefs and a thousand waiters. Maybe you got to meet the Bollywood beauty who reigned as party goddess. Or caught an antipodean sex kitten onstage, who was paid between—reports vary—$1 million and $4 million to spice up the event. And now—la, la, la, la-la, la-la-la—you can't get her out of your head.

Today, you're relaxing on the terrace of the resort's $25,000-plus-a-night suite. You arrived via a six-lane tunnel or a three-mile-long ultraquiet monorail, and you passed a fantastical thirty-five-foot-high glass lobby sculpture before entering your private elevator. A coterie of international chefs with seven

Michelin stars among them have set up kitchens on-site. You also enjoy a dedicated butler at your beck and call 24/7. Should you wish to move about the grounds (although why would you?), you can zoom ninety steep feet down a slide that drops you through a sharky lagoon and walk through an aquarium without getting wet.

A South African is responsible for this megaproperty, while the Dutch—who else?—reclaimed the land upon which it was built, putting an end to a putative beach shortage. Before you stretches a brand-new community of villas and luxury shops. On the coast in the distance, those high-rises follow a sort of Magnificent Mile. Your view also takes in the full sail of a newish hotel with starburst stature. By the look of things, you may never have to explore farther than your balcony.

You are at the center of the universe. Well, when you enter this geodesic sphere in a moment, you will find yourself at the center of a universe. The hundred-foot-in-diameter Epcot-like orb before you serves as the devotional core of a utopian hamlet. After you've absorbed a bit of the temple vibe, you can sit under an enormous sacred tree, a member of the fig family, and ponder whether to move to this unorthodox community. While this society espouses a humble creed and lifestyle, it's devised a whopper of a high-tech contraption. A computer on the rooftop rotates a lens that directs sunlight down to a marble chamber with nothing in it but white merino wool carpets and a crystal ball—not a Wizard of Oz crystal ball but a 2,400-pound globe polished by Zeiss and delivered here at great expense. The larger of the 1,400 stainless steel disks that shroud the dome weigh almost 500 pounds apiece. Applying the gold leaf required calling in a master gilder all the way from Germany.

The globe was the vision of the matriarch who founded this collective in the sixties. Born a Sephardic Jew, she became, in her adopted country, a disciple of an early-twentieth-century nationalist provocateur turned spiritual leader. Half of the several thousand adherents here have non-native names like, say, Gilles, Francesca, or Wolfgang. These expats come to study dance, sculpture, and painting. They practice organic farming and use solar energy, and some live in thatched huts. If you wish to stay on, you can always become a short-term volunteer. However, you'll need to leave your big-city ways behind, since drinking and smoking are not tolerated (never mind that you might detect a whiff of hippie about the residents). On the plus side, the friendly restaurant touts "ridiculously low prices."

Less than ten miles to the south lies a Francophone former colonial territory that itself is an enclave. Until recently, it was a sleepy place; today, a few eighteenth-century villas have been converted into restaurants and small hotels, and a luxury train makes a scheduled stop here. The city's oceanfront promenade leads to some tranquil and inviting beaches (who could resist swimming at Serenity strand?).

The dome you came to see, just completed in 2010 after forty years of labor, fits and reflects its environment well—yet some detractors have called it a golf ball. As with all utopian ideals, the reality is far from perfect.

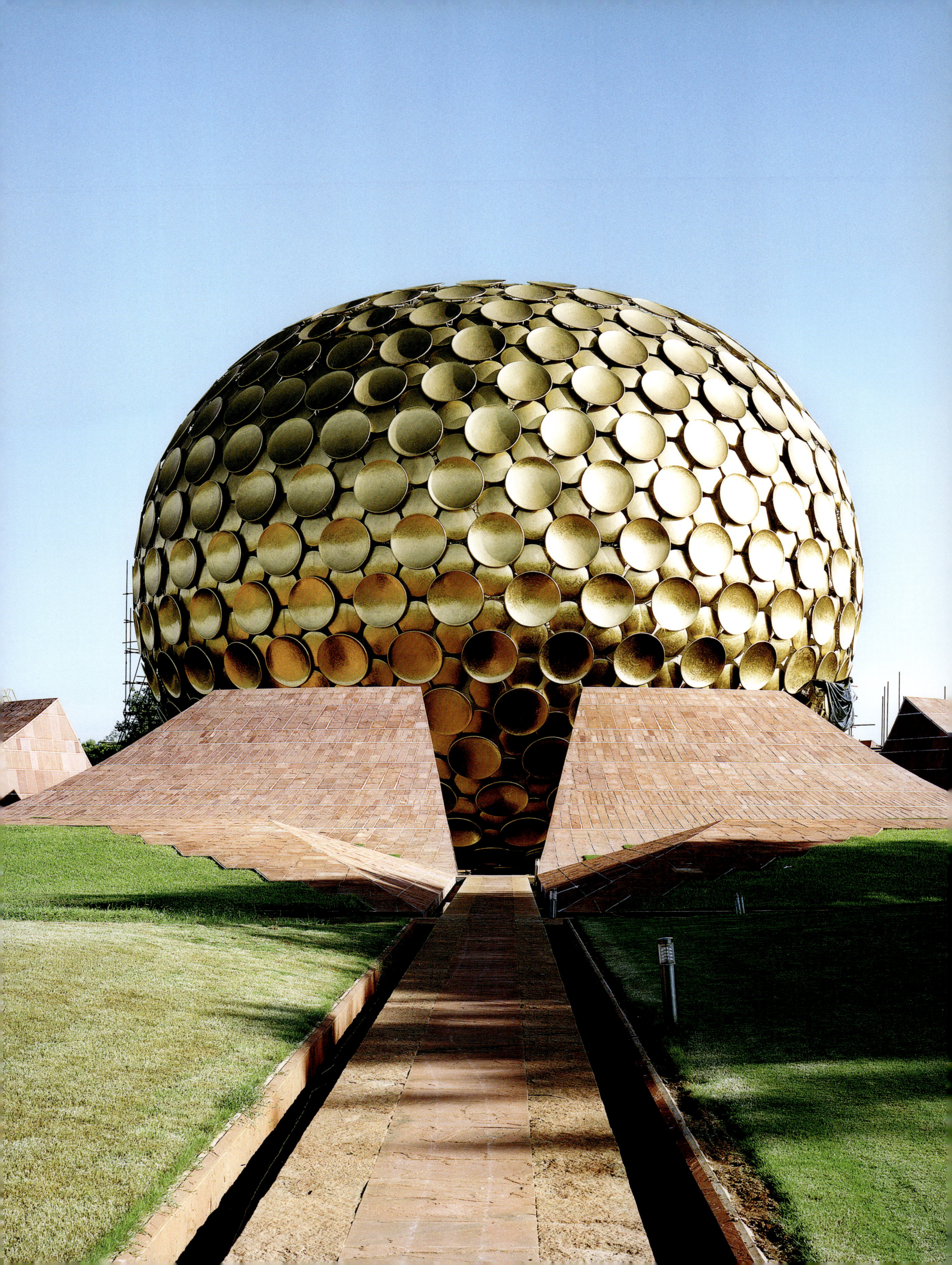

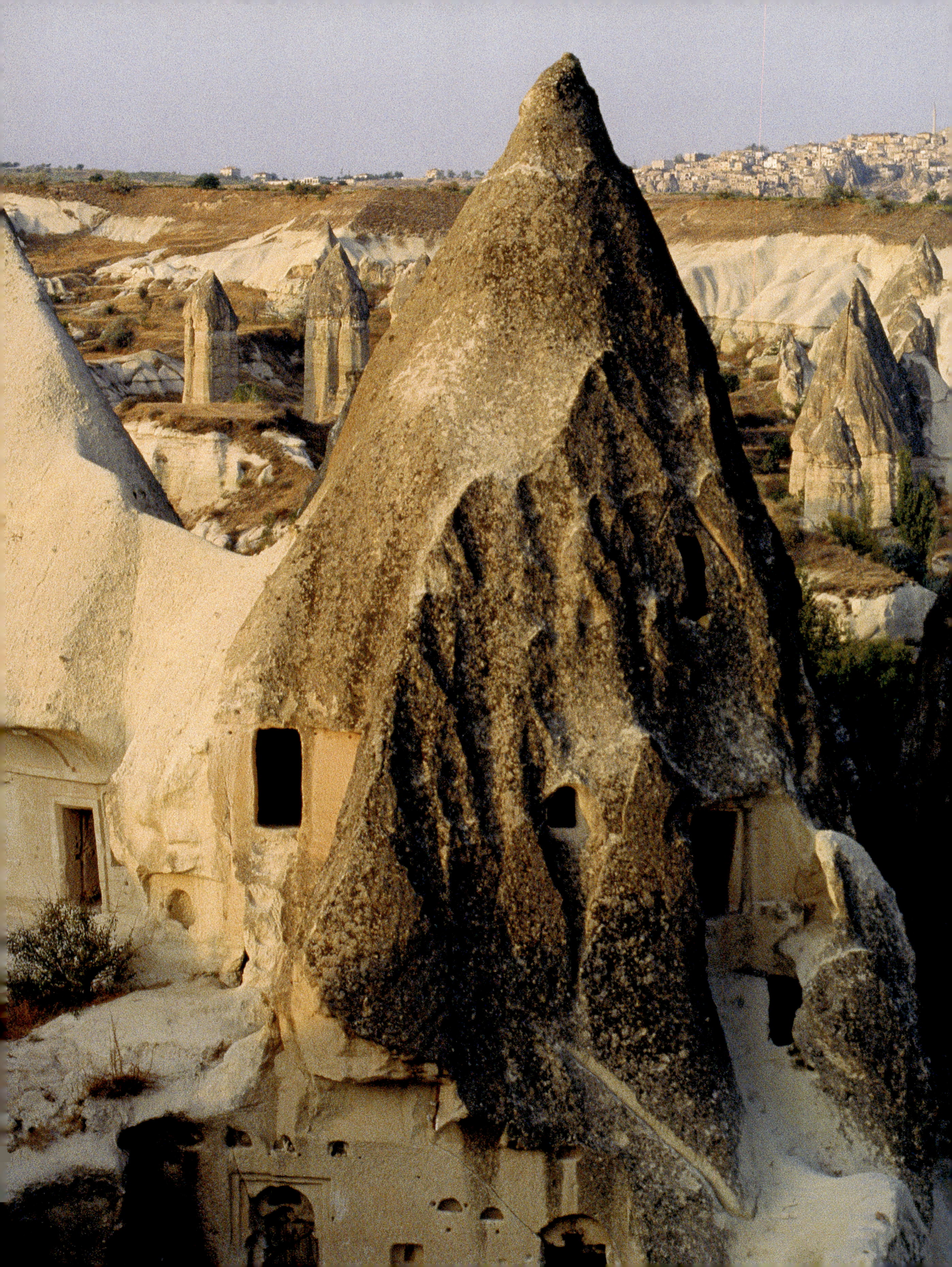

You are at the outskirts of an ancient village, 4,943 miles from the head of the Appalachian Trail. The recipe for this surreal landscape would be difficult to reproduce (kids, don't try this at home): Flood a valley with the magma from three volcanoes, shake vigorously (read: earthquake), and leave uncovered for several millennia. The result—soft volcanic rock sculpted into eccentric shapes such as these—draws thousands of visitors each year, most from April to November, when temperatures rarely dip below the freezing mark. The Jesuit scholar Guillaume de Jerphanion proclaimed this "the most fantastic of all landscapes," despite its austere countenance. The three conical formations shown here (the native name for this village translates to English as "three castles") were once gutted like Halloween gourds to provide refuge in an area where wood is scarce and the weather extreme. Today they are tourist traps and pigeon cotes, the guano from which is used to fertilize groves of apples, pears, plums, and walnuts. This area was a satrapy of the Persian Empire before being taken by Alexander the Great in 333 B.C. Three hundred fifty years later this region fell to the Romans. Indeed, it was just 130 miles north of here that Caesar, with customary humility, had declared: "I came. I saw. I conquered."

The two-hundred-foot waterfall facing you across the moor is the last cascade in a series of twenty. Treasure supposedly hidden behind it by a settler hundreds of years ago has never been found. Although ten thousand falls are scattered around this island of glaciers and mountains, many without a name, this one goes by the word itself—the local term for waterfall—combined with the name of the town (home to a legendary folk museum) about sixteen hundred feet away. This island is a touch smaller than Kentucky and has less than one-tenth the population. The first settlers arrived more than a thousand years ago, a time when the only land mammals here were foxes, and the people remained ethnically homogeneous until recently. Such purity may be the root of a national law requiring immigrants to adopt a local name before being granted citizenship. Two-thirds of the inhabitants call the Bay of Smokes (eighty-seven miles northwest of this spot) home; strong beer, however, is just a drink that, since 1989, has flowed freely—much like this colossal body of liquid thundering to the fore.

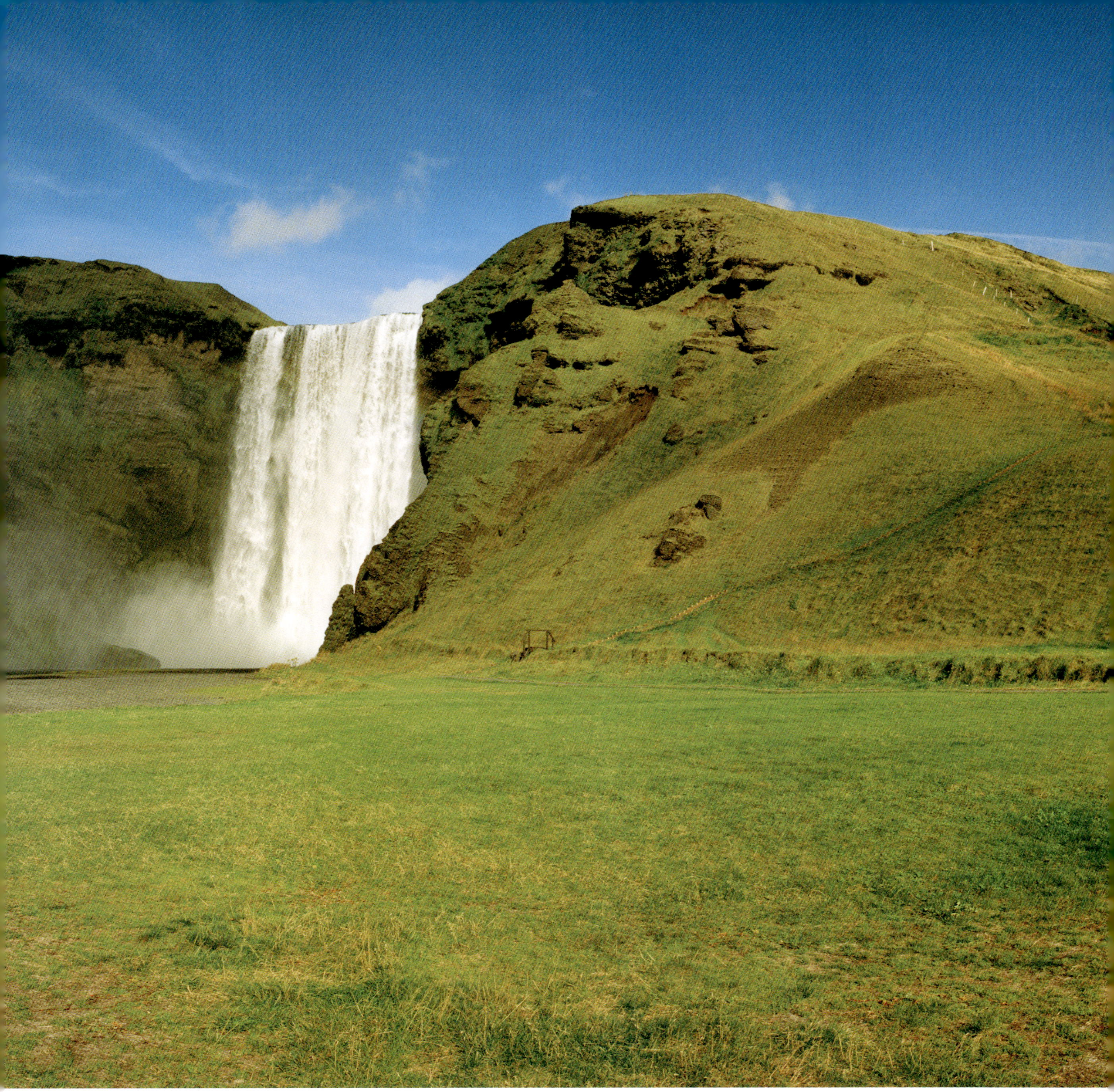

t is hot. The sun bakes. Chalk crunches under your feet. You're faint from last night's fete in the main square of a town that lies behind thick medieval ashlar walls. A cathedral mirage ripples before you. Aluminum stings your eyes. You want to crawl back to town and cool down in a deep stone wine cavern. Slowly you take the path into the winery. Funny, the word they use . . . it's what New Yorkers call the place on the corner where they get their daily bread and milk.

Last night you wandered the two-thousand-foot-high town with the big-city-airport name. Men with saddle leather tans told you the wine region has gotten rich since the old goat died years ago. They filled one "little cup" after another and recited "The Cicada and the Ant" and the "The Old Man and Death." A parable with backbone, you think of the latter. You downed cups until sacramental red splashed the cobblestones. Then, you got up from your comfortable wicker chair. You followed the "hill walk" around the village to the poet's bust. You do not know what time you got to bed in your awfully clean hotel. You can still smell the red peppers that hang from balconies. An Englishman, you read, compared the national music to the "beating of a frying pan, to call down a swarm of bees." Hardwood shells clack softly in your headphones. The mountains divide the cool north from the dry plateau. You wonder if separatists hide up there. Their name makes you think of an estimated time of arrival. That's crazy … they really are a swell people. An old man with stubble and long, sunburned hair tells you the river divided two empires and gave its name to the peninsula. A regional capital has a horse statue with mighty cojones. Go to another town, he says. Calm caped men there perform smoothly and beautifully. Make the pilgrimage north to a titanium master's museum.

You remember that the creator of the winery lives in the Alps. You know his works in the Midwest, and in his hometown on the sea. You eat "thorns" and your strength comes back. The fog in your head burns off. Clarity and vision return. It's time for the tasting. Time, as you learned in Acapulco, to *curarse la cruda*.

You have not come upon a place of worship for mermaids or divers, even though this partially submerged tower is the pinnacle of a church. The edifice was the tallest in a small village of about five hundred souls that existed unremarkably for years in a valley surrounded by mountains. In the 1830s, the people built the sanctuary adjoining the tower, which, despite being waterlogged, celebrates its six-hundred-and-forty-fifth anniversary this year. But the unstoppable force of progress molded the hamlet's destiny: A hydroelectric project completed in 1950 resulted in this postapocalyptic landscape—a dam and its artificial lake, the watery grave of the ancient village. The residents lost swaths of agricultural land, and they resettled on the slopes-turned-shore at the new water level.

There is, however, a happy ending to this tale of woe. The surreal sight has become a popular tourist stop, and the surrounding area attracts hikers and mountain bikers with its alpine scenery and rugged climbs. These waters are less than 10 miles from the borders of two countries—one to the north, the other to the west—yet 360 miles from the nation's capital. Such positioning may explain why the language local folk speak is not the national tongue but an idiom officially spoken elsewhere on the continent, causing most places (including this lake) to have names in both. Its province is one-half of an administrative region and has an abundance of wineries (there are forty vines for every person), fresco-filled castles, and Gothic churches. The country—a touch larger than Arizona—was once described by a British poet as "a paradise inhabited by devils." You might find yourself agreeing, as you ponder a church drowned for a dammed lake.

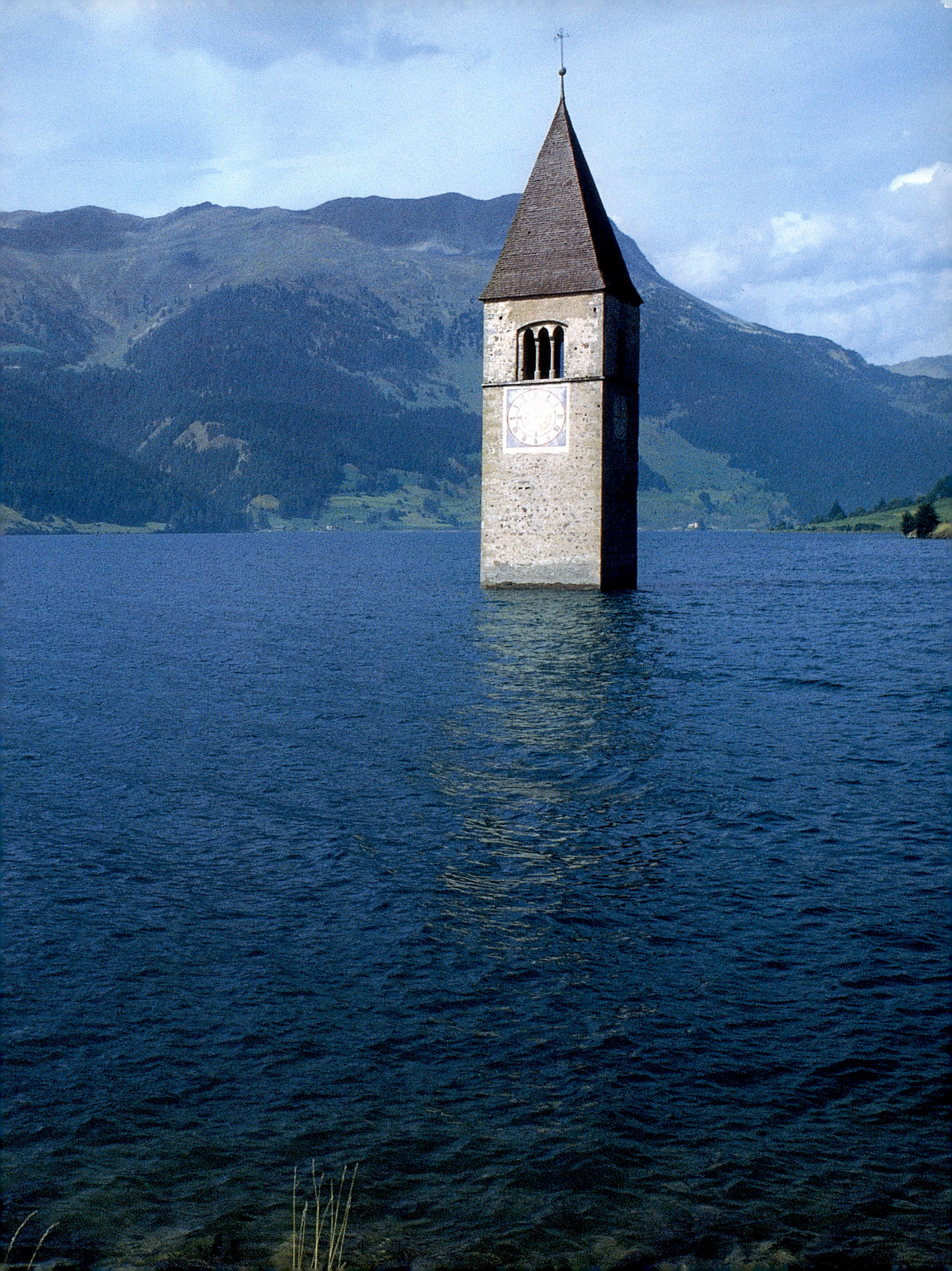

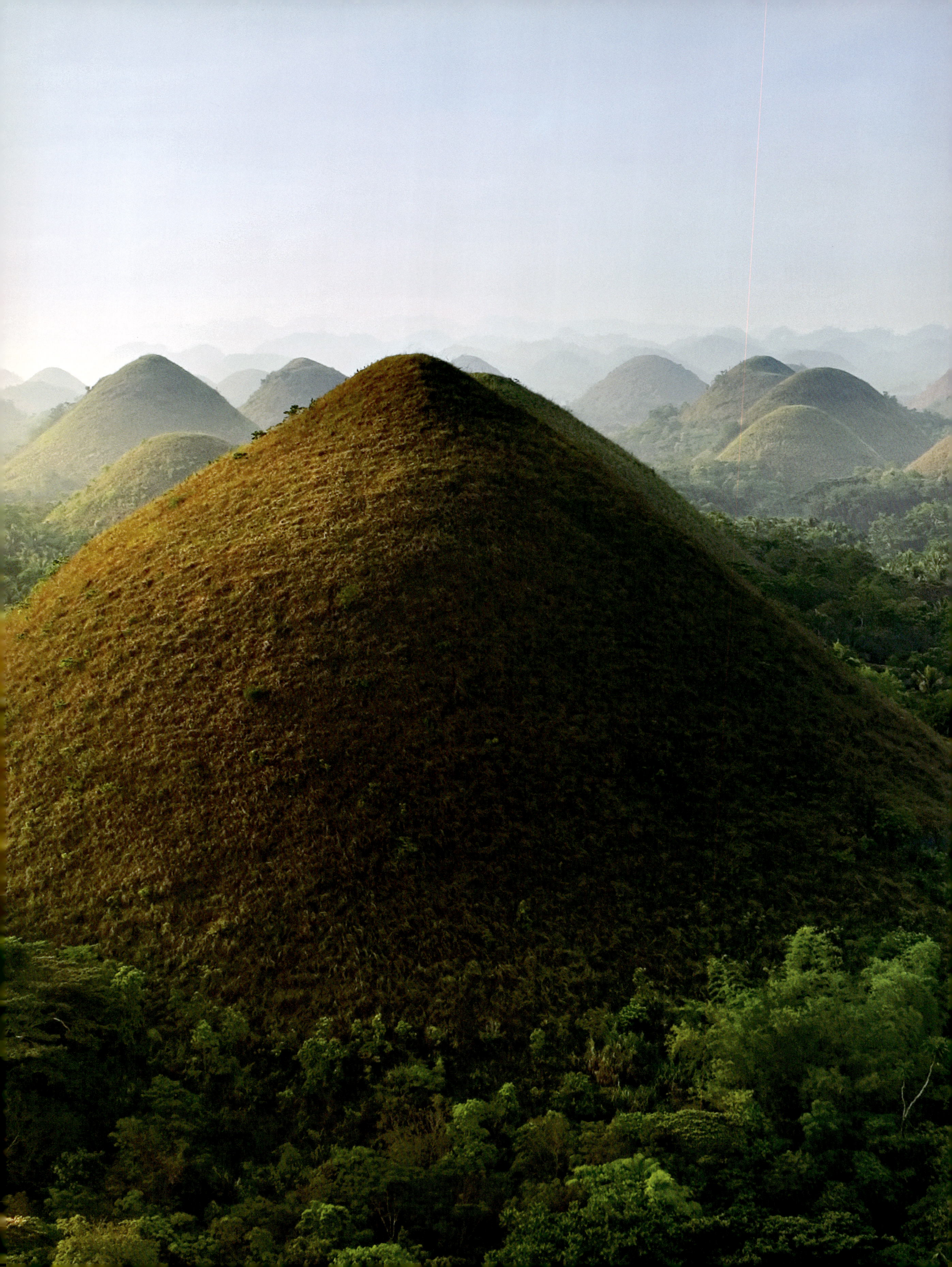

Our ocular perception is ambiguous and malleable, cognitive psychologists say. We see what we want to see. Maybe you divine ginormous anthills in the haycock shapes before you, or great Indian mounds of the Midwest. Or did your visual cortex just trick you into thinking that the landscape belongs to a wondrous new California mini-ecosystem? Then again, you might fancy you're frolicking through an adult Teletubby world. (But what to make of those visitors who blog that they see breasts? Calling Dr. Freud . . .) In the dry season, when the hills turn completely brown, phone the Hershey company and tell them they can shoot a Roald Dahl–esque advert in a place where truffle-filled Kisses are sprinkled as far as the eye can see.

Anywhere between twelve hundred and seventeen hundred of these hillocks dot a twenty-square-mile area (what prevents them from being counted accurately is anyone's guess). In the wet season, the slopes are blanketed by cogon, a grass that recently migrated to North America and grows so fast that it makes kudzu look like a houseplant. You have arrived here from a town whose name might have inspired you to hum the "Habanera" on the way over: anything to distract you from having to cuddle with four or five other passengers on the back of the moto-taxi you took; anything to put some pep in your stride as you trudge up hundreds of steps to the viewing platform.

You are in the middle of an island in the middle of an archipelago. The Spanish once called the inhabitants the "tattooed ones." Today, most of the people here look to Rome for spiritual guidance, while a small number face the Kaaba. The oldest of their many charming churches is made of coral stone. In another kind of sanctuary, you'll discover a palm-size nocturnal primate whose freakishly enormous eyes give it an ET visage. Locals adore their festivals here; if you're lucky, the one devoted to yams will feature a no-holds-barred eating contest.

Legend has it that these hills are a lovelorn giant's tears. In truth, they're made of marine limestone. Authorities are now packaging the island as an eco-tourism destination—but what isn't these days? If you find the claim a stretch, you be the one to tell them that they're making mountains out of molehills.

In the summer of 2008, millions of visitors walked across the new marvel before you to a sixty-acre fairground. A famous troubadour sang about intense precipitation at the opening ceremony of the three-month-long event, but even so, the fair's theme—the fragility of the planet's H_2O supply— didn't much register on our poll-addled brains. You are admiring this nine-hundred-foot span from a small island that bears half the load. The architect, whose work you've gotten to know well in recent years, was given a cool $77 million to interweave four pods, which double as exhibition spaces. The 29,000 exterior panels are meant to evoke sharkskin, while the entire structure is said to look like a gladiolus in the process of opening. Or maybe you see more of a caterpillar inching forward. In any case, the interiors do have a cocoonlike feel. One guidebook calls this city "the nicest of places." How boring is that.... For a more stimulating experience, you might search out some seasoned local guides. Listen closely as they warn you that the temperature in this hot place can drop below zero degrees centigrade. Their city was named for an emperor, they'll explain, and maybe they'll even share civil war stories. Certainly, they are grateful for the thumbs-up reception given their new railway station.

This region, where a revered brick-and-tile architectural style evolved, has a royally powerful past. An eighteenth-century painter who depicted the terrors of war on paper was born thirty miles to the south of the city (you've seen his name in your supermarket). A vicious battle in the last century destroyed a nearby village, which was deliberately left in ruins as a memorial.

One critic declared this bridge a Ponte Vecchio for our age. The traffic won't involve jewelry, though. After the fair a bank took over the span. Talk about a walk on the wild side.

Be careful how you step, for you are 18,500 feet above sea level, on a mountain that shall remain nameless. The range before you extends three hundred miles and slices the borders of four countries. The product of an immense geologic folding that began 65 million years ago, these towering peaks and glaciated valleys form a natural northern border of a young nation. If you were to make your way south, your explorations would take you through gentler valleys that were home in the twentieth century B.C. to a literate civilization that thrived on sea trade until it met a sudden, unfathomable end. In the twentieth century, the society grew and collapsed again, its population swelling by almost two percent a year despite an infant mortality rate of nearly one in ten. Whereas literacy was once burgeoning, today just more than half the country's adults can read and write. The land is plagued by deteriorating infrastructure and political violence. The outlook for the mountain people you may have encountered on your climb up seems equally grim—they struggle to survive, eking out a meager nomadic existence as farmers of barley, oats, and millet. What does the future hold? Some in this region seek to ensure progress through military security. But caution is the key—one slip and it's a long way down.

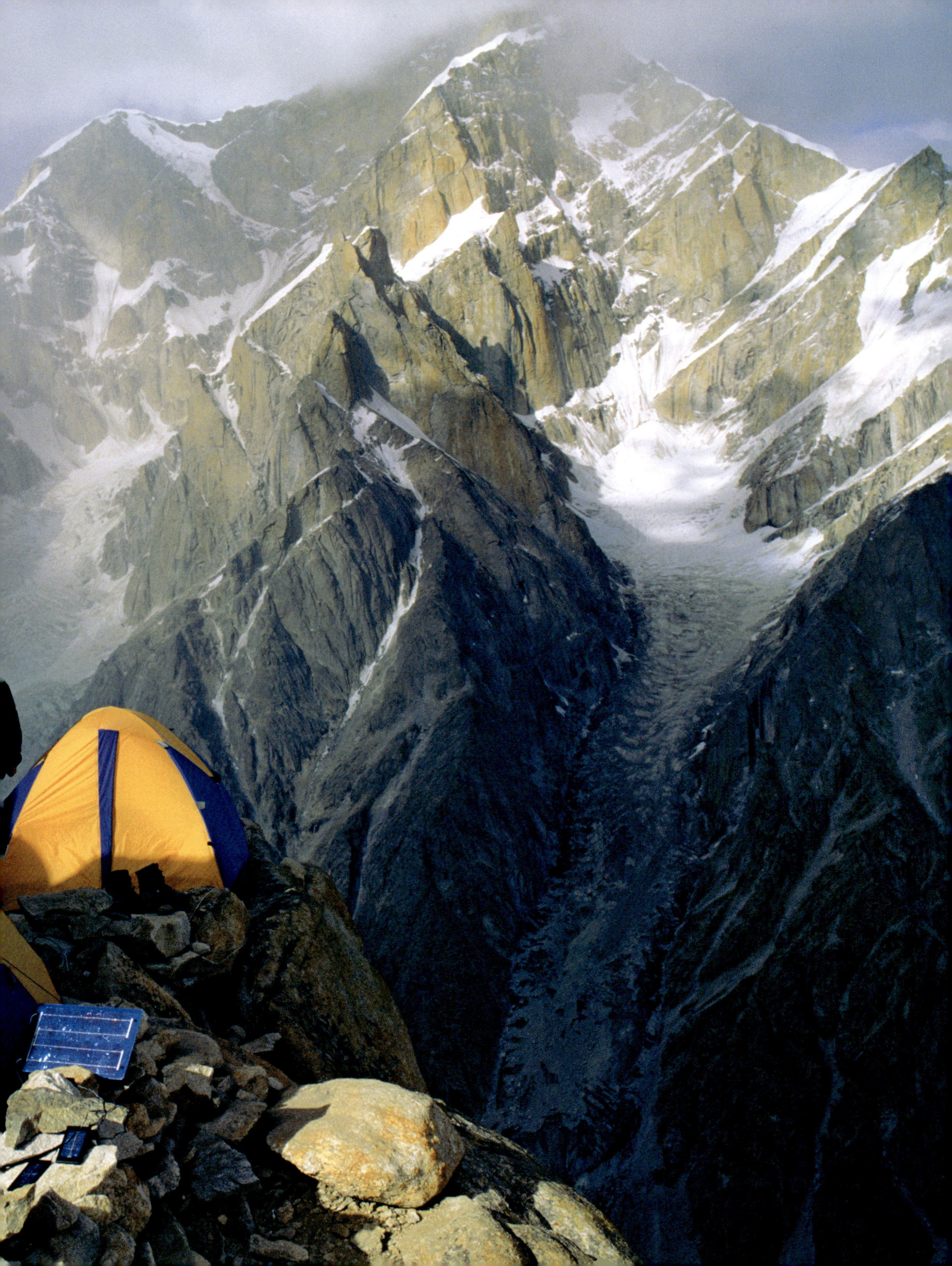

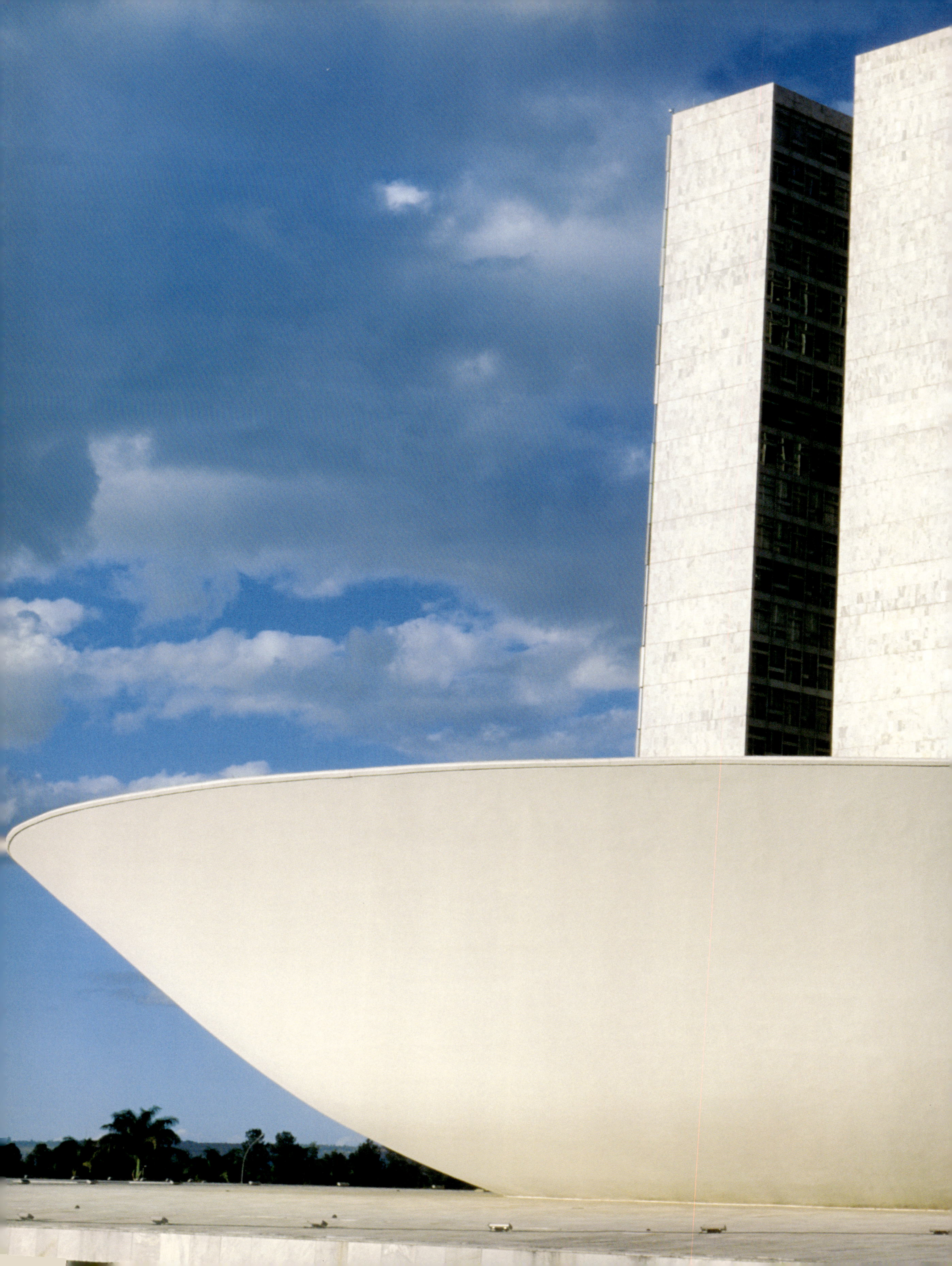

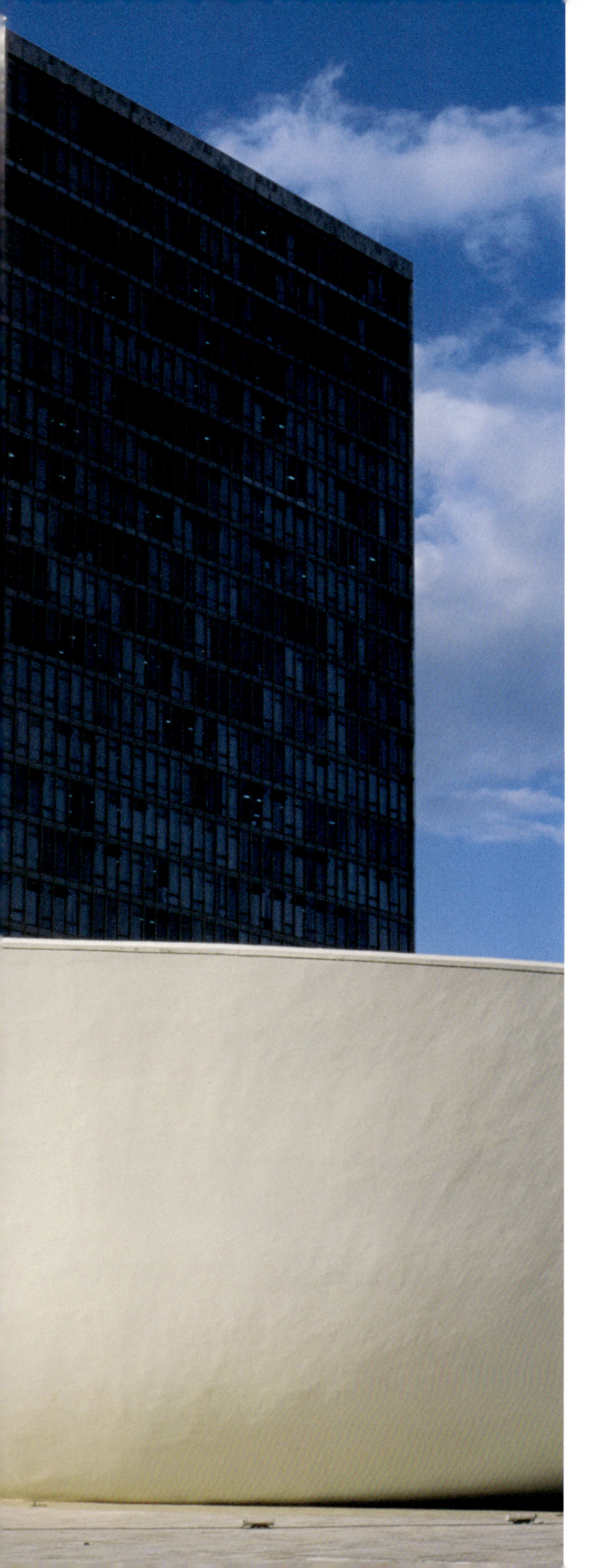

Just add people and stir. The monumental twins rising before you are part of the congressional building of this country's capital city, which was created ex nihilo fifty years ago and has since attracted more than two million inhabitants. A democratically elected president—you might think he was Polish, given his name—conceived this futuristic outpost on the plains as a sort of promised land, one that would unify the nation and sever its old-world ties. The military swooped in some years after the inauguration of the city, however, and a junta camped out for twenty years. The nation ultimately emerged as a federal republic, with colorful leaders including a one-time minister of culture who is a world-renowned songwriter and guitarist. If you're lucky, he might be in town singing in his mellifluous native language.

Most likely, you began your journey to the capital in the coastal metropolis to the south that happens to be the birthplace of the architect responsible for these towers. A winner of his discipline's Oscar nearly twenty years ago, the maestro returned to his hometown some time ago, and his work is enjoying a revival as he approaches his ninety-ninth birthday. Perhaps you even passed him in his celebrated neighborhood while on your way to admire the "dental floss" beauties cavorting on the beach. Or maybe you spotted him in a café, parked in front of a TV: Like his compatriots, he no doubt has his eyes on the pitch as his country prepares every fourth summer to kick derriere—or should we say winter? And surely you toured the spaceship-like contemporary art museum that he designed a decade ago on a promontory across the bay.

Staring at these administrative buildings, you are the victim of an optical illusion: They don't really sprout out of the bowl—which is the chamber of deputies—but share an esplanade with it and with a dome that houses the senate. Gazing upon the surrounding urban landscape as it began to take shape, one journalist described it as "a strident chord in a desert of silence . . . [a] Daliesque perspective to an improbable horizon." Many observers have since proclaimed the entire master plan a catastrophe: Its citizenry is trapped by the sweltering heat in air-con isolation and is forced into cars by distances too vast to walk (sound familiar?). Perhaps the whole conceit was a delusion. If it's utopia you seek, dream on.

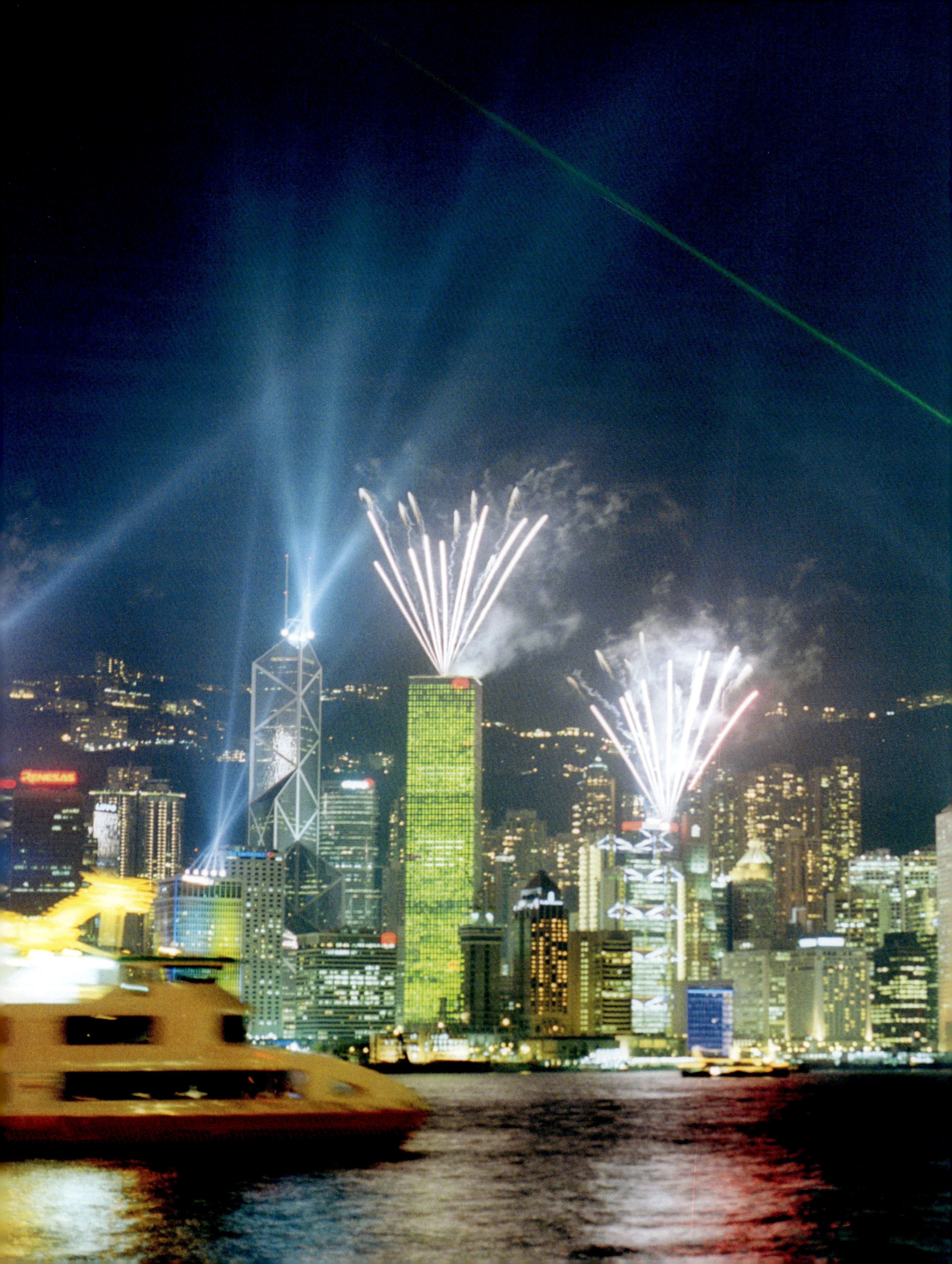

Early in the last century a viscount wrote that this city "illuminated . . . is wonderful. Imagine a giant Monte Carlo with a hundred times as many lights." He was prescient. Today, the town is a thousand times brighter, and laser light shows like the one you're enjoying are a nightly spectacle—the pyrotechnics an occasional bonus.

You are joyriding on one of the myriad ferries and hydrofoils that crisscross this great harbor like so many paddles of ducks on a pond— an apt metaphor considering that most visitors have a fowl experience here (with some even taking a dim view of the savory cuisine).

The district behind you is a stepchild of the glittering one before you, which a mid-nineteenth-century lord called "a barren Island with hardly a House upon it" (not so prescient, that guy). The vertiginous cityscape was drafted by a who's who of international architects, whereas the larger territory spreads out in a geographic jumble of islands and channels, inlets and peninsulas, that will call to mind Rorschach's inkblots when you fly over it.

For entertainment, join the punters at the horse races, or catch a performance by one of the caterwauling, synthesized pop singers (second only to kick-ass movie stars in popularity in these parts). You're visiting a land of luxe and of contradictions, where sky trams and endless escalators are public transport but seventy percent of the region remains blessedly undeveloped. Indeed, you can hike in twenty-three parks and visit wetlands, car-free islands, and some forty beaches. The largest island hosts a new high-tech airport and a theme park yet has a peak where many seek a path to enlightenment.

You won't have to look hard to find historic gems such as gas lamps and a refurbished redbrick market tucked away in the shadows of these glitzy edifices. And that clacking sound you hear as you wander? It's double-decker trams trundling along streets with quaint Victorian names. Step into one of the popular smoky game parlors if you want to ring in the new year with a real bang.

Y ou are about five thousand feet above sea level, on the side of a mountain—whose name is six letters long— popular with hikers, bikers, and downhill skiers. But that you know, having hiked three hours from the village below (the less ambitious take the chairlift). You are taking some shade under part of a modernist concrete structure, standing below the pathway that leads to its entrance. Commissioned by a local businessman to honor his wife, designed by a local architect, and built in the 1990s, this curious geometric vision uses the curve of a double staircase (those steps in front of you) to embrace a mountaintop refuge. Once you enter, you discover a chapel with several frescoes, including one of two large hands joined in a sign of offering.

This house of prayer sits alongside a restaurant and a children's playground in an alpine region where the official language is one of a handful of national tongues. The region, whose name also has six letters, is home to about four percent of the country's population. An American traveler described the nation—long praised for its strong, bankable economy and peaceful society, where most of the citizens are divided into two branches of the same religion—as "a large, humpy, solid rock, with a thin skin of grass stretched over it." Here there's always a reason to put one's trust in the hands of the Almighty.

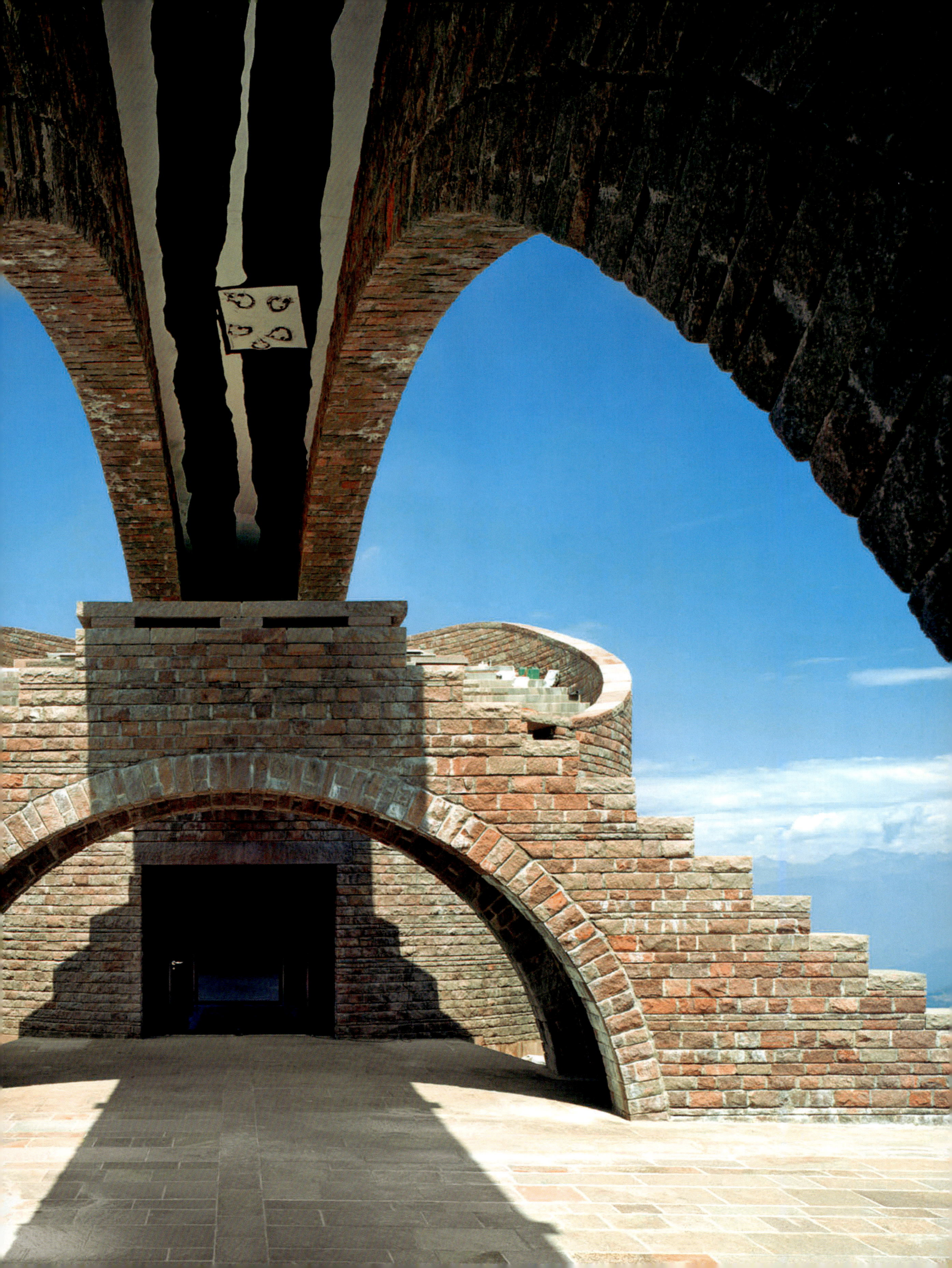

Y ou have come upon a solitary ancient dwelling aglow with the sun's fading light. Crafted from the sandstone of the remote outcropping on which it sits, this remarkably well-preserved ruin—whose name means "Big House"—served as a home to three families who belonged to a people remarkable for their seeming ability to survive without water. This culture flourished around here for four hundred years, before a volcanic eruption in the eleventh century blanketed their land with lava and rock and sent them fleeing. Decades later, they returned (as did neighboring societies), only to leave again after a little more than a century. If you were to roam the surrounding fifty-six square miles, you would discover that this outlandishly positioned house is but one of more than 2,600 remnants of these civilizations. The largest one, called Long Cut House, has about a hundred rooms and many stories; it stands a couple of miles behind you.

For centuries, the ruins were visited only by jackrabbits and antelopes. Then, in the 1800s, nomads began camping in them with their flocks of sheep.

Later, looters ravaged the ruins for pottery and timber. Finally, about seventy-five years ago, the wrath of locals intent on preserving these archaeological remains brought about the creation of a 35,422-acre monument.

Today, this national treasure draws 500,000 visitors a year. Many stop as they travel between a geological spectacle to the northwest (where to stand at the edge "is to enjoy in a moment compensation for years of uneventful life," according to a twentieth-century historian) and the seat of the second-largest county in this nation.

The diverse terrain in these parts ranges from arid desert valleys and plains to expansive forests with raging mountain streams. The average elevation is four thousand feet, the humidity is low, the sunshine is abundant year-round, and it's far from the madding crowd, with only about five or so people per square mile. All of which might explain why someone thought to build a house in what seems, at first glance, to be the middle of nowhere.

Hey, weekend warrior, from the looks of that column of rudimentary huts before you, now is your big chance for a bivouacking adventure in the woods. You know, get some survival training, learn to dogsled, swim in ice holes. When you're ready to really cut loose, just rev up that 1000cc snowmachine.

No, you're not anywhere near Wasilla, Alaska; rather, you're in a region whose cultural scope is multinational. Recently, when troops from a coalition practiced war games west of here, it was much to the displeasure of indigenous local herders. "Utterly unlearned," wrote a sixteenth-century English poet and ambassador about the ethnic group, and "for practice of Witch-craft and Sorcerie, they passe all Nations in the World." He wasn't nearly as slanderous, however, as an early-nineteenth-century mineralogist: "When inflamed by spirituous liquor," he claimed, "their intoxication betrays itself ... in raging lust, and total violation of all decency in their conduct."

Hardly dissolute today, these people are admired for their centuries-old handicraft skills; one artist even fashioned a silver trinket for a recent space voyage. To be sure, their countrymen at large have talent too, which they display in ruthless bouts of spouse toting and cell-phone throwing. Booyah!

If you return to these woods in the middle of summer, you can pick boletes and berries—it's a public right, after all. You can also enjoy a boat cruise on an enormous holy lake. Right now, though, you're about to check into a hotel where, in addition to these podlike accommodations, there are log cabins and tepees. To get to this frigid terrain, you took a twelve-hour train ride from the capital, followed by a four-hour drive. The reward for your efforts is a dinner of sautéed ruminant in the ice restaurant, or perhaps the chance to witness nuptials in the crystalline chapel. Despite the numbing nighttime temperatures, you'll be warm and snug in your pod as you scan the skies for a spectacular solar wind show. The whole shebang will leave you with an inner glow.

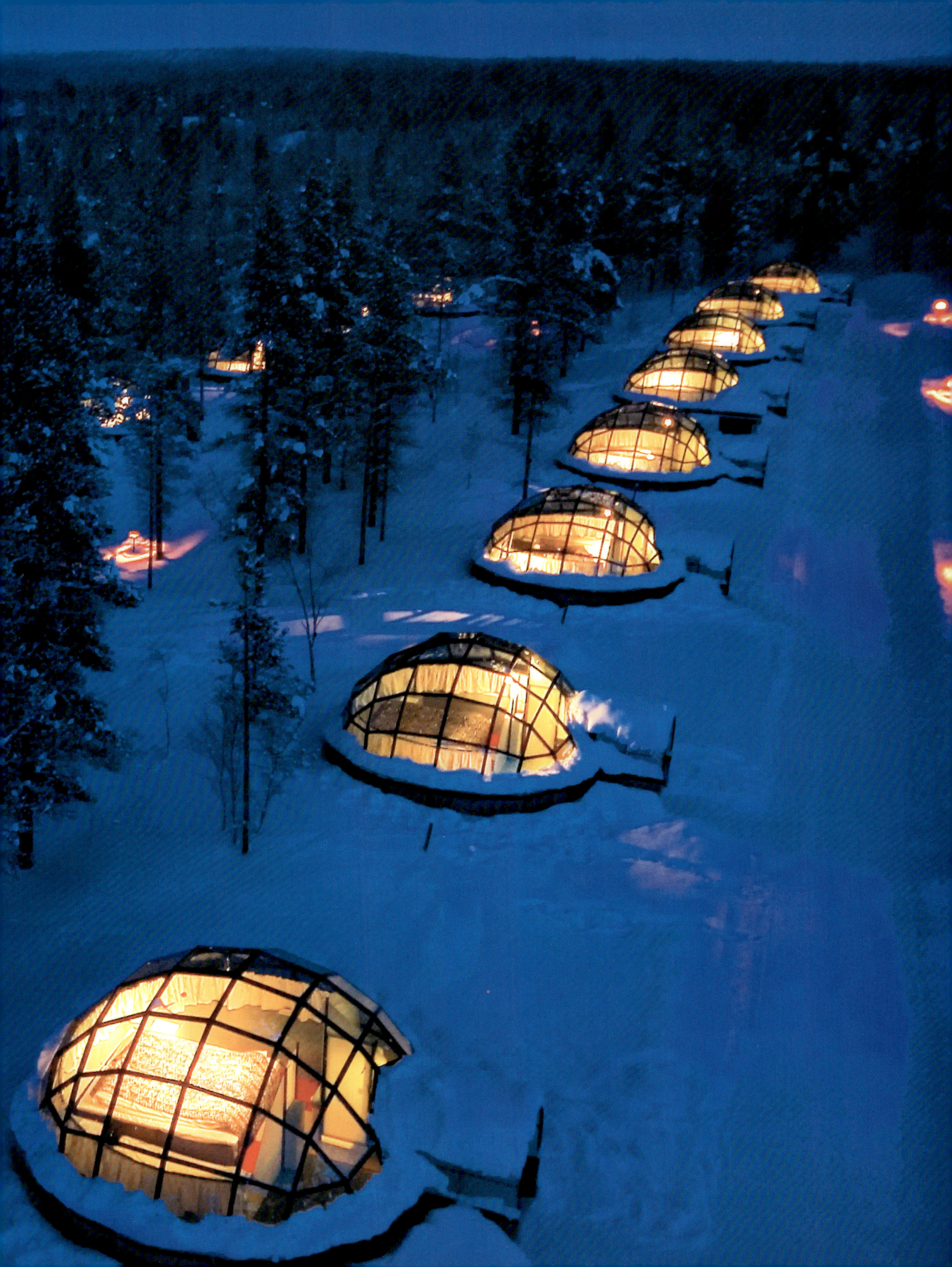

You are standing in a square at the heart of a city where byways, religions, and cultures have long collided and merged. Legend holds that an illustrious emperor arrived here in the third century B.C. His renunciation of war in favor of a spiritual pacifism established the "beautiful town" (the city's name at the time) as a haven of tolerance and a destination for pilgrims. Although the religion he embraced waned in influence, the city thrived—rulers in the seventeenth century went on a building spree, raising the multitude of sacred structures that surround you. Today, separated from a sprawling capital by a river, the city continues to embody its founder's credo. Since the late 1950s, it has harbored refugees from a neighboring land, whose work has made the city a leading center of handicraft production.

The acceptance of other cultures is fitting for this tiny country about twice the size of Ireland. For three thousand years, peoples have mixed here, settling amid its deep valleys and gargantuan mountains and spawning unique hybrids of religion and tongue. Yet not all the mingling has been welcome: With colonialists who had provoked a war here in 1814 remaining in power next door, the nation closed its borders for more than a century. Nearly fifty years ago, it partially reopened them, but not until this decade did it allow outsiders access to all areas. Tourists are now arriving in increasing numbers—making the crossroads before you once again an appropriate symbol for this ancient land.

Beep-beep! Is that the Road Runner zipping through the landscape, toward dwellings stamped ACME that will crumble with the push of a finger? Actually, it's a golf cart, and you're on the grounds of a much-celebrated resort. The guests are likely to be going to one of two golf courses or a tennis academy, all of which consistently rank among the best in this country.

To get here, perhaps you drove through the intersection of Ho and Hum in a tiny nearby municipality whose atmosphere is so tranquil that the founders could have called it Sans Souci—in fact they did, in a more prosaic manner.

Surely you noticed en route the copper-plated behemoth that dominates the town center. One of the world's largest sundials, it measures ninety feet in diameter. The thing not only tells time but heats water (a superfluous function, perhaps, in a place where temperatures can hit 122 degrees).

Eighty percent of the land in this territory is publicly owned, and the three-million-acre national forest abutting the resort is the country's fifth largest. Nearly six million people come here annually, apparently not put off by the forest's name, which translates as "stupid" in one local language. Right, Kemosabe?

If you can't sit still—beep-beep—the resort will organize day-trips on vintage trains or steamboats through the famous natural splendors that fill this region with the sonorous name, or take you for a drive on a fabled highway. It will even guarantee that there are no wily coyotes lying in wait.

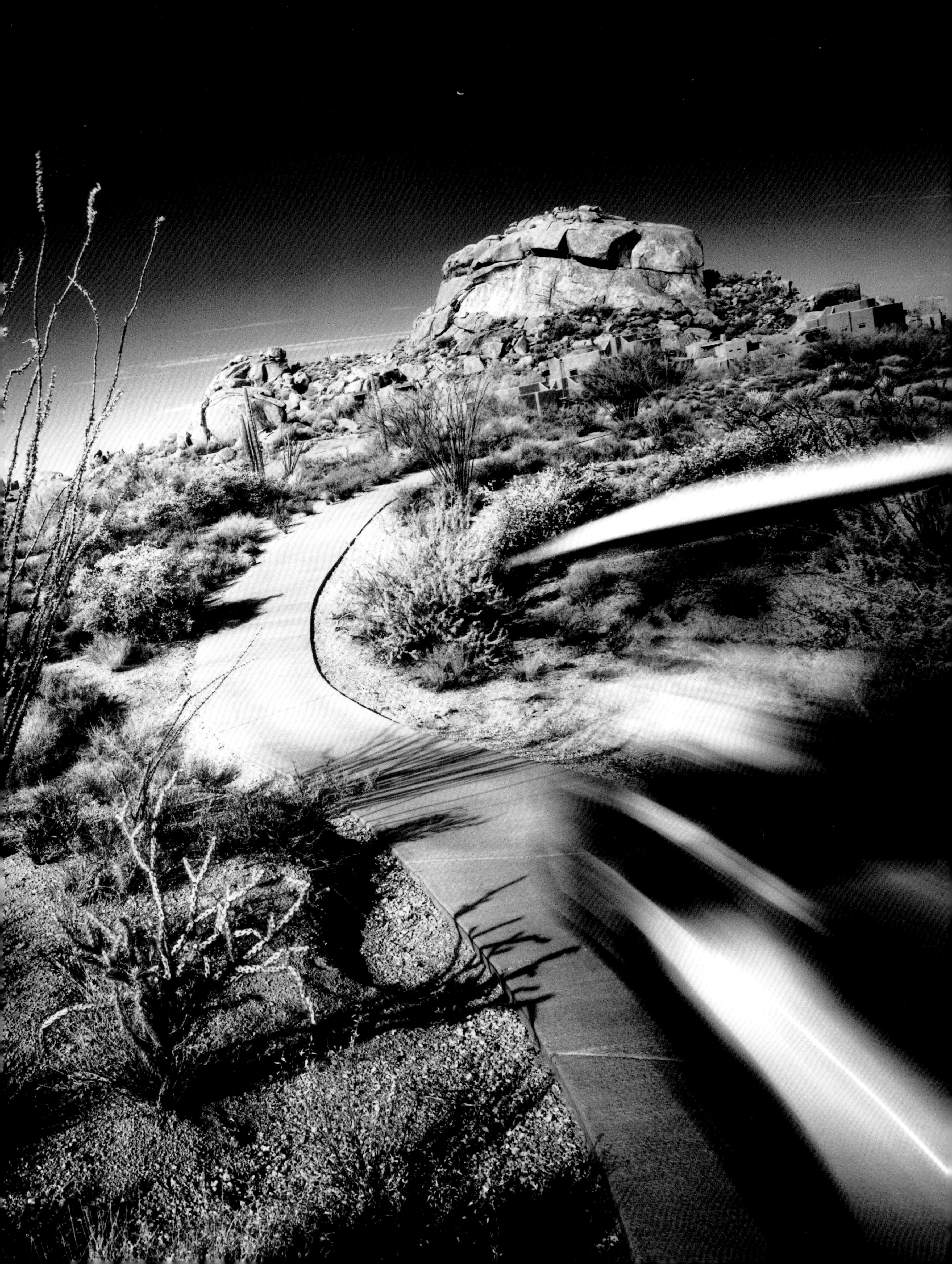

W**ell now, isn't this a fine mess.** A day of languorous river cruising is about to come to an abrupt and shattering end: Your vessel is on a collision course with a glass-and-steel leviathan. As you wonder at this glowing 320-ton latticework ensemble—the love child of Buckminster Fuller and Frank Gehry, perhaps?—you realize that it is a man-made island and that you can swing around it, under the bridge. Tragedy averted, you might prefer to continue downstream, the burg you are passing through being rather unknown anyway. But reconsider. Even if this place lacks your favorite things, it is the country's second most important city, with a quarter of a million inhabitants, and is packed with charm. Those towers in the distance, for instance, grace a church that is but one of many Baroque splendors, while on the left bank, a castle, a theater, and a cathedral crown a historic center which was recently granted World Heritage status. Forty thousand university students guarantee swinging nightlife; indeed, the school claims the continent's only jazz studies program.

A famed eighteenth-century political philosopher (who you could say was always humorous if not funny) wrote of the people in this province, "Very many of them have ugly swelld Throats: Idiots & Deaf People swarm in every Village." Today, the inhabitants' physical and spiritual health is much improved, thank you—maybe owing to the ancient thermal baths, the exceptional vineyards, and a major pilgrimage site, all of which you'll find less than an hour away. You might begin to suspect there is something in the water: Evidence, after all, includes a nearby stud farm that produces a prize breed of horses and a homegrown stud of the nonequine variety, who recently lent his name to the town's stadium.

You're about to skirt the complex's café/bar, but the folks inside would no doubt urge you to dock. Over drinks they would proudly tell you that this novel edifice was constructed early last year to celebrate the city's turn as the continent's cultural capital and that the rest of the structure is given over to exhibitions, an open-air theater, and a children's playground. So drop anchor and explore awhile. You can always go with the flow later.

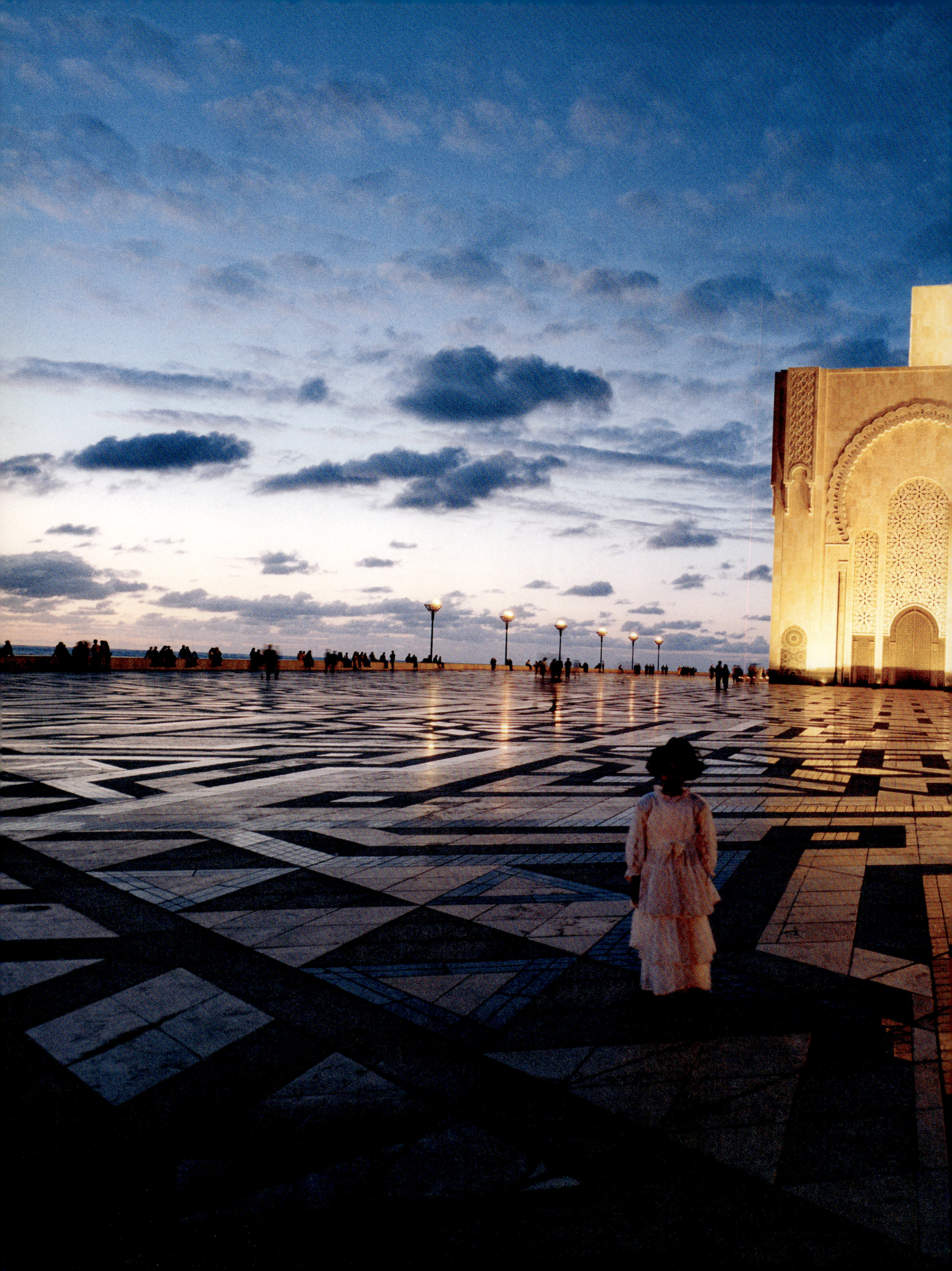

You are standing before an architectural triumph, a literal synthesis of centuries-old craftsmanship and state-of-the-art technology. One of the biggest religious monuments in the world—big enough to house the cathedral of Notre-Dame comfortably—it was constructed by order of a king who wanted to accomplish what a twelfth-century sultan had failed to do. In this city of extremes, where Art Deco boulevards coexist with sprawling tin-shack slums, it is also a symbol of a much-hoped-for urban renaissance.

Phoenician traders were the first recorded settlers of this area, arriving in the seventh century B.C. Latter-day citizens have drawn their heritage from a cultural fusion—not only from the major European powers that have ruled here, but also from an ancient race of warriors with obscure ethnic origins and fiercely insular tribal traditions. This colorful past has attracted numerous writers and artists to the country since the 1700s. Visiting in 1920, Edith Wharton wrote of "the dream-feeling that envelops one at every step." It's still here, along with the realities of the twentieth century (upon arrival, some express disappointment that so much modernity is in evidence). In particular, the city in which you find yourself is the prisoner of its own enduring image as a hotbed of romance and intrigue—an image that says less about this land of dreams than it does about Hollywood's power to create them.

The ancients came here to worship, seeking a higher spiritual plane and enlightenment. You are merely up in the air, jousting with thermals and gazing at a striking assemblage of temples. These intricate towers—whose walls recount an epic story in relief—are part of a complex named for a nearby village. Constructed about eleven hundred years ago, during an era when new religions were taking root in a land of dynastic kingdoms, they celebrate a military victory. The central structure was once the tallest building on this island, standing a grand 154 feet. Though dedicated to a multifaceted god, it is called Slender Maiden—in reference to a statue in the tower, said to be a virgin who was turned to stone for resisting marriage to a local prince. Concealed for centuries by grass, trees, and volcanic ash, these temples were rediscovered in the early 1800s and subsequently restored.

This spiky architectural feast lies on an island in a country of many hundreds of islands. The nation is rich in nature's bounty—nickel, copper, gold, silver, gas, oil, and fertile soil—so financial fortitude would seem assured. Even the name of the major city nearest this site (about eleven miles away) means "prosperity without war."

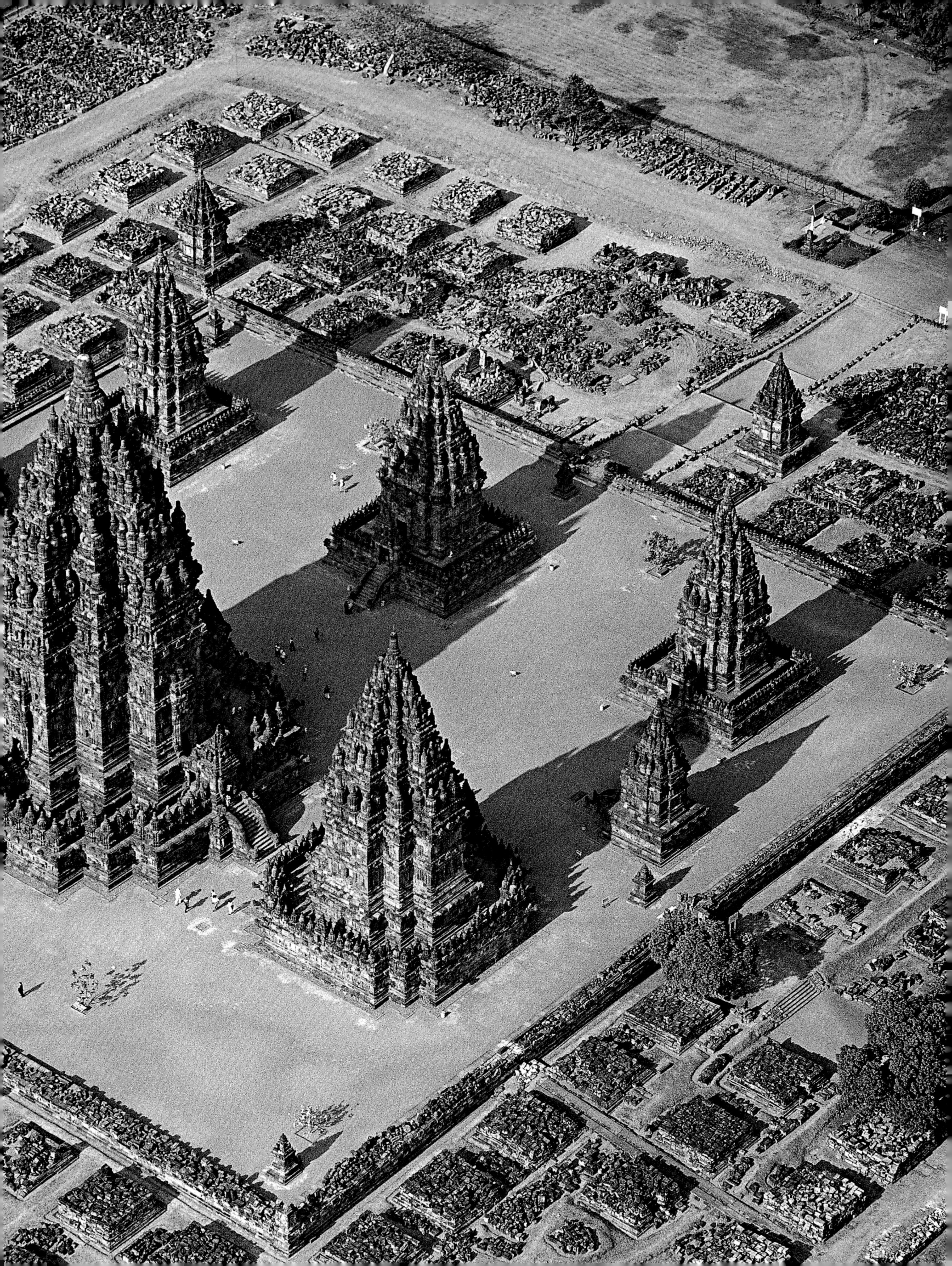

A rchitecture," Goethe wrote, "is frozen music." You're looking at a masterwork just a few notes short of completion (those temporary crimson piers were jettisoned when the bridge premiered at the end of 2004), a highly modern composition that was microcalibrated using Global Positioning System technology to splice together its seven massive sections.

According to an English novelist, every road in this country has "a touch of despotism in it." Perhaps this span can be said to add a touch of utopianism, designed as it is to alleviate the most notorious bottleneck in the nation. Driving over this river of many gorges, surveying the spectacular karst landscape, you might exclaim, "Where in tarnation am I?" The flora is rupicolous, the villages tufaceous, and the caves cheesy. Consider detouring for a stretch—to kayak, parasail, fish for brook trout, or even hunt for Plesiosaurus bones.

The structure, whose stays are as elegant as spun silk, towers over a town of 21,000 that was founded by a religious minority; its name you'll recognize as one-half of the title of a popular epicurean guide. Stop in at the local museum and give it the white-glove test. En route to a sunny land to the south, you'll also pass a larger city, which an American novelist once described as "agreeable as certain women are agreeable who are neither beautiful nor clever." Forged in the idiom of the region's ancient viaducts, the bridge is clearly a contemporary hit: 300,000 visitors have already toured the work site. The firm responsible for construction guarantees a life span of 120 years, which is nearly the age of its tour de force in the nation's capital. As the German polymath might put it, you're viewing an aria for the ages.

I
t's just you and the fat man out here on this deserted river terrace, the site of an ancient monastery uninhabited since the fourteenth century. The caves are this spot's *raison de visiter*—seventy-seven wonders carved into the distant sandstone mountains early in the fifth century. More wondrous still is that they've survived at all, enduring nearby earthquakes, destruction by local villagers who broke off pieces of the walls to fertilize their fields, and lootings by German archaeologists in the early 1900s. One of history's most traveled trade routes passes close by, renowned since the first century B.C., both for its access to the country's most coveted export and for its part in importing other religions. The concept of centricity figures

heavily in this culture (indeed, it is often said that you can bore through the center of the earth to arrive here), and socializing often revolves around food and its elaborate preparation—as one might expect, given the girth of the figure above. Yet visitors have not always been so appreciative. As one turn-of-the-century traveler observed, "At a little distance [this nation] appears fair and attractive. Upon a nearer approach, however, there is invariably much that is shabby and repulsive." Then again, when staring at a landscape as stunning as this, one might reasonably beg to differ.

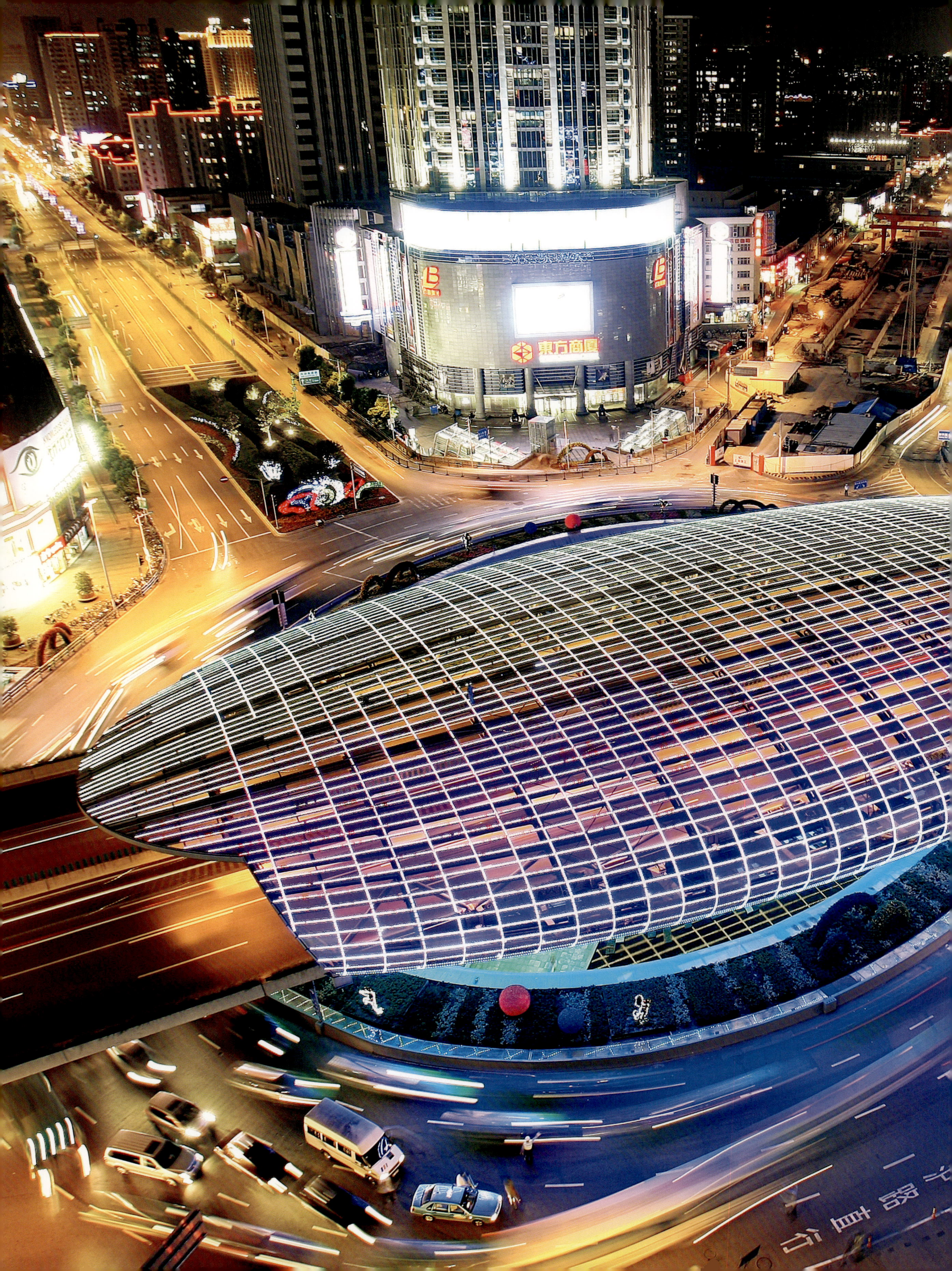
東方商厦

Five broad avenues feed into the roundabout before you, above which an elevated highway slashes through a glittering pod. This novel, dynamic crossroads looks fairly quiet at the moment, but it was clearly designed for a people on the go. Every day, tens of thousands of pedestrians ride the escalators here to shop underground. No surprise, for you are visiting the most bustling noncapitalist city in the history of global economics. Welcome to Shanghai!

Okay, we gave you one. Now the real work begins.

If you arrived in the Paris of the East by way of Pudong Airport, you may have crossed a six-lane cable bridge to enter the district you are now touring (and if you got trapped behind some of the hundred thousand vehicles that do so daily, the term *shanghaied* probably has a whole new meaning). Or perhaps you followed another route, winding along a river in order to marvel at the heralded towers that once housed consulates, banks, and trading companies and gave the city its prewar buzz. In that case, you surely stopped in an eminent old hotel for drinks and to swing to the beat of its popular septuagenarian jazz band (when you find yourself imagining former guest Noël Coward scribbling upstairs, it's time to pay the tab).

However you arrived at this crossroads, you are a long way from the narrow lanes and alleys that still lend the city some charm. You're also a good distance from the malls, boutiques, and posh hotels that flank a celebrated road, as well as from an area with a French connection and from a flowery park with a new contemporary art museum.

"The Suburbes contayne as many houses as the Citie," observed Father Matteo Ricci in the early seventeenth century. Indeed, this outer district—one of nine that make up the city proper—has more than a million inhabitants. Until recently, it was also largely industrial, full of factories that date back to the "international" era. Now, in addition to shops that range from an exotic food mart to a Wal-Mart, art galleries have opened and more than a dozen universities are helping to turn the area into the city's high-tech "brain."

While the pod (or the egg, as it's known locally) serves as a sound barrier, its higher purpose is aesthetic: A thousand LEDs change color every ten seconds, and it has been lit up with videos as part of an arts program. You might just be witnessing—dare we say it?—the beginnings of a cultural revolution.

They call this area with the very un-L.A.-like topography South Central. To arrive at this two-hundred-foot-high cascade, you drove southeast from the capital along a coastal highway. En route, you passed horse farms and flocks of grazing sheep, as well as the odd camping tent and turf house. On the final approach, you halted on a bridge that crosses the broad floodplain of a glacial river and took pleasure in a dandy panoramic view of the cataract and cliffs. And you put on your hiking boots.

You've just wandered around this grassy domain that teems with kingcup, cotton grass, angelica, and myriad wildflowers. You crossed a simple footbridge over the creek and came full circle by following a trail that skirts under the cliff and behind the falls. Now, as you lie on a park bench and let the sun exsiccate your damp wool sweater, you are lulled by the steady plash of water into the pool. Eyes shut, you imagine this terrain covered in snow and ice and the wind shaving your face. You hear the ethereal and wistful symphonic ballads of a famous local band through your earphones. Long before you ever came to this country, the indie group's slow-motion, cinemagraphic videos familiarized you with the landscape of black moraines and rhyolite forms. You begin to dream up a heroic narrative which goes something like this:

There was a man named K, the son of S, who was a mighty chieftain and dwelt in a valley. He was goodly to look upon and had a courteous and fair daughter with silky hair down to her waist. After much counsel with his kinsmen, K betrothed his daughter to a rival. When the rival betrayed and attacked him, K turned on his foe and with his sword smote him asunder at the shoulder bone. The man at once fell dead to the earth. Peace held for many seasons, and all the year-round K went on the sheep hunt and sailed the sea and fished for salmon. He gave great feasts for his clan and died of old age.

Your reverie over, you might head down to the ocean and stroll on volcanic sand beaches, or challenge yourself to a twelve-mile hike between two enormous ice caps that lie just beyond this waterfall. On your return to the capital, you will surely detour up Route 36 to see a special Thing in a national park where the roots of this culture burrow deepest. A soak in a lagoon before you hit the airport and you're good to go. It's one pleasure you can bank on these days.

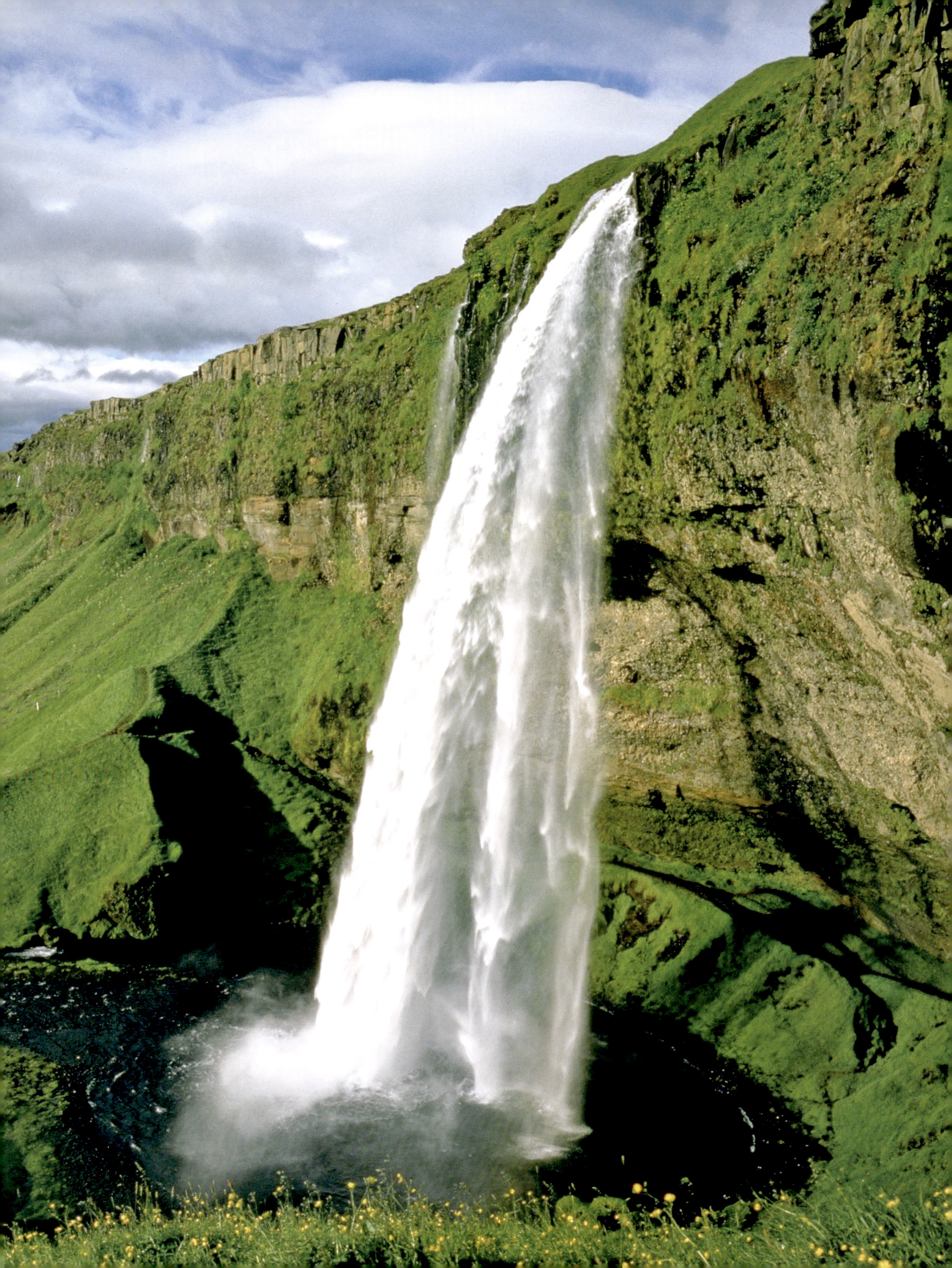

Steady at the wheel. You're zipping along a major highway—the A1, to be exact—at 70 miles an hour when, suddenly, you spot the silhouette of a gigantic winged creature. Although the aftermath of the distraction could prove unfortunate, rest assured: Ninety thousand motorists speed past this patinaed angel daily without having to solicit divine intervention. "A demonic-like figure . . . an infamous heap of rusting scrap," groused one reader of a local newspaper when the statue was erected in 1998. A "vulgar, idiotic piece of sculpture," opined a leading art critic. Ignoring the vitriolic row over its merits, 400,000 visitors traipsed across the field for a close-up view the first year, helping to make this herald of modernity so popular that it supplanted an early-twentieth-century bridge as the foremost icon of the country's north. For his part, the controversial native artist who conceived the figure called it "the complete antithesis of what an angel is, floating about in the ether." Indeed, it springs from the local soil and sea: Its 200 tons of steel rest on piles driven 60 feet deep into a former coal mine (the pithead baths of a colliery, if you want to get technical), and its 65-foot ribbed structure mimics shipbuilding techniques, a nod to the area's once-mighty dockyards. The borough of 190,000 that you are about to enter, part of a conurbation where locals are known by a diminutive of George, is busy shedding its industrial image, turning its river quays into a cultural quarter with a rotating pedestrian bridge and a grain warehouse turned contemporary-art center. You may want to pull over and wander around this monolith, observing it from different angles and perhaps inventing clever Icarian metaphors or musing on the nature of redemption. Better yet, grab a pint in town and contemplate the epiphany of the ten-year-old local girl who said, "It makes me feel smiley."

've got sand in my f---ing brain right now," squealed a ditzy Hollywood star on her MTV travel show. "It was awesome!" She had just taken a tumble trying out the gonzo sport of sandboarding. You, on the other hand, had better move, pronto, or risk a full trepanation courtesy of that Tasmanian Devil bearing down on you.

A Mexican magazine called the arena you are frolicking in "the belly button of world sandboarding." It went on to describe the hot sand in this region as "indomitable, thirsty, and tossed around by an irascible wind." If spending hours trekking up harsh and liftless heights has left you with doubts about the payoff for this abrasive diversion, they'll soon be put to rest as you surf at speeds of up to sixty miles per hour on your gnarly, waxed-up Venomous board. More a fan of riding giant tortoises than of hurtling down dunes, Darwin wrote of his visit to this country, "I cannot say that I liked the very little I saw." Charlie don't surf, and he clearly don't look around enough, either. You are in a southern coastal region whose largest city is two hundred miles from the bean town national capital. You can boat in an oasis with Troglodytes aedon and Amazilia amazilia zipping about, hunt for marine fossils, ride a dune buggy, and explore communities with African roots. If people offer to share some lines with you, don't think narco: They're just inviting you to see mysterious and massive geoglyphs. Wind down your wanderings with a stop at some of the famous grape brandy distilleries, and then hit the slopes again.

Even sober, you'll wipe out a lot on your sandboard—just like Miss Hollywood. As one journalist said, this sport is like "trying to simultaneously do squat thrusts and the samba." Not to worry; you'll get it right. Just be sure to stay on piste and steer clear of any fragile desert plants. Now that would be totally awesome.

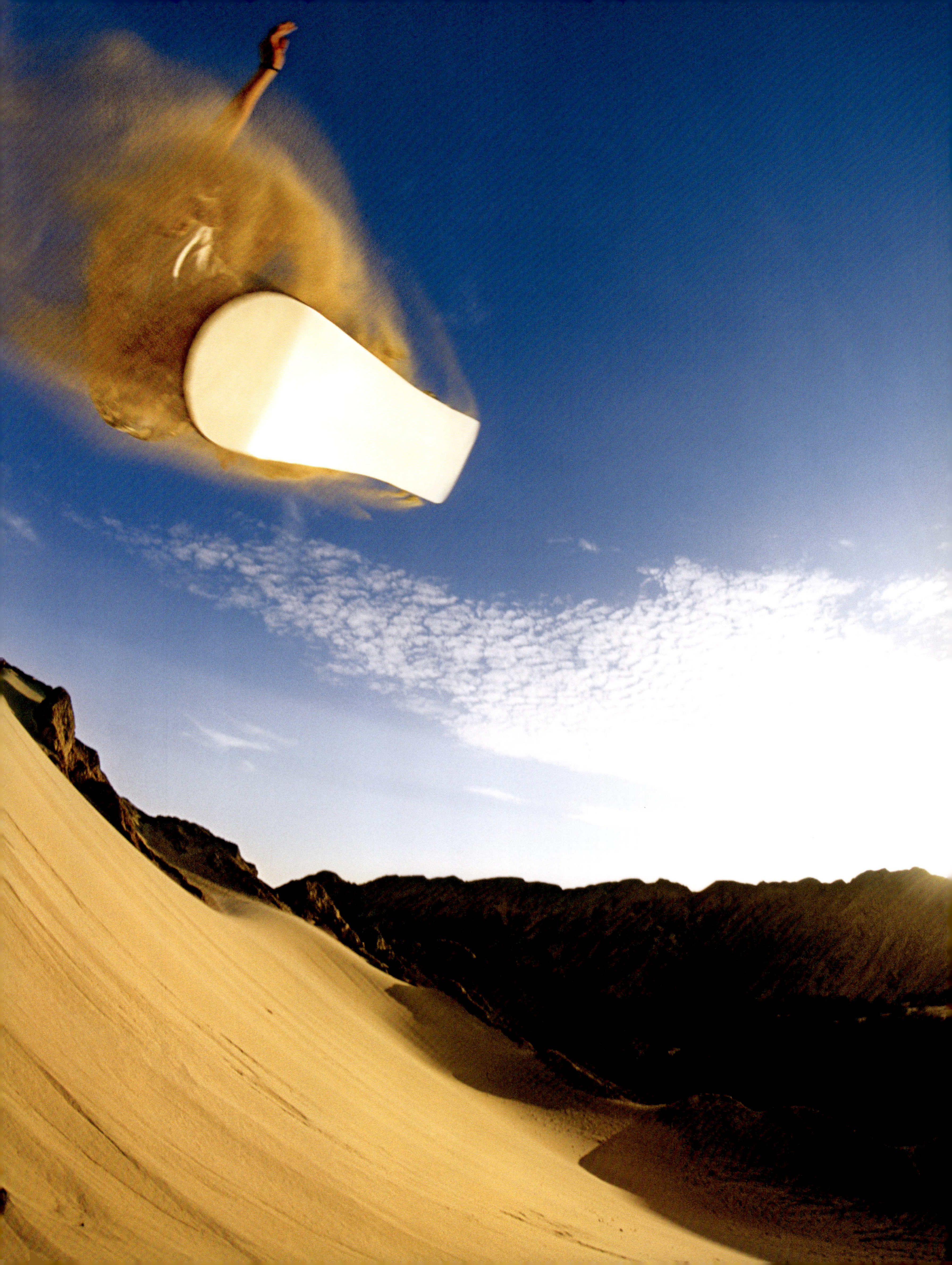

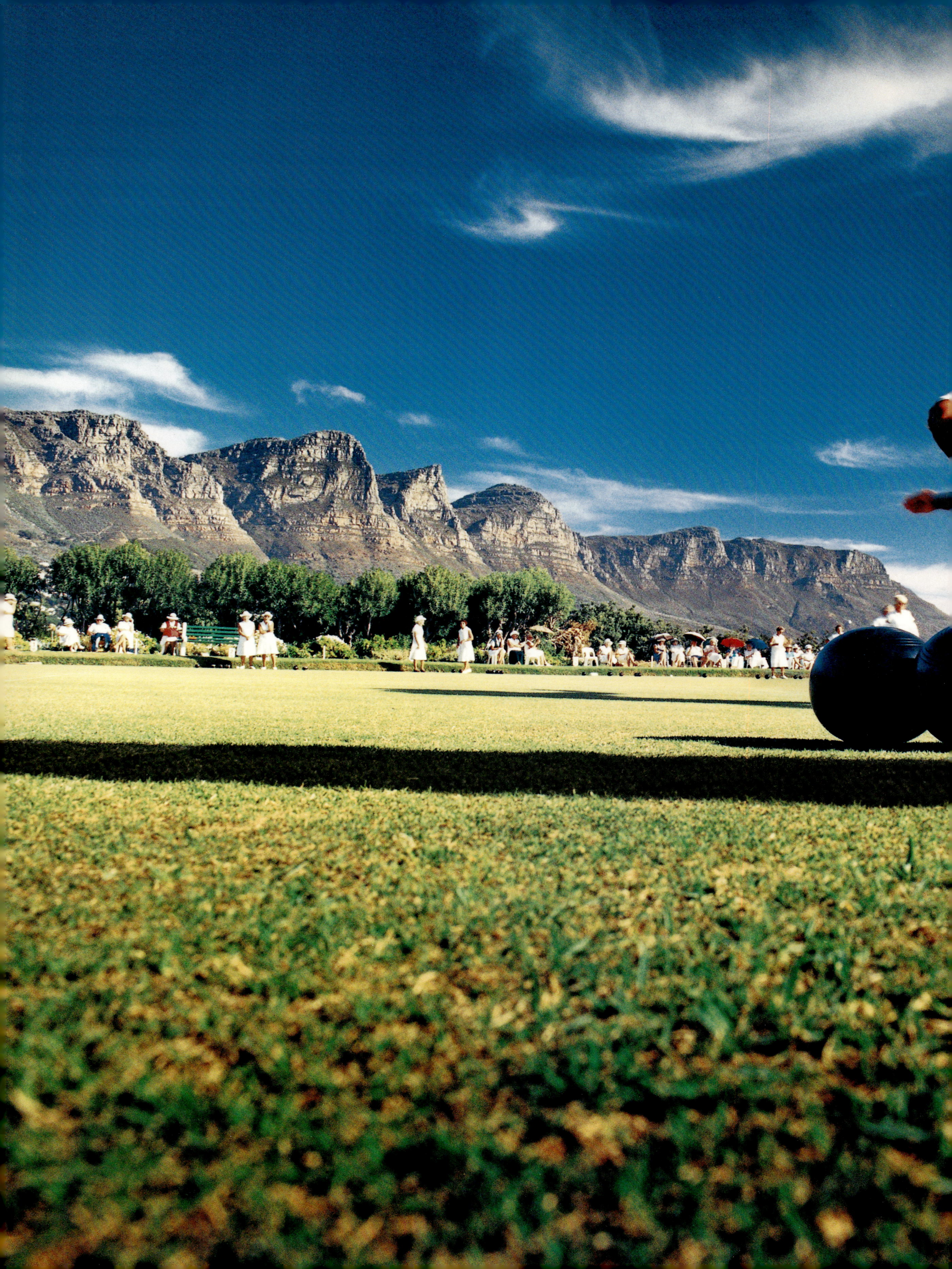

This is not a picture from a bygone era. The tranquil, idyllic scene is present day, and it's a beautiful afternoon for bowling. You are in an exclusive suburb of this country's most visited city, sheltered from the world. But outside influences have shaped this region, from the fifteenth-century European mariners who optimistically christened the promontory thirty miles to the south, to the traders who settled to the north, to their descendants who governed the land. Dazzling geography cradles this little utopia. The bowling club sits between imposing tors (twenty miles to your left stands a much photographed flat-topped mountain) and, according to one guidebook, "one of the most beautiful beaches in the world." The ridge before you is named after a number of biblical figures—an early governor believed he could discern the proselytizers in the contours of the gabled formations— but is not to be confused with big rocks of the same name that live in the sea thousands of miles away.

Beyond this soft, protected green breathes a noisy nation that has eleven official languages. Although it is the world's largest producer of a valuable inert metal, the country struggles against poverty, crime, disease, corruption, and the vestiges of an oppressive political system. Nurturing this ancient land poses a continuing challenge: Perhaps the constancy of these stone sentries will provide comfort and inspiration.

Admit it, the only thing stopping you from rolling down that hill is that you're afraid of getting sand in your pants. You're standing on a scrubby verge, debating with your inner mom whether to climb two hundred feet to the top of the hill. Besides the kids who like to frolic in its soft, powdery grains, frantically slogging up and tumbling down the golden incline, nature lovers climb this dune to enjoy the easterly views of two connected lakes. The more adventurous continue on, to the west, where, after a strenuous two-hour hike, they come upon the shore of a lake that seems to stretch forever. In the distance, they spy only the outline of two small islands: According to local legend, the isles commemorate the babes of the creature for which this national park is named. Created in 1970, the park is split into three sections (one of which includes this sandy ridge) that stretch across thirty-five miles of lakeshore.

Water is a recurring theme in this northern region that comprises a pair of peninsulas and thousands of miles of shoreline. Visitors might well be forgiven for taking Coleridge's famous phrase "water, water everywhere" out of context to describe this verdant area, for you are never more than six miles from a lake or stream. A nineteenth-century sociologist noted that "Milton must have travelled [here] before he wrote the garden parts of *Paradise Lost*"—fitting words, for the land is also replete with rolling hills and forests and, today, the nation's largest number of state parks. This spot is about 620 miles northwest of the country's capital and about halfway between the center and top of the world. Thankfully, you just have to get to the top of that ridge. We dare you: Last one up is a rotten egg.

G ood news. Objects in the water appear larger than they are. While the sucker in front of you might look huge and menacing, light refraction exaggerates his bulk (you remember Snell's Law); he's really a mere five or so feet long. Like his requiem brethren cruising in the background, he's also a picky eater (and is himself prey to even larger sharks), so unless holiday bingeing has plumped you up to the size of a fat, juicy pinniped, no worries, mate.

You've taken the plunge in reef-rich waters that belong to a country composed of seven hundred calcium-carbonate islands; you're just off the fourth-largest isle, where dozens of resorts share space with a re-created indigenous village, a nature center, pine forests, mangrove swamps, one of the world's biggest underwater cave systems, and plenty of flamingos. This pelagic predator is looking to make sushi out of the ubiquitous Albulidae family, and you might enjoy grabbing a reel after your dive and competing with him for a few of those hard-fighting fish, which draw top sportfishermen to these many banks and channels.

The 300,000 people in this archipelago nation (you've long admired a handsome native son with a French surname who won an Oscar in the '60s) seem to have a knack for creating hybrids: a popular rum drink blends coconut, coffee, lemon, and pineapple flavors; and a few years ago, local musicians mixed calypso, reggae, R&B, and hip-hop beats and barked out a song that became the "Macarena" of the new millennium (does anybody care who unleashed the canines?). Even the local folk religion is syncretic.

Visitors who just can't exorcise a famous chilling 1975 ostinato from their mind can play it safe here and swim with dolphins or observe the undersea wonders from glass-bottom boats. But you know you're in the hands of well-respected dive operators. And you know the truly scary things lurking in these waters are fuchsia wet suits.

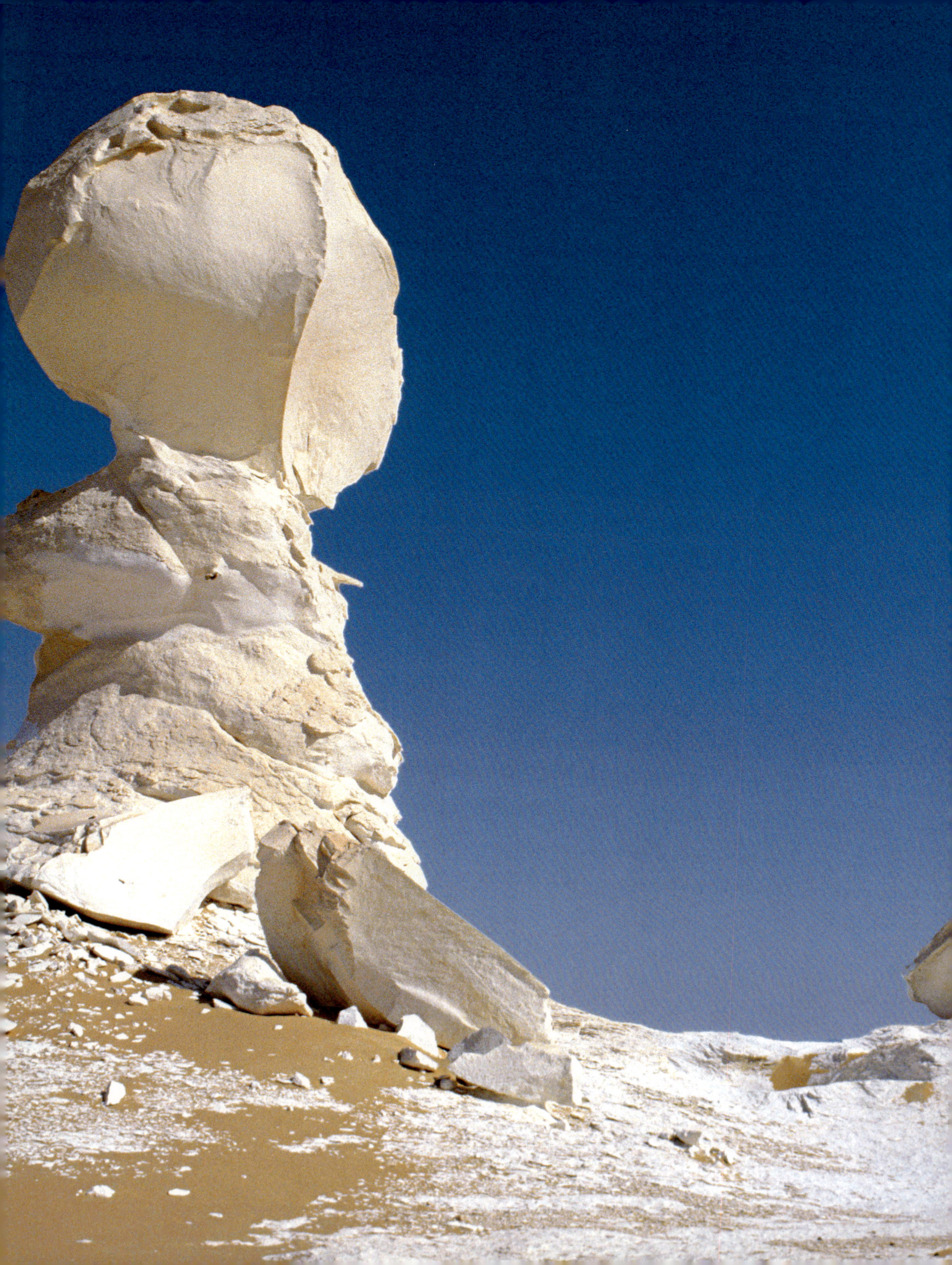

A fifteen-foot desert snowman? Not quite, but the truth is nearly as strange. These incandescent limestone formations, sculpted by aeons of fierce wind, distinguish the otherwise-barren expanse that constitutes two-thirds of this country. The arable land that does exist is scarce but highly productive; indeed, it once served as ancient Rome's breadbasket. (Ironically, the country must today import nearly half its food and is the third-largest recipient of U.S. foreign aid.) Three hundred years before the Romans, an imperialist conqueror, hoping to confirm his divinity, journeyed across this near-rainless realm to consult with a beastly deity. Nowadays, inhabitants turn to a single god, practicing a faith that was introduced by seventh-century invaders whose language still dominates the area. Miraculously, the ancestral tongue of this great nation is preserved in the liturgy of a second-century sect, whose modern adherents often sport a distinguishing tattoo. While surveying the terrain, travel writer John Carne noted, "There is a sameness in the character of the . . . scenery, [but] it is such as is to be seen in no other land." Thankfully, that sameness is punctuated by five vibrant oases, the smallest of which is situated nineteen miles to the south of here. So if you prefer paradise to being parched, you'd best be on your way.

Y ou are standing in big sky country, in front of a ponderous structure that appears to emerge, miragelike, from the monochromatic rock-strewn terrain. Although you're probably not thrilled to wind up in such an unaccommodating place, that unadorned edifice is in fact a high-tech residence: Completed in 2002 at a cost of twelve million dollars, it features a cinema and a glass dome that hovers over a swimming pool and a palm garden. But you can't just check in—the rooms are reserved mostly for researchers who trek here from all over the globe, principally from another hemisphere, where their organization has its headquarters. Atop a peak to your left are a number of much taller buildings which house some very delicate equipment, known collectively by a three-letter acronym that rhymes with the name of a sandwich featuring bacon.

The 8,500-foot-high mountain on which you're standing is 80 miles south of the country's fourth-largest city, and the drive here follows a stretch of famous highway that skirts the best beaches on the nearby coast. This region is perhaps the world's driest (which accounts for the significant discoveries of petroglyphs and mummies), and yet every few years the landscape explodes in a riot of flowers. The nation itself erupted in 1973, torn asunder by a vicious coup that inflamed passions worldwide. After an election years later, a celebrated native novelist proclaimed that "the old dictator still holds the democratic government hostage." For decades the superannuated strongman was a living ghost.

Despite the fact that you're in the middle of nowhere, one bright spot is the nightlife, which is out of this world—provided you stay away from the national drink, a fierce grape brandy (the stellar residents don't see eye to eye with those who tipple). The place starts jumping at dusk, but sunrise brings a total eclipse of the smart.

Looks like a subaqueous duel is about to break out—time to go a little bubble à bubble with the masked man staring you down. Actually, he's a latter-day Mike Nelson, and the two of you have launched your sunset sea hunt in a cathedral-walled cove—more of a mini-fjord, really—that was scooped out by glacial action and then carved by the sea. This is just one of many such karst formations that plunge from great heights into the water along this twelve-mile stretch of coast.

You've dipped in near a many-hued village that is known for its decent white wines, though you are more likely to associate it with a currant crème liqueur. In the late nineteenth century, the town's quarries supplied stones for a canal that was to alter the global geopolitical canvas of the day as well as form the base of support for a new-world lady. Not long after, a number of painters—adherents to a beastly movement of sorts—unfolded their easels and made a name for themselves here.

Should you have the stamina to swim around a cape some miles to the west, you would come ashore in the country's second-largest city, the hometown of one of this nation's top sports heroes, who famously just kicked off his retirement by going out as a bit of a head case. The name of the geographic subdivision you are in refers to the mouth of a river, one which Byron, Wordsworth, and Longfellow all extolled. With an eye toward history, another writer described the delta as "a wedge of Greece" and as the place that premiered "the great war song of the Republic." To arms, citizens!

While the marine environment here is fragile, the parched terra firma is even more so: In fact, the risk of fire is so great that access is not permitted in the summer months. Though autumn is the perfect season to lace up your hiking boots and trek across the craggy landscape, don't rush to shed your tank and fins. The Paleolithic drawings in a nearby underwater cave may be strictly off-limits, but several millennia's worth of enticing shipwrecks beckon. Diver down!

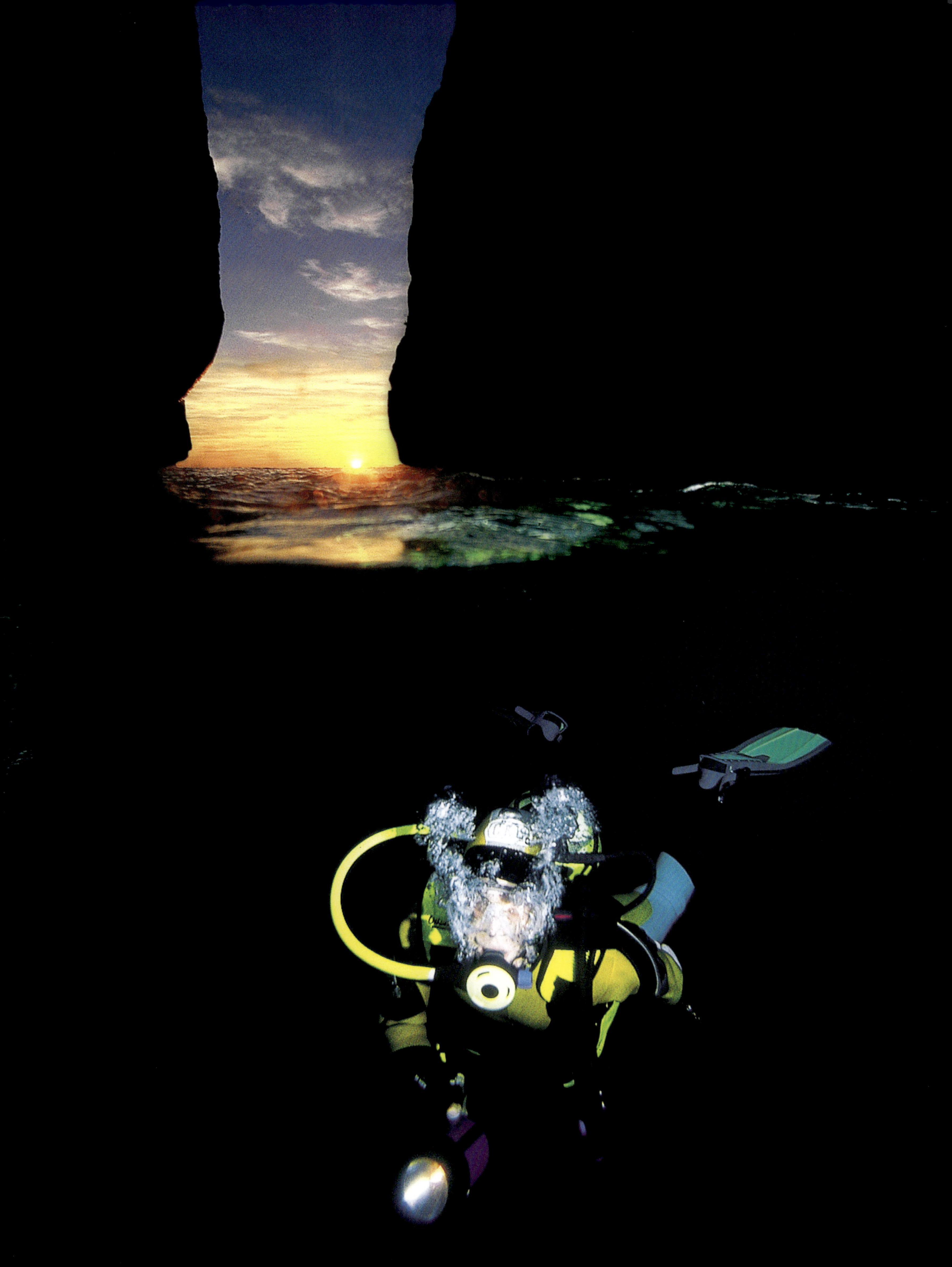

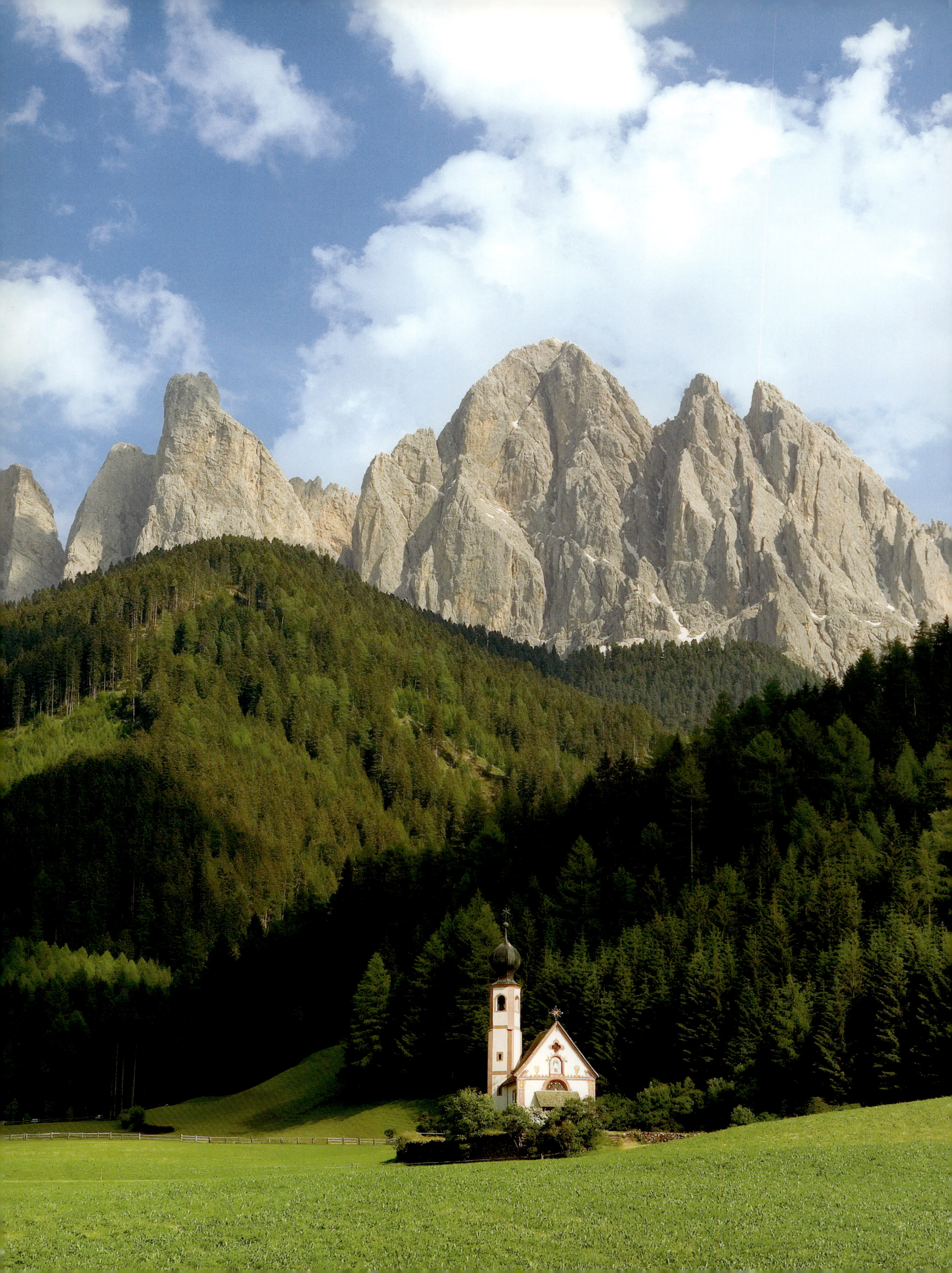

This is where it ends. You are going no farther. If your wanderlust isn't sated after exploring this cloistered fifteen-mile-long valley, you need professional help. So go ahead, snap away with your iPhone and show 'em back home why not to expect you anytime soon.

Six hamlets here form a township of more than two thousand inhabitants. Although you are touring the north of a country, you are currently at the southern edge of a cultural realm where ninety-nine percent of the locals speak a mother tongue different from the national language (listen carefully and you might even catch a few folks conversing in a third language, ancient and extremely rare).

Virginia Woolf's father, a prominent early mountaineer, observed that the peaks in this range "recall quaint Eastern architecture, whose daring pinnacles derive their charm from a studied defiance of the sober principles of stability." Perhaps his notion was inspired by staring at this Baroque church, erected in 1744.

The valley is located in a 25,000-acre natural park that enjoys a quiet renown—apt for such a sleepy environment. One of the world's most celebrated mountain climbers was born here and cut his crampons on the vertiginous ten-thousand-foot peaks you see before you. Maybe with luck—and binoculars—you'll spot chamois in the heights. Most likely, you'll stick to admiring the insane variety of wildflowers and majestic forests of pine and fir trees or to visiting the mineral museum. The biggest danger is getting slammed by a mountain biker careening around a curve or, if you hang out for a few more months, being upended by an out-of-control tobogganer.

Perhaps you came north to escape the crushing crowds at a glam fashion show or in a World Heritage Site lagoon. After stopping in a provincial capital, you traveled twenty miles northeast on the A22 to get here. From converted farmhouses to hunting lodges, you found no lack of rustic accommodations. If you'd like the keys to the church, incidentally, inquire at the neighboring twelfth-century farmstead.

Freya Stark, who knew her mountains, wrote, "To me, the great and simple lines of the granite are ever the most satisfying"; the range possesses "a domestic loveliness; old age can walk about in their meadows, where no distance is too unmanageable.... Few countries in the world look more happy or more beautiful." You really aren't going back, are you?

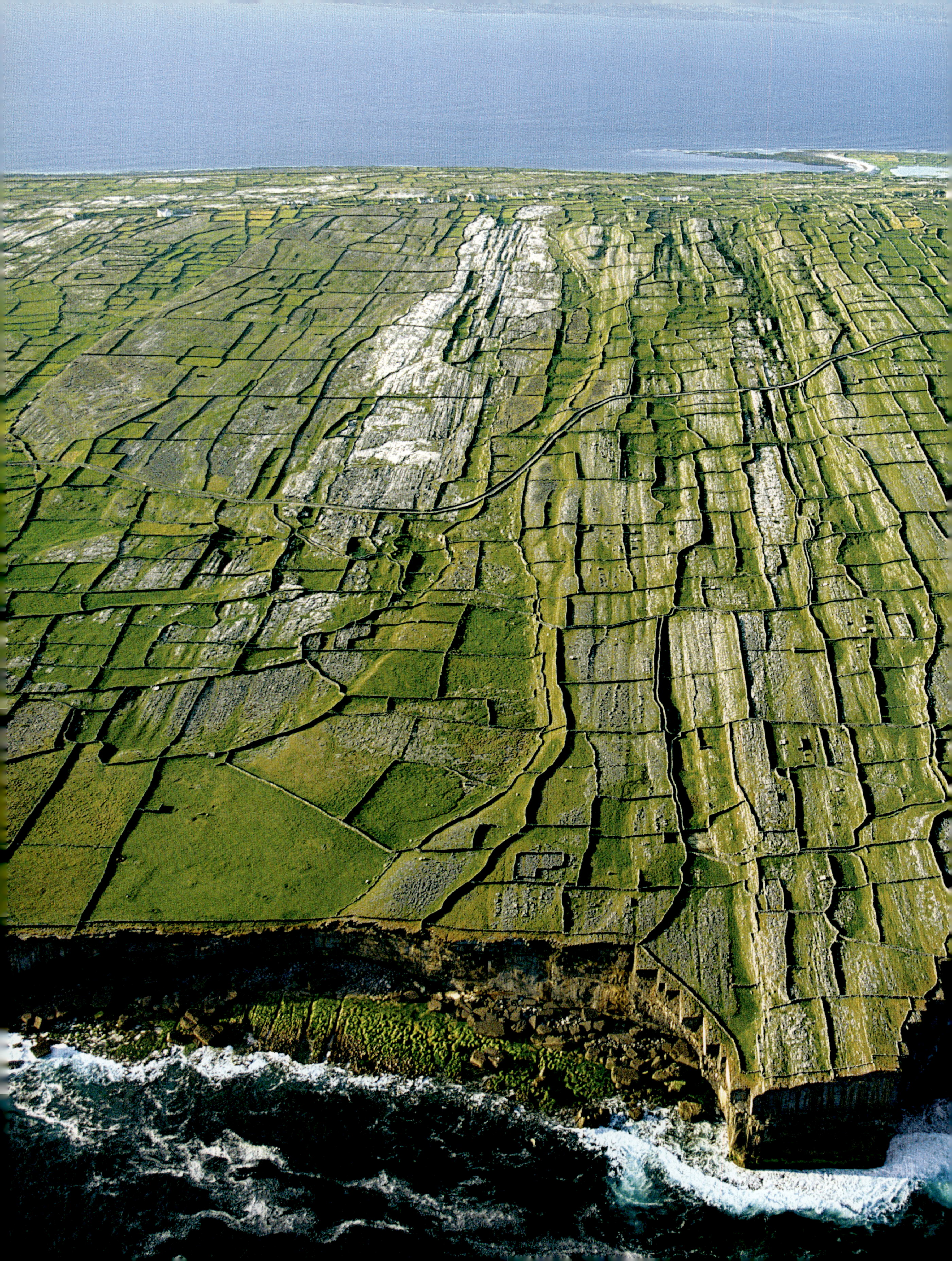

You are passing over what could be mistaken for a Mondrian painting (*Composition V* turned on its side, perhaps?), but this canvas is in fact a sixteen-square-mile island. The relentless ocean winds and waves that carved the precipitous three-hundred-foot cliffs right beneath you rake the naturally stony land barren. The lines you see are neither cracks in the terrain nor haphazardly planned roadways, but stone walls erected by canny local farmers to protect their small pastures from the punishing elements. To grow their crops and graze their cattle, they nourish the land with seaweed and sand.

Life here has changed little over the centuries, the isolation fostering a robust indigenous culture: The native tongue remains the language of choice, though the accommodating locals can switch effortlessly to a more universally spoken one. Agriculture and fishing are still the main livelihoods on this isle, along with tourism, especially in recent decades. (From June through August, up to two thousand day-trippers arrive by plane or ferry, tripling the population of year-round residents.) Visitors come here to examine old stones prized from this unforgiving earth: remnants of two-thousand-year-old stone forts, early monastic ruins, and a Lilliputian (seventy-square-foot!) thirteenth-century church.

This island is one of three—the others are to the southeast—whose collective name suggests a popular garment made of sebum-saturated hair. These three bits are but fragments of a small country on an island—partly occupied by a neighboring government—that humans settled only after the Ice Age. The capital city, about 150 miles almost due east, has long been known for its lively watering holes, literary heritage, and period architecture, even while the nation's history is an epic of turmoil and trials: invasion, rebellion, civil war, and foreign rule, all against a background of poverty, starvation, faith, and abandonment. If one were to believe the words of an itinerant British writer, the national character echoes the nature of the place, for the "men and the landscapes seem to be the same, and one and the other seem ragged, ruined, and cheerful." Yet here in the wind, this little island provides a big picture of the eternal—stubborn, small green plots finding sustenance in the nonetheless stony soil.

A n orderly country, yes," a nineteenth-century Brit wrote of the nation you are visiting, "and the people in it steeped to their lips in every abominable vice." Harsh. So what would he make of this entrance with its undulating cherry-red canopy, aptly dubbed The Tongue? He'd follow you right in, no doubt. As for the building itself . . . A swank boutique? A velvet-rope nightclub? Nope. It's a new eight-hundred-person-capacity auditorium by the same architect responsible for every other grand edifice in this public park. A prominent old lefty, he built a domed exhibition space, a planetarium, and fine modern and contemporary art museums more than fifty years ago in collaboration with a renowned landscape designer who shares a surname with the philosophical father of all lefties. The architect has declared this hall one of his favorite creations, but its construction entailed the controversial felling of a swath of trees. (How ironic that the indigenous people once called this land "place where there were trees.") The building was completed shortly before the master draftsman celebrated his one hundredth birthday.

Jesuits founded this city in the sixteenth century, and wannabe barons later pushed into the hinterlands to cultivate crops and search for gold. When Kipling passed through, it was drawing millions of immigrants from around the world—Italians, Japanese, Middle Easterners. Eventually it was dubbed the locomotive pulling the country. Now, in fact, it pulls the entire continent. This makes it all the more surprising that the council in this ultra-consumerist city with a Times Square hustle has banned billboards.

You are in a sports-mad nation where, as one guidebook explains, athletic heroes are Homeric—and you surely know some of these idols by their colorful one-word nicknames. Currently, several hometowners are thrilling their compatriots with their NBA play. As for high-octane sports, the city has produced so many top Formula 1 drivers that you may wonder if the residents are weaned on petrol. Tonight, whether this venue fills with rock, hip-hop, or the lively sounds for which this land is famous, get your hand stamped, plunge under The Tongue, and enjoy the "abominable vice" of your choice.

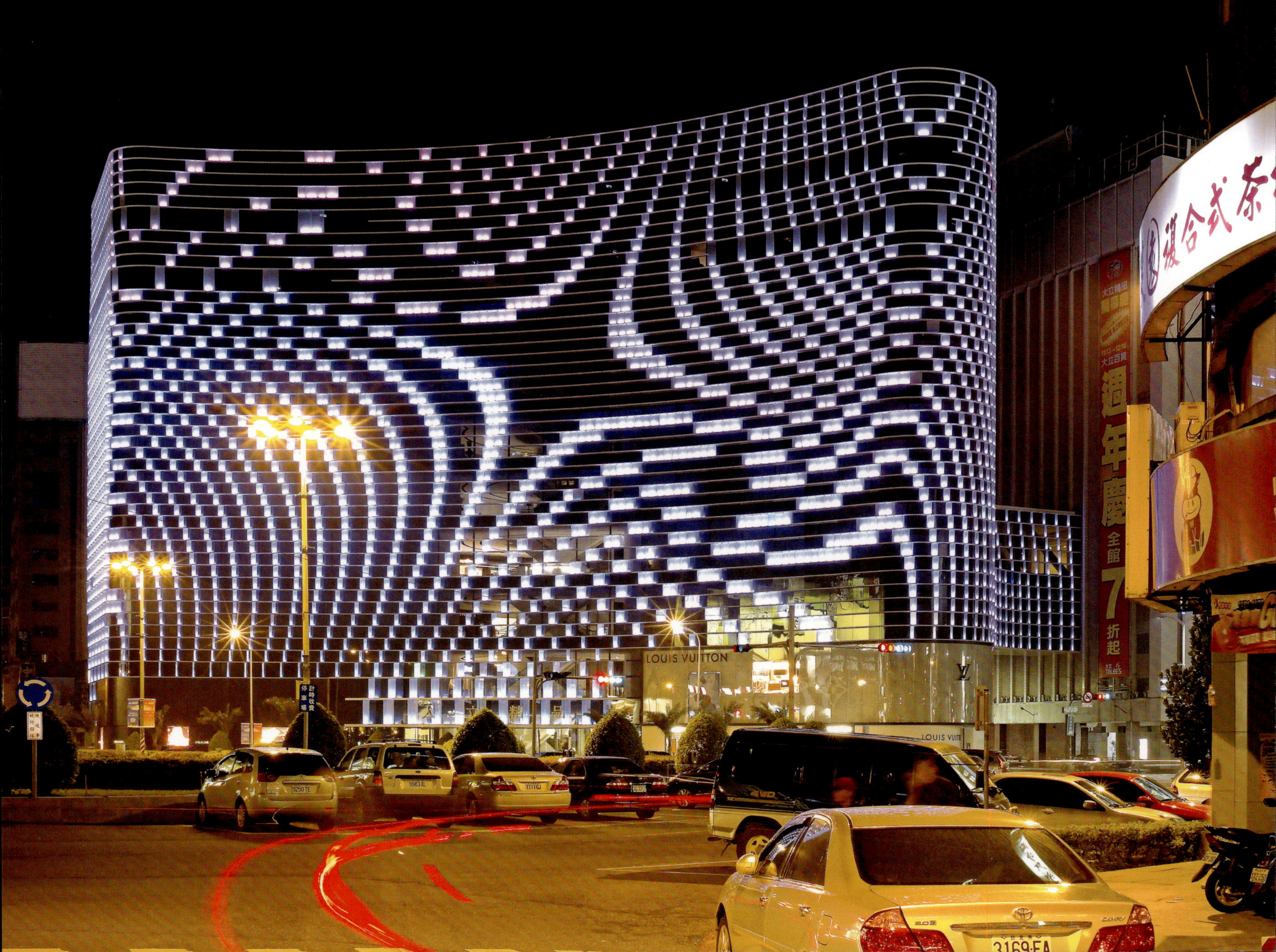
LOUIS VUITTON
週
年
慶
全
館
7
折
起

You're looking at the house that Louis built...with help from Prada and Gucci. The superluxe galleria before you opened in the fall of '08 and has added some Vegas flash and swagger to a staid downtown block. This port city was heretofore better known for welcoming convoys of containerships than for hosting purveyors of hoity-toity wares.

A Dutch design firm with a multinational name is responsible for the twelve-story structure and its pseudo-moiré facade. It took engineers two years of experimenting to make the lights dance correctly across the concave exterior. Job well done: Internet postings of the ever-changing luminous choreography have made a video darling of the building. The real star of the show, though, is the interior, where staggered escalators spiral in a Guggenheim-ish way up the core of an atrium. The wide all-white space-age landings that lead to the shops look ready-made for George Jetson to shuttle in on his aerocar.

You zipped from the nation's capital down the west coast to this city in ninety minutes on a new high-speed train. You rode the new metro, constructed for a mini-Olympics, across town to meet your destiny with consumer bliss. Once you've had your fill of shopping, you might enjoy a simple walk along the local Love Canal (which was recently cleaned up) and a stop at the café in the former British consulate. Townspeople have a strong preference for beef, so you can always dip into the restaurant on your right—see, it says "steak house" right there on the sign. If you're looking for a change of pace, the surrounding county has hot springs, aboriginal homelands, and a town famous for its beautiful hand-painted paper and bamboo umbrellas. The thirtieth anniversary of the brutal squashing of a pro-democracy movement in this city was recently marked. Ultimately, the incident helped to usher in a new beginning for the nation... and, it appears, new purchasing power.

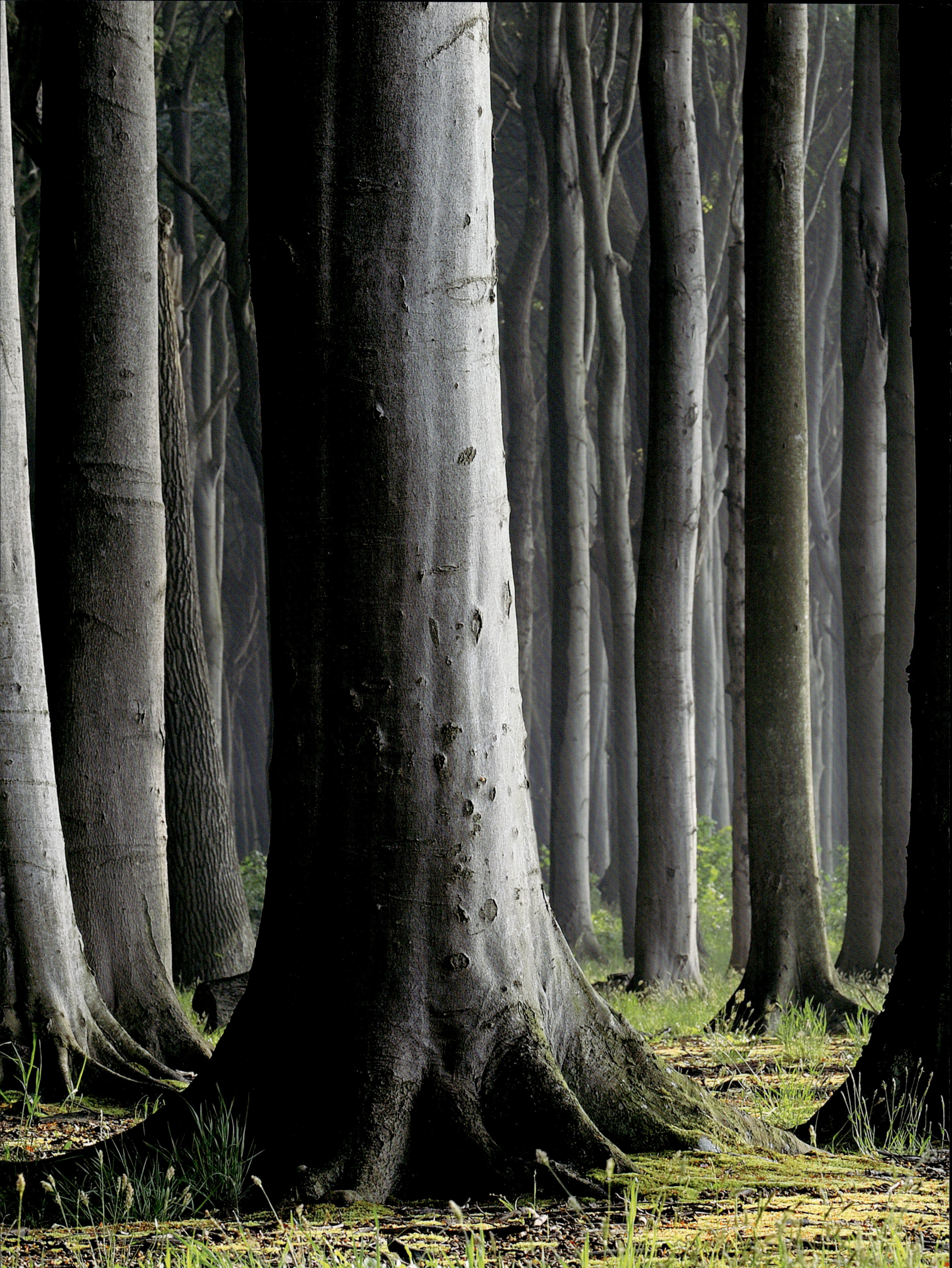

Ghosts in the Trees. You've just hit on a title for that gothic thriller you're going to write after wandering in this eerie 450-acre woodland. Robust ocean winds relentlessly buffet the trees before you, causing their tangled branches to lean seriously sideways. It's a phantasmagorical world that Tim Burton or M. Night Shyamalan might have conjured. Locals, for their part, describe it as the place where the wind mows the grass.

You are looking at a protected remnant of vast bygone forest. If the land were allowed to revert to its natural state, these broadleaf trees would eventually cover two-thirds of the nation. This dominating species is deeply connected to the history and psyche of the people—their word for *book* is derived from the name of this tree, whose wood was once used as writing tablets. You are likely familiar with its catkins and its burred shells that hold twin pyramidal nuts.

Descend the forty-foot cliff behind you and you'll find yourself on a two-mile beach. There you can repose in iconic "strand baskets" that you'll recognize from the introspective works of a Nobel Prize–winning writer who came from these parts. The nearest town, whose name first appeared in monastic writings in 1264, has fewer than two thousand residents. (Its recent claim to fame is that a family-owned enterprise made a precision tool used to rescue those Chilean miners.) The district you're visiting stretches for nearly forty miles along this tranquil, duney coastline, once belonging to a powerful league (of a nonathletic sort). Your first encounter with a ghost was in the famous castle in the regional capital, where a pranksterish sprite is said to live.

You're touring a bike-friendly country, so hop on a hybrid two-wheeler and pedal the meandering forest paths. And when dusk falls, stroll along the beach and ponder this mysterious semi-dark sylvan reserve. Who says tales of spooks came to an abrupt end here twenty years ago?

It might take a good rub of the eyes to dispel any fears that the blob before you in the crepuscular light is not a T-1000 shape-shifting android. You can bet Ah-nuld will be back one day, but for now the only thing terminating around here is the funicular car in which you've just ridden. You have arrived at the top stop, and belvedere, of an eighty-million-dollar narrow-gauge railway whose station motifs echo glacial moraines and luminescent ice formations. The project has drawn, well, glowing tributes.

The railway track slopes at times a vertiginous forty-six degrees over a nine-hundred-foot ascent, but no matter the angle, you're sitting pretty in small cabins that pivot. Dreamed up by a Koolhaas acolyte, this designer transport system opened in 2007. The eight-minute, mile-long trek begins at a metro station just outside the Old Town, then proceeds to the Lion House and the zoo before depositing riders next to gondolas that head up the pistes in the distance. Along the way, the funicular exits a tunnel to cross a curvy cable-stayed suspension bridge (whose minaretlike towers suggest that the architect was returning to her roots). Speaking of spans, the name of the provincial capital you are in refers to an ancient bridge over a strategic river. As you stroll the cobblestoned streets, you will no doubt gaze many times at the city's erstwhile icon, an imperial town house whose Gothic oriel has a gold-plated roof. You'll wonder if that gilt hue is what inspired a visiting nineteenth-century English novelist to envision "mountains holding up cups of snow to the fiery sun, who glares on them in vain." Perhaps his celestial prose in turn inspired the physicist who set up an observatory on a peak here in the 1930s to study cosmic rays (and later basked in his Nobel Prize).

Now is the season to enjoy vigorous walks in the woods. Not to worry: Your reception at this ice station promises to be anything but frosty.

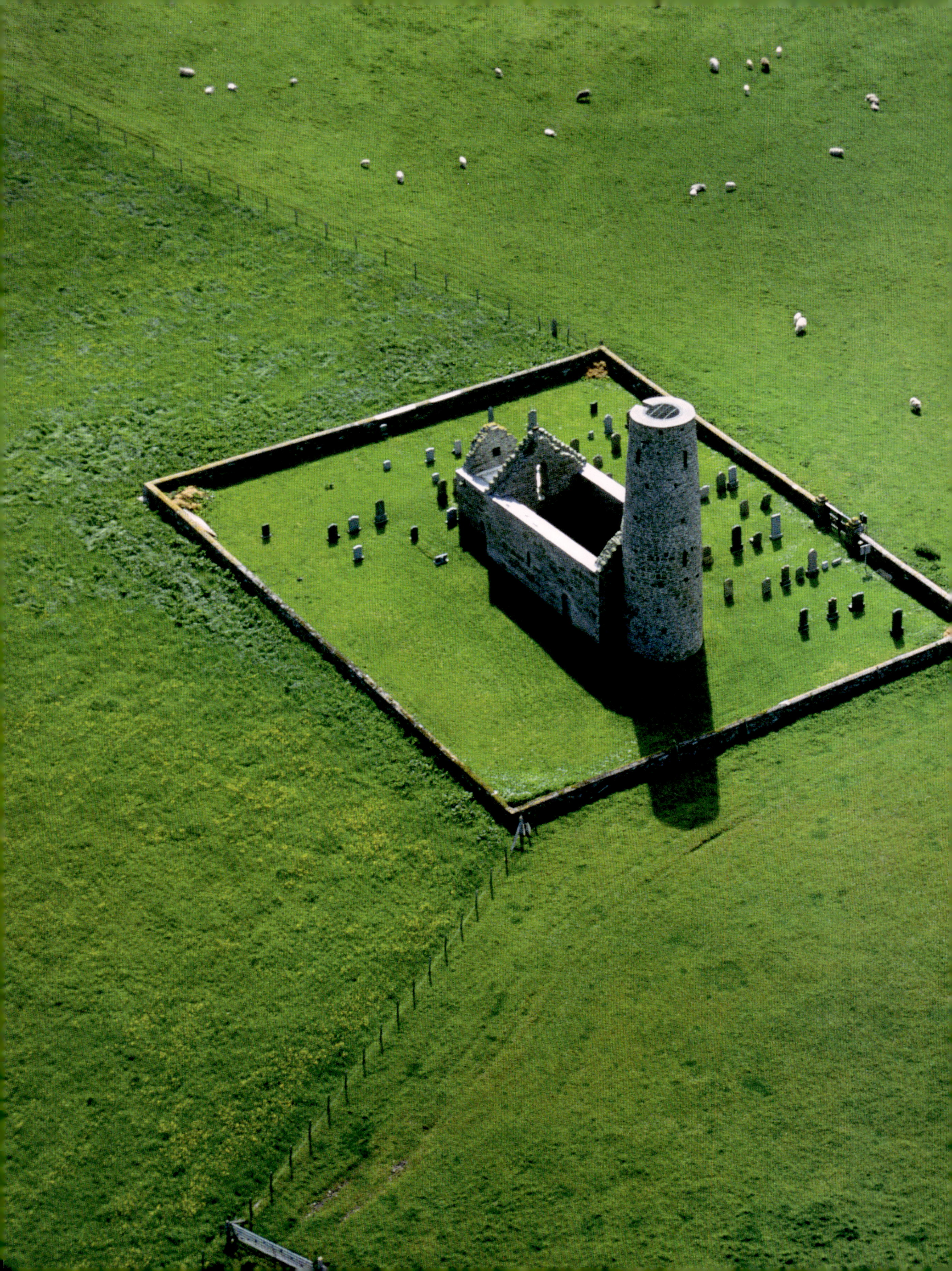

You might assume that this ruined stone church and graveyard anchor a vast hacienda, where livestock graze on a pampas-like expanse that stretches to the horizon. In truth, you hover over an arrowhead-shaped island that covers a mere sixteen hundred acres and lies in a turbulent sea. An inner isle within a circle of seventy, it is situated just off a larger island that itself is off the Mainland of the chain, which in turn—bear with us!—belongs to a country that belongs to a larger island nation. Getting here is akin to taking apart *matryoshkas*, those Russian nesting dolls: After all, you have reached the core—the very soul—of this island chain, for it is here, on this tiny parcel of land, that we can distill the story of its founding.

Nine hundred years ago, a nobleman whose name suggests greatness was martyred on this spot (the church was built around the time he gained sainthood). A gentle ruler in an age of great violence, he had journeyed here to discuss peace with a jealous cousin. But, as history records, the cousin came "with evil intent" (and a vast number of men) to deliver a murderous sucker punch. The nobleman forbade his few men to defend him, asking only that his executioner "hew on my head a great wound, for it is not seemly to behead chiefs like thieves."

This tale inspired a local bard in the 1970s to create an innovative novel of guilt, goodness, and sacrifice, and shortly thereafter, a well-known composer turned the work into a modern opera. Together, they founded a popular summer arts festival on the Mainland—named after the martyr, of course.

Today, fewer than fifty people make their home within the tight radius of these ruins, a fraction of the population in the 1800s (the most sensational news here of late was the discovery of a rare bee species in the nearby wetlands reserve). Over the centuries, however, a who's who of ancient tribes has passed through the entire chain, leaving behind everything from languages to rich archaeological sites. The islands lie closer to the ancestral homes of these tribes, in lands to the east, than to their own nation's capital to the south. Even the round design of this tower came from another island nation. Multiculturalism evidently had a rich pedigree long before we coined the term.

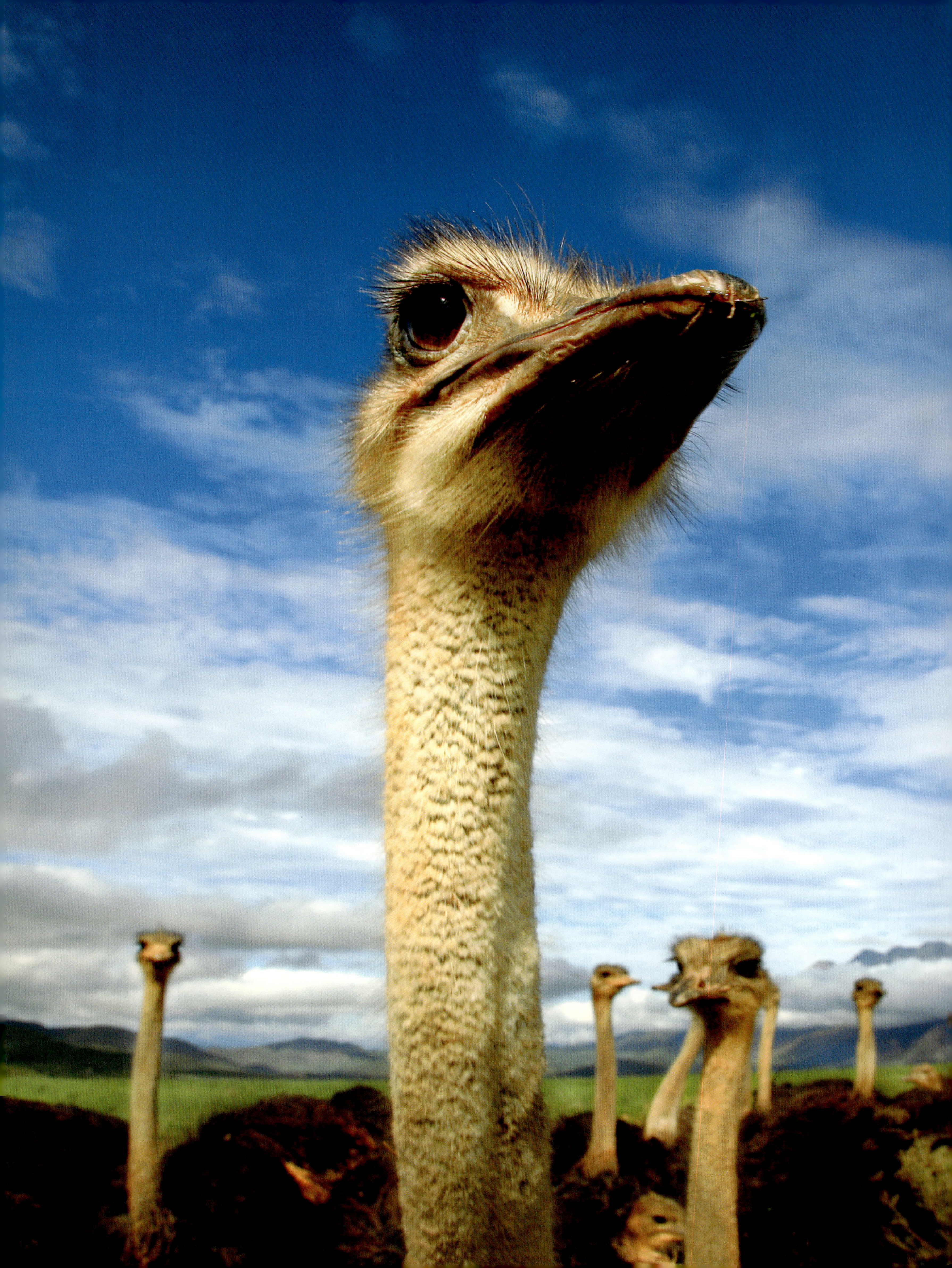

You might not want to get too attached to the cute and curious critters inspecting you. As domesticated ostriches, they are not long for this world. But follow these fellows back to their tourist-friendly farm, and you can pet and ride them ... or savor their flesh. Today they are valued for their lean meat and fine leather, while in the nineteenth century a worldwide mania for their feathers led to the emergence of a massive breeding industry in this country. By the time of the Great War, that lucrative market had lost its plumage.

You've encountered this pride near a legendary pass in a mountain range whose name suggests that you're about to enter a tenebrous realm. (Other ranges in this nation's southwest have names like Witch River, Dragon Stone, and Sour—what were those rugged settlers ingesting?) With sandstone and shale anticlines tilting ninety degrees, this range is a geologist's dream, and a World Heritage Site. The unpaved road that bisects it and links the so-called Great and Little parts of this semi-arid region was built in the 1880s by convicts whose stone huts still stand. The road's original retaining walls are also in place, a tribute to the engineer, who built more than twenty passes. If you'd rather climb the highest peak (five thousand feet), take the thirty-seven-mile, five-day trail, and book with the guides who boast of having beer cooling for you in a river. A hike to the cloud-shrouded summit is not complete until you've seen the sign that reads "The Top."

A prolific Victorian novelist visited the main town here and declared, "I wish some of my readers would write the name of the village in order that they may learn the irritation which may be produced by an unfortunately awkward combination of letters." Not long after his remark, a war broke out between speakers of his language and the one he was mocking. From this town—whose sumptuous sandstone palaces came courtesy of the ostrich booms—you can explore caves and visit a cheetah breeding facility or take off on a famous wine route.

One love. Mellow island tunes on the radio had you swaying all the way up to these lime-green waters. You sipped from coconuts handed through the window by roadside vendors. Now upon arrival, you adjust your unisex sarong and wiggle the winter out of your sandaled toes. You feel all right. Scrrraaaatch ... Wrong sound track, wrong reverie.

Sure, you're going to have a blast frolicking under those cascades, but don't expect to find jerk chicken on the menu tonight. You've interrupted your drive along a forty-five-mile river for a stop and a swim in a fifty-five-square-mile national park packed with more than eight hundred plant species. Who knew that this decidedly nontropical country could be so lush and idyllic? As you float lazily in your inner tube, you'll want to read up on how karst and tufa deposits created these dazzling pools. Later, you might get a hoot out of watching the deliciously dreadful spaghetti-esque westerns that were shot here for a northern audience.

As you continue your riverine journey, you'll pass a string of old water mills and fortresses and an island monastery. Eventually, you'll arrive at a town near the riverhead that was liberated from a not-so-neighborly neighbor to the east. When you reverse course, you'll finish at a coastal town with an immense domed cathedral. You may be asked if you know the sexy local actor who starred on an American TV medical drama until it was retired after fifteen seasons. Next you'll visit a nearby peninsula town where your most strenuous activities will be admiring the hilltop church and lifting an espresso cup to your lips in the many outdoor cafés.

Just around a bend of sorts begins one of the nation's more touristed stretches, where yachts are anchored off rocky islands and a honey-colored-stone town draws crowds. But you can deal with that—you feel all right.

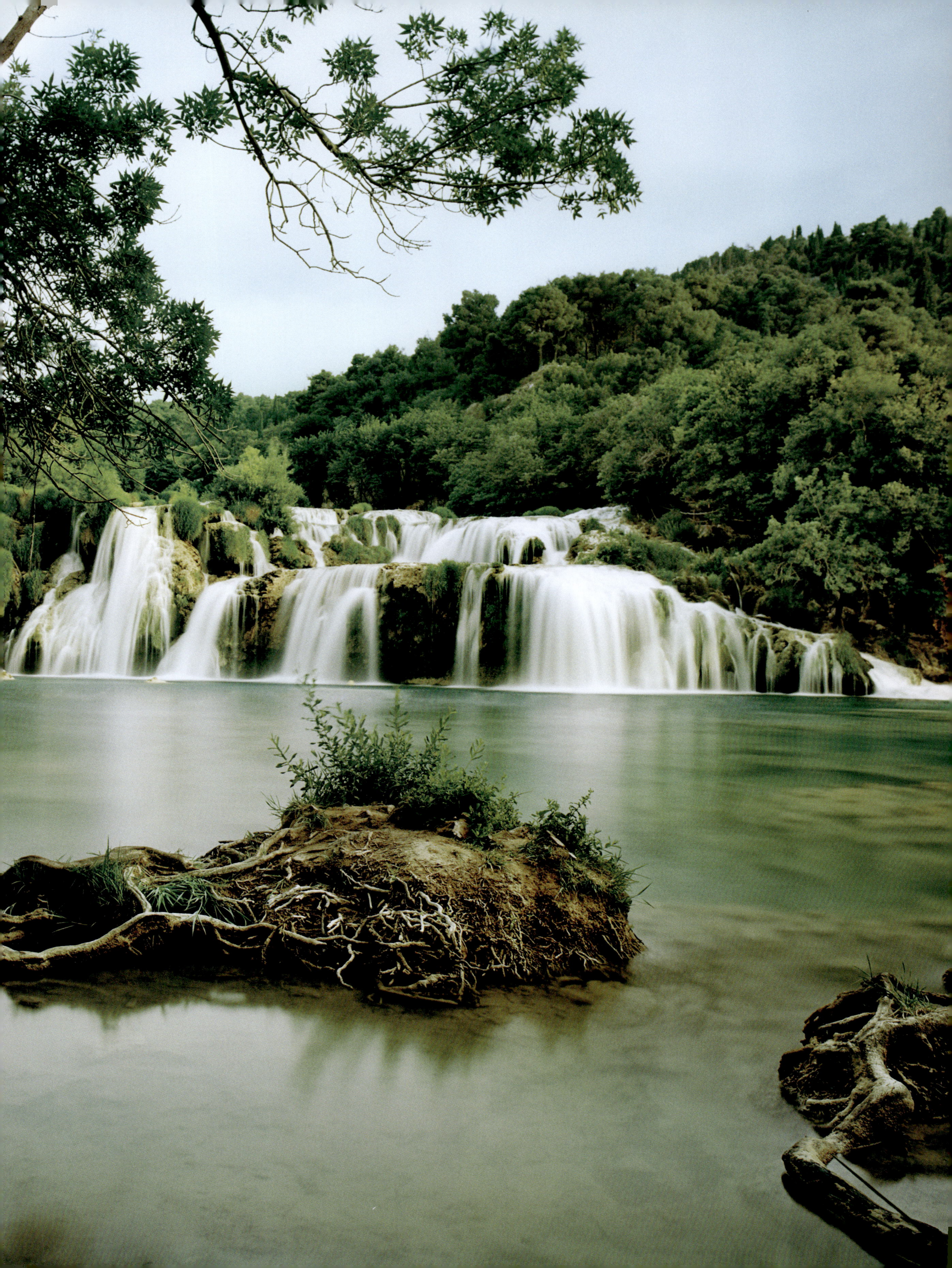

Wham-O, *Vertigo*, 707s, Rice-a-Roni, NASA, *Dr. No*, Fidel and Nikita, Barbie and Bardot… A superflux of impressions from a simpler yet restive time fills your mind as you gaze at this megalithic Tinkertoy.

Ceci n'est pas un atome, you might declare correctly. It is, in fact, a rendering of an iron crystal, nine atoms magnified to way more than a thousand million times their actual size. The structure was erected on a plain at the erstwhile edge of a capital that is in—but not of—a distinct region (you might cheekily suggest "Okely-dokely-doo" as its Simpsons-esque motto).

While the edifice wasn't intended to outlast the event for which it was built, it quickly became a landmark and was left alone—so much so that it took $33 million to buff it back into shape. Regrettably, its visionary architect, who died in '05, missed the unveiling of the renovation.

Don't waffle; take the high-speed elevator to the top for the city's best views, then follow the escalators from sphere to sphere. If you wish to blow $1,300 on a souvenir, ask if any of the original aluminum panels are still for sale. You might also sit in the restaurant, crack open the classic *Tintin in Tibet*, and sip the specialty beer on whose label clever brewers have drawn a molecular latticework of beer kegs. Do not, however, be so roguish as to mimic the brazen little statuesque character downtown.

After you've toured the exhibition devoted to that optimistic era when modernity and progress were all the rage, you'll think the future never looked so retro cool.

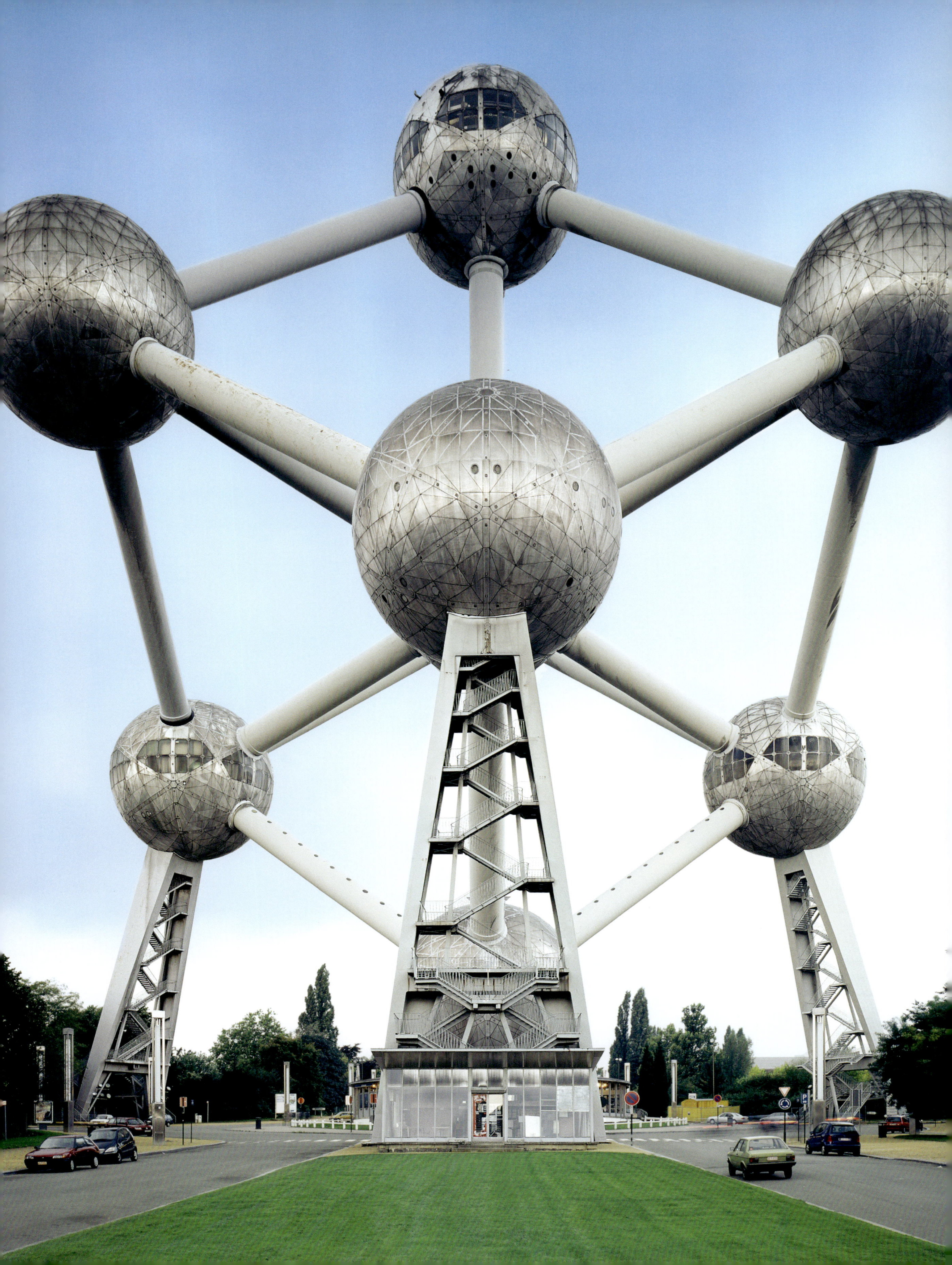

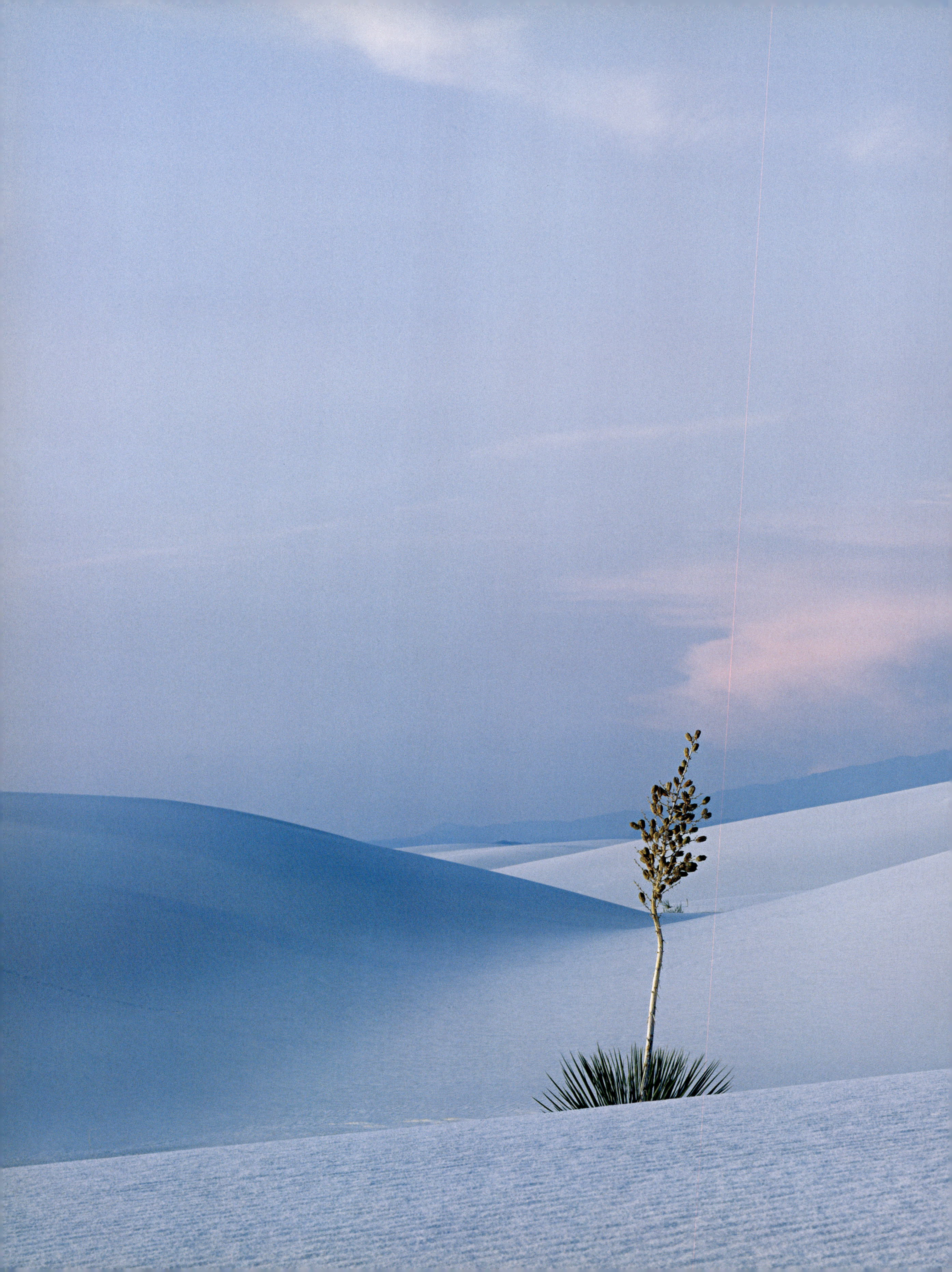

You're stranded amid hills of granulated gypsum punctuated by gnarled desert blooms that stand like lone sentinels on a snow-swept tundra. Neighbor to a foreign territory that shares its name with a diminutive household pet, this dune field is a hundred miles northwest of the area's top tourist attraction: an outlandish labyrinth of caverns (remnants of a prehistoric reef) housing a subterranean chamber more than twenty stories high. Blessed by nature's sublime gifts, this district has also suffered the wrath of lava flows and witnessed the horrifying power of nature's smallest building block, the atom. Fortunately, nuclear tests are no longer performed sixty miles north of here, but deadly missiles are still detonated outside a nearby town (whose name in English means "big cottonwood"). After living two years in the north of this realm, D. H. Lawrence confessed that it was "rather like comic opera played with solemn intensity. All the wildness and woolliness and westernity and motor-cars and art and sage and savage are so mixed up, so incongruous, that it is a farce and everybody knows it." Two thousand years ago, the locals up north built houses of clay, instituting a form of architecture that continues to adorn the landscape. This ancient civilization later gave way to a society of fierce nomads, who still dwell on their ancestral land; nowadays, they're permanently settled and even operate a fashionable ski resort. But neither time nor man seems to have left any trace on the powdery slopes that surround you, an everlasting monument to this land of enchantment.

In the 1930s, a renowned American anthropologist described her visit to the island you are touring as "journeying in a dream through the landscape," where scenes "repeat over and over in astonishing and unpredictable rhythms." She might have added that there's enough chlorophyll in this panorama to oxygenate the entire archipelago-nation. No matter how you describe these terraces—chartreuse, smaragdine, aestival—they're the greeniest green that you ever did see.

With myriad iridescent birds and monkeys, the province is après "Le Douanier" Rousseau. As you wander this splendid viridity, it's hard to believe that you're never far from a host of luxury resorts, restaurants, cafés, and bars. This island of three million people welcomes half as many visitors annually; they come to raft the white-water rivers and experience rich indigenous arts, chief among them painting and crafts, a complex percussive music, and a textile-printing technique that you might have practiced in your youth. Just don't take umbrage at the famous marionette performances.

Tell your friends back home the name of the nearby village that serves as your base (the region's cultural center, it lies fewer than twenty miles north of the capital), and they might think it sounds Arabic—a reasonable assumption given that most people in this country face the Kaaba to pray. But it's not. The word means "medicine" in the local tongue. In fact, the province is sui generis, the only place in this nation where the predominant religion comes from a country to the northwest (albeit practiced in a slightly different form).

Life here revolves around the rituals of rice cultivation. Villagers make obeisance to the goddess of rice and prosperity and consult high priests on irrigation planning. The American anthropologist commented further on "a great variation in . . . color as one small plot ripens an hour or a day behind the other." So go slow and take it all in, as she did. Even if you overdose on verdure and arrive home with a temporary case of chloropsia, your friends will be green with envy.

The jagged ridge below you appears to be rising out of a netherworld. And it's no CGI fantasy. Colossal rainstorms that swirl around the great sea on the horizon have eroded these sunbaked, gypsum-rich hills for millennia. Subduction zones, flysch sediments, tombolos—you can really beef up your geological vocabulary in this topography, which has more folds and faults than a Hollywood cosmetic surgeon could dream of. You are traveling along a coast that extends from a geopolitically vital strait west of here to a major city in another country to the east. In antiquity, a great king forced a number of his warriors to march home through this littoral, and it's said that as much as three-quarters of his army perished in the harsh conditions. A little more than a century ago, a British explorer wrote, "The coast-line . . . is six hundred miles long. On it there is one tree, a sickly stunted-looking thing . . . which serves as a landmark to native craft and a standing joke to the English sailor." By the looks of things, no one has initiated any sort of arboreal crusade since he visited.

When you deplane in this country's largest province, keep your eyes open for prehistoric rock drawings and a surprising amount of wildlife: desert locusts, chikaras, and rare masked boobies as well as the marsh crocodiles that live in the nature reserve on the eastern border. Hopefully you'll get a glimpse of the vibrant costumes worn by women from the dominant ethnic group, who are known by a name that means "wanderers" (they've been called ichthyophagi as well). If you go up north to the provincial capital and make the short leap across the border, you can cheer on tens of thousands of your fellow citizens promoting political stability. Which will underscore how wobbly this part of the world remains thirty years after a fourteen-month standoff dominated the news. The only stability, it might seem, is one president's Members Only sartorial taste.

Modern geologists can easily account for the topographic anomaly you see before you: For thousands of years, waves have crashed upon this craggy shoreline, slowly but surely eroding the rock until only a thin arch remains. An ancient poet cast a more fanciful eye on the landscape: He was inspired, some say, to make this island the home of his notorious sea nymph, who for seven years held a famed wanderer captive in her rocky lair. Indeed, pathos somehow seems more appropriate than science on an island from which, in 1551, pirates kidnapped and sold into slavery almost the entire population. Three years would pass before new settlers could be persuaded to make their home here. Today, however, such strife seems worlds away, and you'd be hard-pressed to find a more relaxed twenty-six square miles anywhere on the globe.

This easy pace is in sharp contrast to that of the major island in this nation, known almost as much for its frenetic drivers as for a history that Evelyn Waugh called "unconscionably romantic." From its earliest settlement some ten thousand years ago through World War II, the country has been a geopolitical pawn, controlled variously by Phoenicians, Romans, Arabs, Normans, Germans, the French, the Spanish, an order of knights, and the British. The result is a cultural mix—Christian religion, Semitic language, Egyptian superstition—that's as unusual as a bridge of rock suspended above the sea.

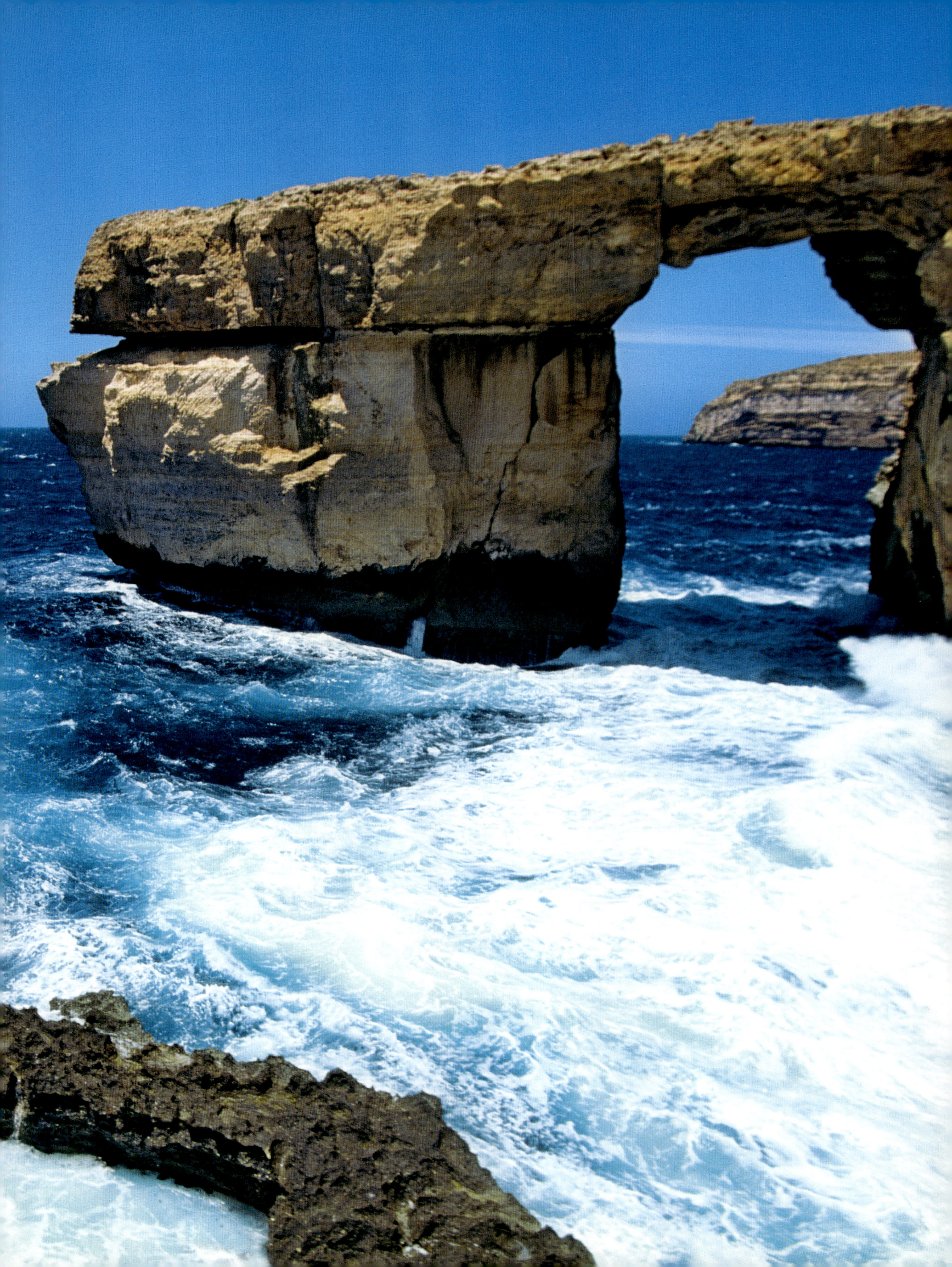

A haven at last! At five thousand feet, a perfect spot to take your ease and have a cup of tea. You've hiked up a hill to this village of the same name; at the bottom, which you left two hours ago, lies the nation's third-largest city. Explore the crafts shops here and then spend the night in a bare-bones lodge. Just before sunrise, make the fifteen-minute climb to the top.

That is, if you can hold out till then. The view here is just a tease for the 360-degree panorama awaiting you above. That pyramid crown to the left is but one peak of a mountain resembling the tail of an aquatic animal. Once *en haut*, to the south you will see a turquoise lake (created by an angry deity to drown a town that had scorned her in her vagrant's disguise). To the west are the remnants of a fort, the seat of a king's rule two centuries ago. Catch your breath on the grandstand at the pinnacle—where the only other signs of human activity are the ruins of another fort, a TV tower, and a shrine.

Mountains cover more than half of this country (which is just a little larger than Arkansas). The most celebrated straddles the border 182 miles to the east and has been described as "easy to climb, just a little too high." The tiny nation is distinguished not only by its highs but by its lows: Almost half the population lives in poverty. There's no doubt which extreme you're here to experience, but, alas, you will eventually have to come down.

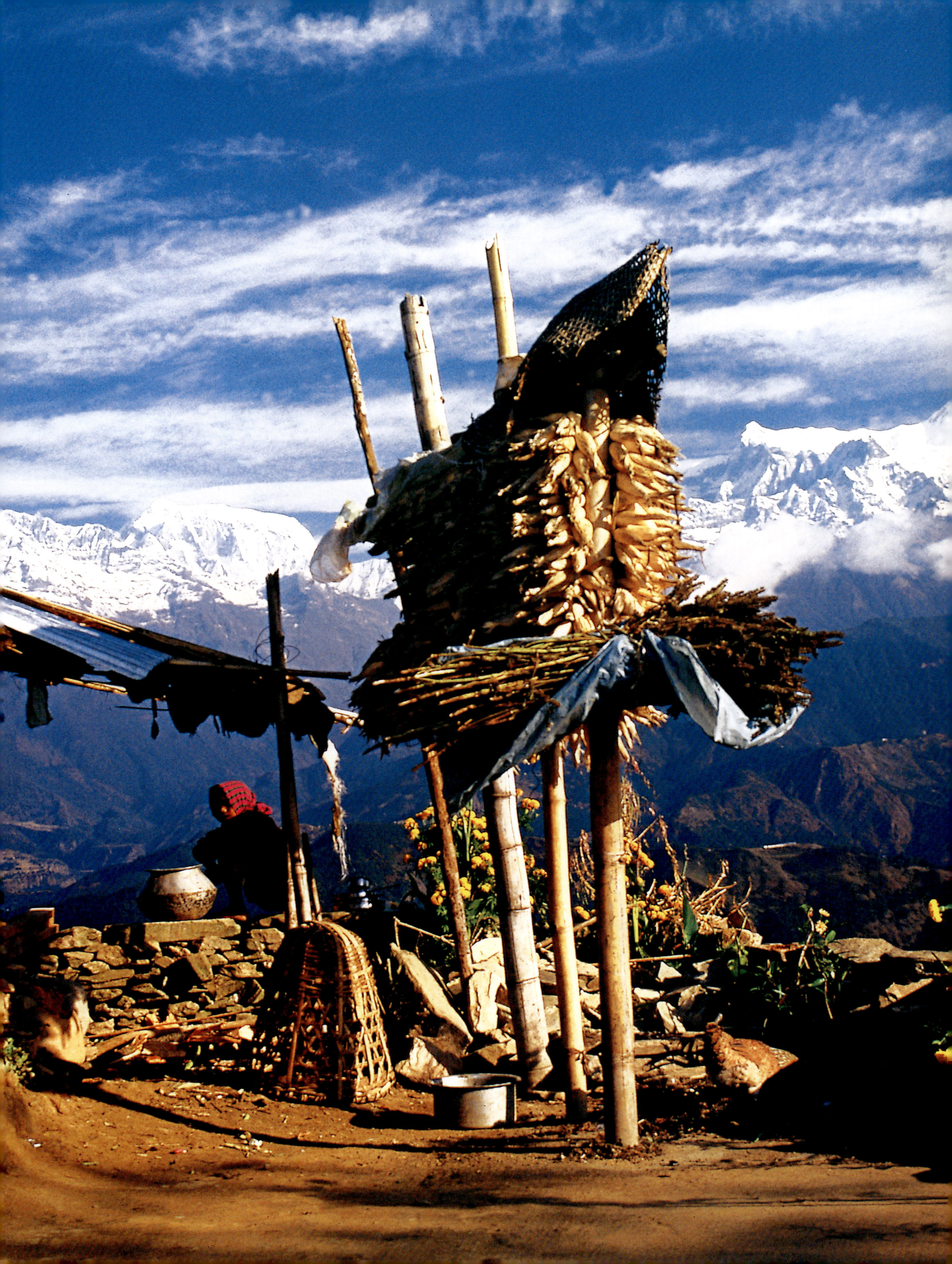

You are standing in a former watchtower, 165 feet (and 226 steps) above street level, surveying a town that has looked this way for five hundred years. The view is romantic, as is the local history and even the road that connects the town to others in the vicinity. Residents proudly tell stories of legendary bravado: One recounts the feat of a former mayor, who in the 1600s bet a would-be invader that he could down three and a half quarts of wine in a single draft—with the burg as the wager. The man's hearty thirst saved the day.

A revered English novelist was more impressed with the nation's intellectual prowess: "I know [the countrymen] to be, in their great mental endowments and cultivation, the chosen people of the Earth." (At times, they too have thought so.) Just slightly smaller than the state of Montana, this country has had a greater impact on its continent's modern history than any other. In 1989, it was again the site of one of the twentieth century's defining moments.

Crowds have long been an integral part of the fabric of this land: Since 1810, revelers have gathered once a year in the state capital, 132 miles to the southeast, for a sixteen-day party; after World War I, thousands rallied in a city 45 miles to the east in support of a charismatic leader; and today, two million tourists visit this town of twelve thousand inhabitants each year. Nowadays, the nation is a heavyweight in the global economy. And even the medieval town you see here is keeping up with the times—it has its own Web site!

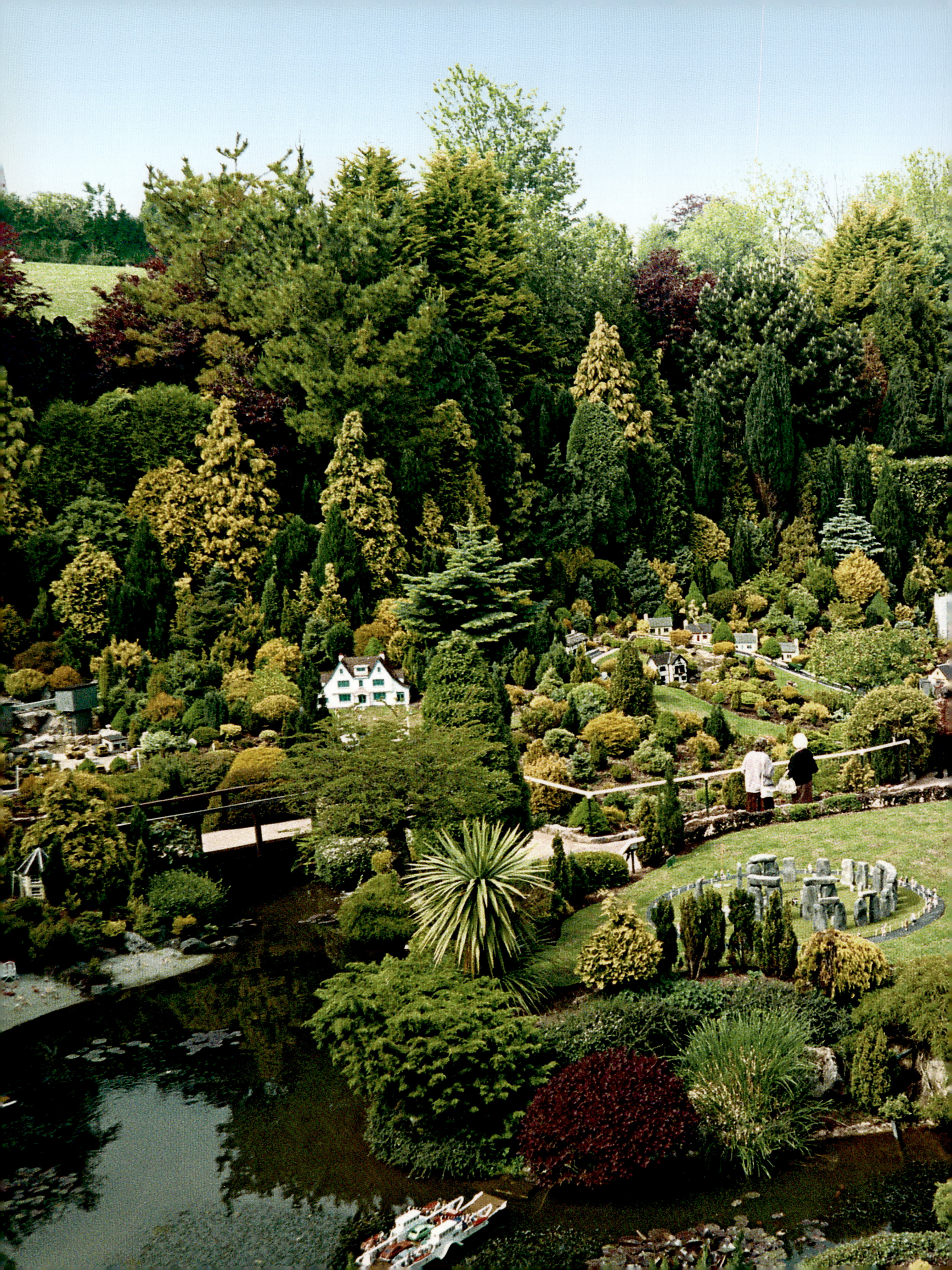

P erched on the brow of a hill, you are looking at a village that is an almost perfect representation of the country it's in. The Tudor architecture belies its age: Although the buildings are made of traditional materials, this hamlet was built in the 1960s. Life in this neck of the woods is beyond tranquil—you may stroll around to admire the stone tower of the church across from you, the koi swimming in the lake below, the beautiful landscaped gardens, the neighboring farm, the trains as they cross the bridge to your right, or one of the world's great cultural icons.

The surrounding area is a suburb of a town to the south, 162 miles from the capital, that has been officially part of the local Riviera since 1983. A pleasant climate, semitropical gardens, and a sheltered bay have helped popularize the seaside resort, even though a native poet described winter in this country as "ending in July to recommence in August." The town has inspired its share of national treasures—one a writer famous for mysteries, another the Minister of Silly Walks. Cows roaming this southwestern canton's picturesque meadows produce a local treat that is lapped up by visitors as well as by citizens of this, according to the poet, "low, newspaper, humdrum, law-suit Country." Vis-à-vis the village here, he got at least one thing right— it's a pretty quiescent scene.

Fourteen centuries ago, your mission at this building would have been worship. It is one of numerous temples and fortresses, among the oldest of their kind, that stand watch over this former capital. Some, such as the one before you, are structures; others are caves carved into the steep and rocky red-sandstone ridge that rises on the southern end of town. They were created by a succession of dynastic kings who ruled during a period of great diversity, from A.D. 540 to 757. Indeed, the style of these buildings incorporates elements that reflect both the dominant religion and the smaller sects that were allowed to flourish here.

Today, the town's prominence has waned, and it is just one of many farming burgs in the southern part of a modern state. But like the mélange seen in its ancient temples, this country is as varied as it is populous. Often characterized as virtually a continent unto itself, it encompasses a multitude of races, languages, and customs; a landscape that runs from the flattest plains to the sharpest mountain peaks; and a history marked by the rule of competing kingdoms as well as a faraway colonial power. Independence came more than half a century ago, birthed by a legendary pacifist and a bloody separation. Today, as is true in so many developing nations, diversity and population thrive while infra- and superstructure struggle to keep up—not the most accommodating arrangement for travelers. But it is the richness of the mix that makes this part of the world unforgettable.

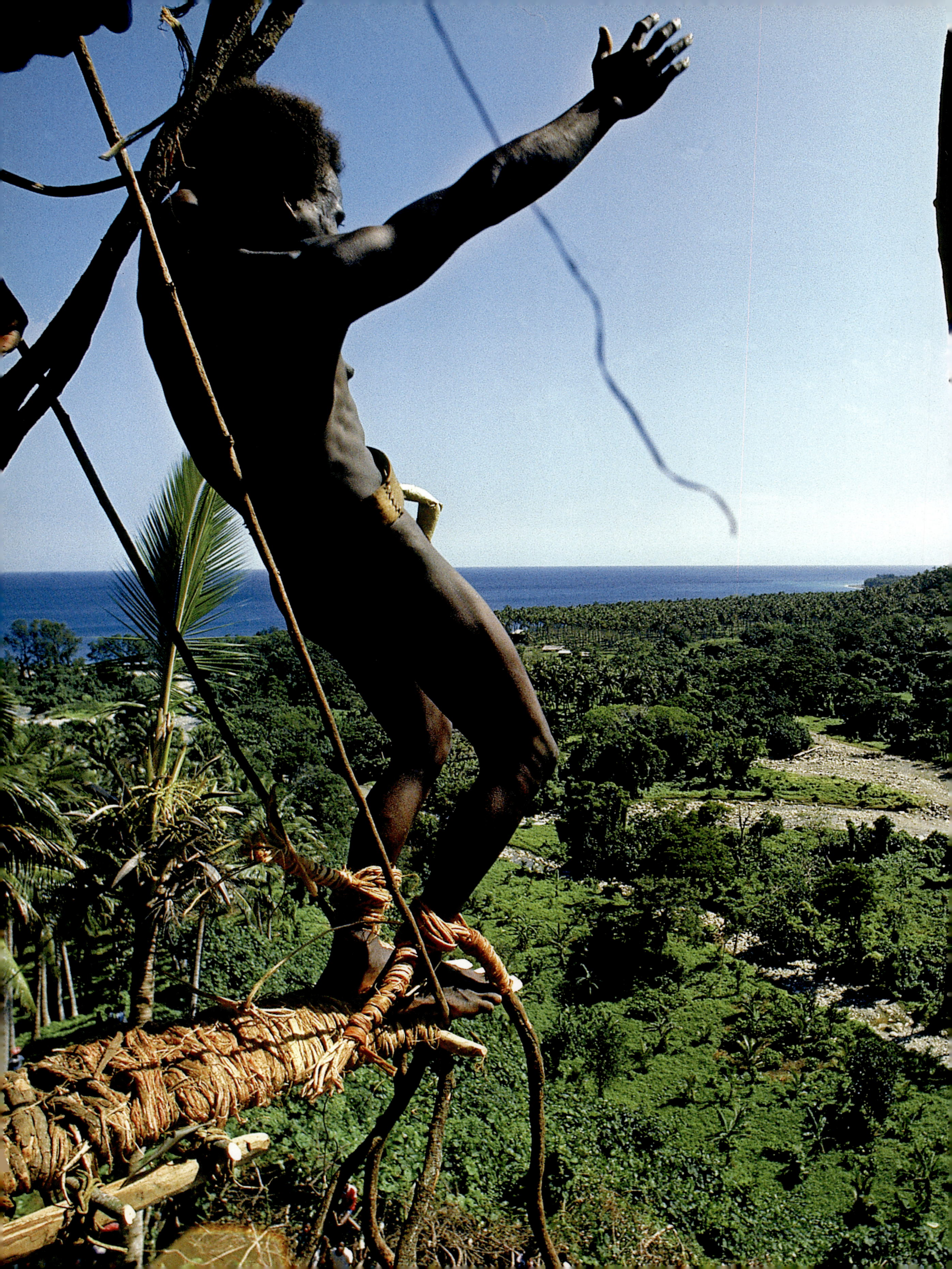

Warm enough for you? Though you may be feeling the breezes if you chose an outfit to match your confrere's, anticipation of what's to come is likely making you sweat. The platform supporting you, made of a tree's branches lashed with lianas, is about seventy feet off the ground. Below, the villagers chant and dance, and the excitement builds. The fellow addressing the expectant crowd is actually looking to preserve the food supply: The idea is sort of like bungee-jumping for a cause. His plan is to leap into the void, vines tied around his ankles, and have his head just graze the ground—in so doing, he fertilizes the earth and ensures a bountiful harvest. The villages around the south of this island practice the ritual, with boys as young as seven taking the plunge in their passage into adulthood.

Food has an important symbolic role here: Although the island was named for a Christian feast day, its people believe that they owe their existence to the fruit of a coconut tree. And while local custom and belief still prevail (for instance, a man must not swim beneath a woman's canoe), explorers, sandalwood traders, labor recruiters, and missionaries have eagerly influenced national identity. In the nineteenth century, the country—comprising many islands—achieved independence from two foreign rulers. Their legacy lives on in two of the nation's three official languages (the number of indigenous tongues, meanwhile, is fifty times that).

But right now, you don't need to speak the local patois to understand the drama around you. Chances are it will stay with you—even a few hours hence, on some of the world's finest reefs, when you hold your breath and dive deep into yonder sea. An epiphany, a leap of faith!

T he flight from the capital to this stunning chunk of granite on the horizon lasts a brief twenty minutes. Soon you'll be begging the pilot to tilt the chopper and circle the island a few extra times. After all, you've shelled out eight hundred dollars for this air time, and at forty bucks a minute you have the right to hover and pirouette. Well before the rotors stop whirling, newcomers gush, "This is paradise! The Garden of Eden!" So feel free to make up your own *Fantasy Island* tropes as you go— a few days in a place this riotous could make a cliché-meister out of anyone.

With a vowel at the end of its name, this lush isle is the feminine version of its nearest neighbor—a relative it practically smooches, so to speak. At the turn of the century, a South African couple developed a luxury property here, where soon after a knight honeymooned with his young bride. (You can be pretty sure they didn't return when he was sixty-four.) They weren't alone: This place is for the birds . . . literally. It doubles as a private ecological reserve, and scientists come from around the world to study its rare endemic avian species, as well as its giant tortoises and other creatures. At night, you'll be happy to discover, the resort keeps its lights low so as not to disorient the sea turtles that hatch by the thousands on the half-mile-long beach.

This isle belongs to an archipelago-nation (which itself belongs to a continent to the west) comprising 115 coralline and granitic islands spread across 154,000 square miles, an area the size of Montana. Locals come from a cluster of cultures, but nearly all of them are Catholic—as were, long ago, many of the lonely sailors who were driven crazy by the salacious shape of the earth's largest seeds, which drop from palm trees growing in a World Heritage–designated valley on the country's second-largest island, four miles away.

The resort shuts its doors between August and November, giving you plenty of time to dream about the sweet thwacka-thwacka that will escort you here again.

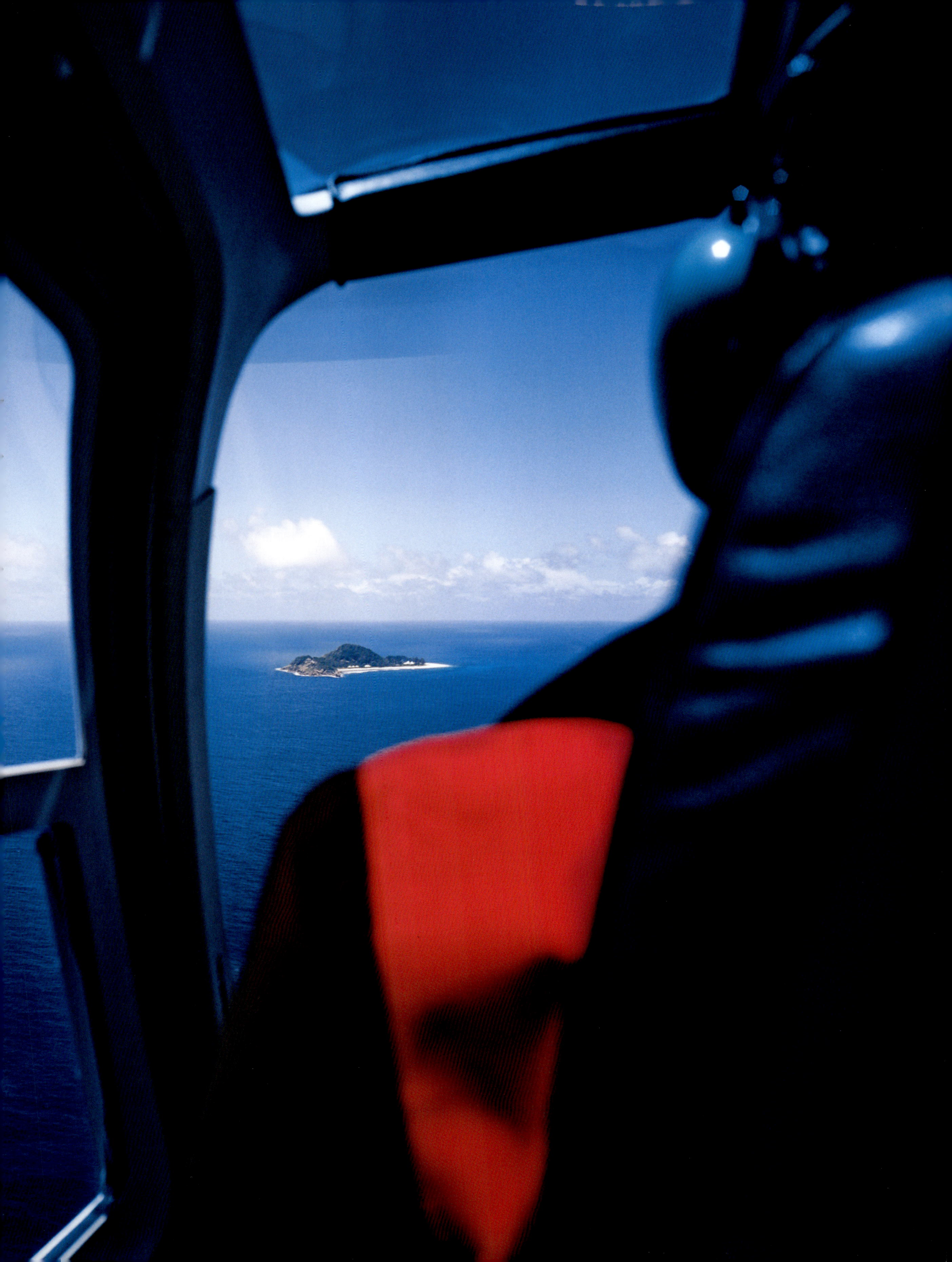

M any early-morning hours of browsing the literary stock of the famous *bouquinistes* that line the Seine paid off. You found a slim volume, *Guide des fontaines de Paris*, and you're now sitting down to sip a café au lait and learn more about the city's stunning fountains. As you dust off your rusty school French, you're thrilled to discover the following excerpt, which takes the reader on a whimsical multi-arrondissement adventure that leads right to the very waters gushing before you.

Si vous commencez la randonnée depuis la rive droite, il faut traverser un pont. Vous pouvez faire une pause au Café de Flore ou aux Deux Magots bien sûr, puis descendre le Boul'Mich. Ou, si vous logez dans un hôtel comme le tout petit Duc de Saint Simon, il vaut mieux descendre le boulevard le plus long de Paris. Quand vous arrivez à la rue la plus longue de Paris, il faut continuer à gauche. C'est là, dans ce terrain qui mesure plus de vingt hectares. Après avoir regardé le bassin plein de petits bateaux à voiles, prenez une chaise et mettez vous à l'ombre des platanes, marronniers, et tilleuls. Rafraîchi, vous allez traverser le jardin et arriver à une avenue bordée d'arbres. Suivez l'avenue vers un autre petit jardin qui porte le nom d'un grand commerçant et voyageur italien. C'est en cet endroit précis que se trouve notre fontaine en bronze avec la sphère céleste en haut, entourée de chevaux, tortues, et poissons. Le Baron Haussmann avait même commandé l'oeuvre (il en existe aussi une copie en plâtre au Musée d'Orsay).

Ne ratez pas le centre scientifique datant du XVIIème siècle où passe le méridien et où M. Foucault avait fait une démonstration publique (billet sur réservation, 5 euro). L'édifice se trouve à quelques centaines de mètres au sud de la fontaine. Il faut manger, n'est-ce pas? La Coupole n'est pas loin de la fontaine. Après le repas, vous pouvez danser la salsa au sous-sol.

If you're anxious to get back to your hotel after a long day of exploration—and translation—you can always hop on the RER or the Métro (lines 4 and 6). Just don't be tempted to cool off in the fountain. Like the sign always says: *Il est interdit de se baigner.*

Remember the little fortresses and castles Mom let you build in the living room, when you'd position the recliner, couch, and coffee table at odd angles and cover them with blankets? Cocooned and protected from the world, you allowed nobody in and nobody could see you. You're about to recapture that *temps perdu*. Made of aluminum and plywood, the mirrored cube suspended before you is not much more elaborate than your childhood sanctuary. And once inside, you won't be seen.

The forest you're in is near a town whose name is similar to the London retail house that sells a coveted signature vinyl bag. Inspiration for this hermetic chamber came from a film about three city dwellers who built a tree-house getaway—a flick that likely didn't make it to your cineplex. This is not just any abode; it's bed, bath, and beyond, with linens milled by a purveyor to the royal court and lighting by a top design firm. Four different architects created several other minihouses (and a sauna) in this copse.

Bloggers fretted about matters such as luggage (how to haul it up and down), waste (where it would go), and the tree itself (would it be harmed). As for the major concern, well, you don't have to worry about the safety of woodland birdies—a transparent film that only they can see has been applied to the glass.

If you grow bored with this serene arboreous environment, consult your hosts. They will present you with a long list of activities. Canoeing, kayaking, and a day-trip to an indigenous village on a lakeshore sound refreshing. But riding Irish draft horses, herding Scottish Highland cattle, and tree felling? You might just as well tour this northernmost county in winter with your snowshoes and dogsled.

This singular domicile is, in fact, an elfin hotel room. And at $600 a night, double occupancy, this 172-square-foot box is rather *cher*. But then, you've been dreaming of just such a secure citadel all your life.

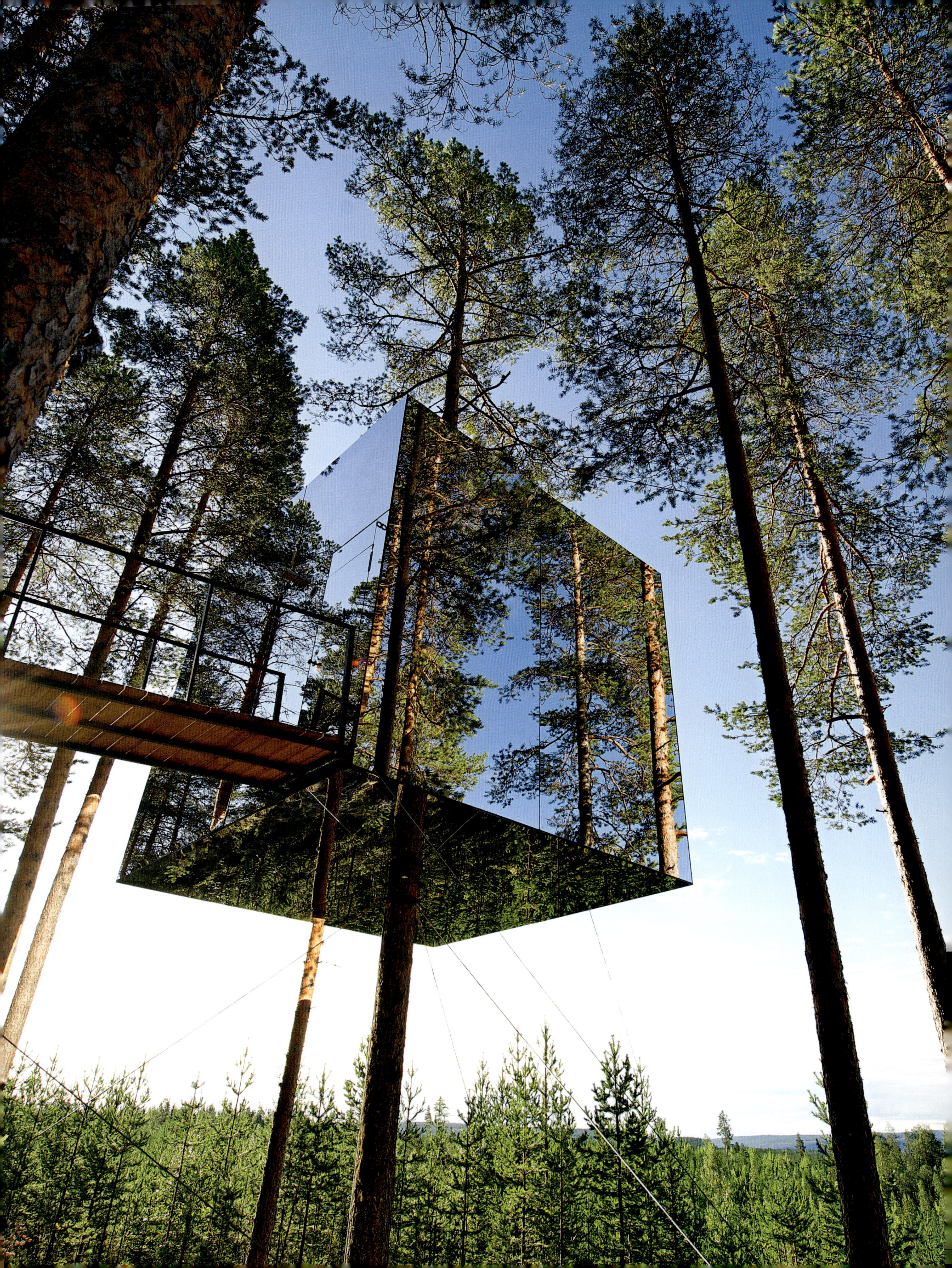

ANSWERS

8 Irian Jaya or Papua Province, Indonesia
Photographer: Anders Ryman
Issue: February 2002

10 UK Pavilion, Shanghai World Expo 2010, China
Photographer: Iwan Baan
Issue: August 2010

12 Atacama Desert, Chile
Photographer: Macduff Everton
Issue: January 2008

14 Yverdon-les-Bains, Switzerland
Photographer: © Paul Raftery/View
Issue: September 2002

16 Sacsayhuamán, Peru
Photographer: Chris Caldicott
Issue: April 2001

18 Dubai, United Arab Emirates
Photographer: Peter Bialobrzeski/Laif/Redux
Issue: December 2005

20 Tarawa, Kiribati
Photographer: Macduff Everton
Issue: July 2000

22 Tokyo, Japan
Photographer: Toshihisa Ishii
Issue: July 2007

24 Work by Anish Kapoor, at the Farm, Kaipara Harbour, New Zealand
Photographer: Jos Wheeler
Issue: March 2010

26 La Digue, Seychelles
Photographer: Chris Caldicott
Issue: September 2010

28 Yunnan, China
Photographer: Frank Lukasseck/Corbis
Issue: August 2008

30 Gansu, China
Photographer: Arif Asci/The Cover Story
Issue: October 2001

32 Julian's Bower, or Alkborough, or Lincolnshire, United Kingdom
Photographer: Michael Engler
Issue: April 2006

34 Blackpool, England
Photographer: © Peter Cook/View
Issue: March 2007

36 Gough Island, United Kingdom
Photographer: Tui de Roy
Issue: June 2009

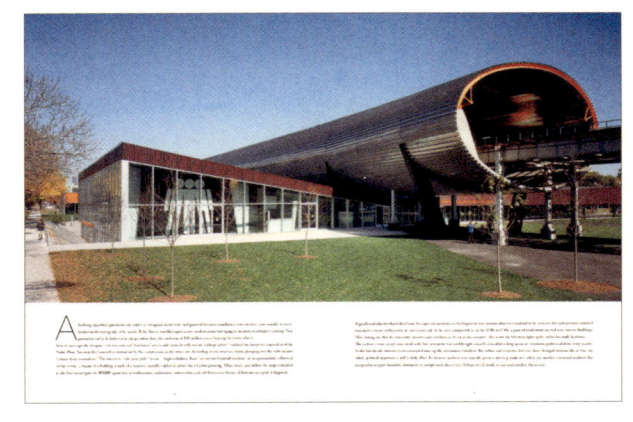

38 Illinois Institute of Technology, Chicago, Illinois, United States
Photographer: Richard Barnes
Issue: February 2004

40

Saxony, Germany
Photographer: Peter Bialobrzeski/Laif/Redux
Issue: August 2007

42

Nile Delta, Egypt
Photographer: © Béatrice Amagat
Issue: February 2008

44

Ales Stenar, Sweden
Photographer: Macduff Everton
Issue: February 1999

46

Dalki Theme Park, Paju or Seoul, Korea
Photographer: Kim Yong Kwan
Issue: December 2004

48

Laguna Colorada, or Potosí, or Salar de Uyuni, Bolivia
Photographer: Massimo Borchi/Atlantide
Issue: October 1996

50

Parc du Futuroscope, Poitiers, France
Photographer: Luc Boegly/Artedia/Artur
Issue: May 2003

52

Great Falls Park, Virginia, United States
Photographer: Skip Brown
Issue: June 2000

54

Pistol River, Oregon, United States
Photographer: Skip Brown
Issue: December 1999

56

Wat Phu, Laos
Photographer: Stefano Amantini/Atlantide
Issue: June 1997

58

Mount Bromo, Java, Indonesia
Photographer: Knut Bry
Issue: November 1994

60

Hierro, Spain
Photographer: Andoni Canela
Issue: March 2005

62

Nasca, Peru
Photographer: Stéphane Compoint
Issue: October 2002

64

Ring of Brodgar (Orkney Islands), Scotland
Photographer: Macduff Everton
Issue: May 1993

66

Trafalgar Square, England
Photographer: © Andy Stagg/View
Issue: March 2009

68

Guilin, Guanxi, China
Photographer: Lois Conner
Issue: January 2004

70

County Wexford, Ireland
Photographer: © Peter Cook/View
Issue: August 2001

72 Western Desert, or Libyan Desert, Egypt
Photographer: Obie Oberholzer
Issue: August 1998

74 Les Baux-de-Provence (or Les Beaux), France
Photographer: Guido Cozzi/Atlantide
Issue: August 1994

76 Curucaca Falls, Paraná State, Brazil
Photographer: Valdir Cruz
Issue: June 2004

79 Golden Rock (or Kyaiktiyo Pagoda), Myanmar (or Burma)
Photographer: Fridmar Damm/Corbis
Issue: December 2009

80 Jarlshof Prehistoric and Norse Settlement, Shetland Isles
Photographer: Grace Davies
Issue: August 2000

82 Xian, China
Photographer: Lynn Davis
Issue: June 2003

84 Mosquito Cays, Nicaragua
Photographer: Jay Dickman
Issue: December 1996

86 Papua Province, Indonesia
Photographer: George Steinmetz
Issue: April 2010

88 Bisti Badland, New Mexico, United States
Photographer: Jack Dykinga
Issue: September 1998

90 Queen Califia's Magical Circle, Escondido, California, United States
Photographer: Macduff Everton
Issue: April 2004

92 Qutab Minar, Delhi, India
Photographer: Macduff Everton
Issue: November 1996

94 Irish Hunger Memorial, New York City, United States
Photographer: © Peter Aaron/Esto
Issue: December 2002

96 Meota Iwa (or Wedded Rocks), Japan
Photographer: Rolfe Horn
Issue: October 2008

98 Skógar, Iceland
Photographer: Macduff Everton
Issue: February 1996

100 Temple of Concord (or Concordia), Agrigento, Sicily, Italy
Photographer: Macduff Everton
Issue: March 1993

102 Atlantis, the Palm, Dubai, United Arab Emirates
Photographer: Jim Franco
Issue: February 2009

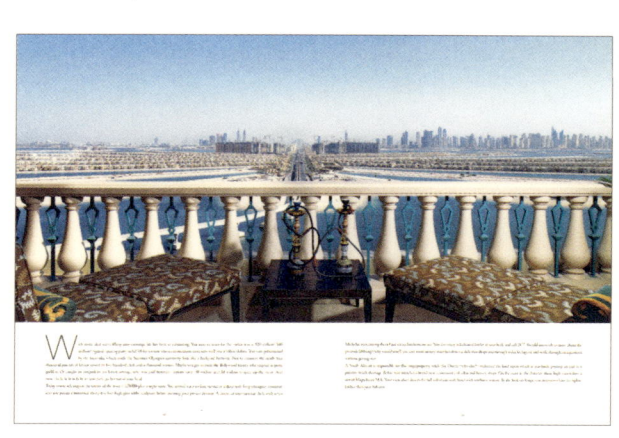

105 Auroville or Pondicherry, India
Photographer: Adrian Gaut
Issue: May 2010

106 Uchisar, Cappadocia, Turkey
Photographer: Guido Mangold
Issue: August 1993

108 Skógafoss, Iceland
Photographer: Macduff Everton
Issue: December 2000

110 Ysios Winery, Rioja Alavesa, Spain
Photographer: Roland Halbe
Issue: November 2008

112 Lake Resia, Italy
Photographer: Fausto Giaccone/Anzenberger
Issue: November 2002

114 Chocolate Hills, Bohol, Philippines
Photographer: Michele Falzone
Issue: April 2009

116 Zaragoza, Spain
Photographer: Roland Halbe
Issue: January 2009

118 Karakoram Mountains, Pakistan
Photographer: Bill Hatcher
Issue: December 1998

120 Brasília, Brazil
Photographer: Christian Heeb
Issue: February 2006

122 Hong Kong, China
Photographer: Hub/Laif/Redux
Issue: January 2007

124 Mount Tamaro, Switzerland
Photographer: Wolfram Janzer/Artur
Issue: January 2002

126 Wupatki National Monument, Arizona, United States
Photographer: Macduff Everton
Issue: March 2002

128 Hotel Kakslauttanen, Finland
Photographer: Courtesy Hotel Kakslauttanen
Issue: September 2009

130 Patan, Nepal
Photographer: Macduff Everton
Issue: June 1998

132 The Boulders, Carefree, Arizona, United States
Photographer: Håkan Ludwigson
Issue: January 2005

134 Graz, Austria
Photographer: Håkan Ludwigson
Issue: March 2004

136 
Hassan II Mosque, Casablanca, Morocco
Photographer: Håkan Ludwigson
Issue: May 1998

138 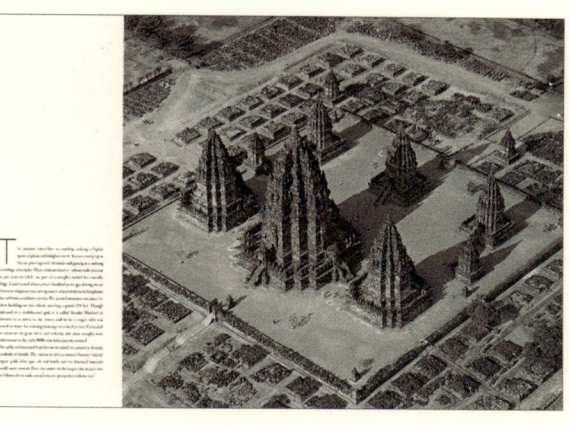
Prambanan Temple, Java, Indonesia
Photographer: © Marilyn Bridges
Issue: November 2000

140 
Millau Viaduct, Millau, France
Photographer: Håkan Ludwigson
Issue: November 2004

142 
Bezeklik Thousand-Buddha Caves, China
Photographer: Josef Polleross/Anzenberger
Issue: August 1996

144 
Yangpu District, Shanghai, China
Photographer: Shanghai Daily/Imaginechina
Issue: March 2008

146 
Seljalandsfoss, Iceland
Photographer: Corbis
Issue: December 2008

148 
Angel of the North, Gateshead or Newcastle, United Kingdom
Photographer: © Sally Ann Norman/View
Issue: October 2004

150 
Ica, Peru
Photographer: Olivier Renck/Aurora
Issue: April 2007

152 Cape Town, South Africa
Photographer: Obie Oberholzer
Issue: November 1999

154 Sleeping Bear Dunes National Lakeshore, Michigan, United States
Photographer: Richard Olsenius
Issue: November 2001

156 Grand Bahama Island, Bahamas
Photographer: Jeff Rotman
Issue: May 2005

158 Western Desert, Libyan Desert, or White Desert, Egypt
Photographer: Josef Polleross/Anzenberger
Issue: May 1996

160 European Southern Observatory, Chile
Photographer: Roland Halbe
Issue: August 2003

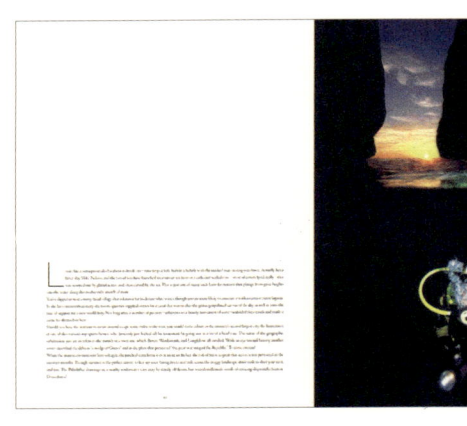

162 Les Calanques, or Cassis, France
Photographer: Philippe Poulet
Issue: November 2006

164 Villnösser Tal or Val di Funes, Italy
Photographer: José Fuste Raga/Corbis
Issue: September 2007

166 Inishmór, Ireland
Photographer: © Yann Arthus-Bertrand/Altitude
Issue: June 2002

168 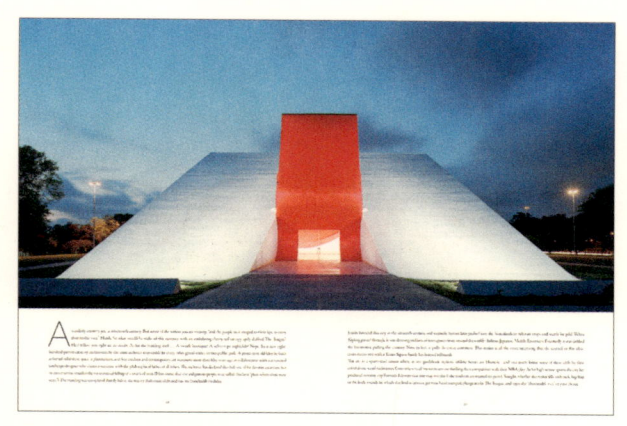
Ibirapuera Park, Sao Paulo, Brazil
Photographer: Nelson Kon
Issue: February 2007

170 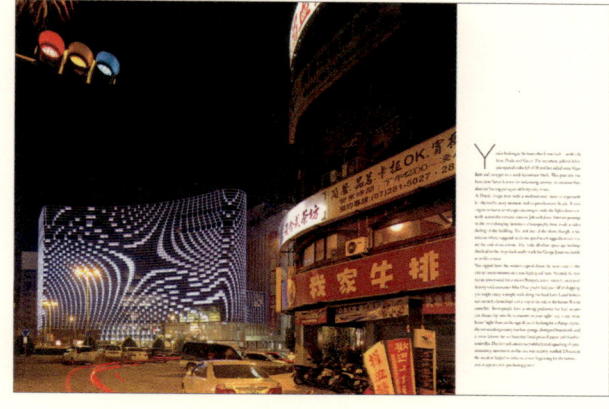
Kaohsiung, Republic of China (Taiwan)
Photographer: Christian Richters
Issue: July 2009

172 
Gespensterwald (Ghost Forest), Nienhagen, Germany
Photographer: Martin Ruegner/Getty
Issue: December 2010

174 
Innsbruck, Austria
Photographer: Reiner Riedler
Issue: June 2008

176 
Orkney Islands, Scotland
Photographer: Jim Richardson
Issue: July 2003

178 
Swartberg Pass, South Africa
Photographer: Florian Selig/goZOOMA
Issue: June 2010

180 
Krka National Park, Croatia
Photographer: Berthold Steinhilber/Laif/Redux
Issue: May 2009

182 
Atomium, Brussels, Belgium
Photographer: Barbara Staubach
Issue: January 2006

184 White Sands National Monument, New Mexico, United States.
Photographer: Jack Dykinga
Issue: September 1996

186 Village of Ubud, Bali, Indonesia
Photographer: Macduff Everton
Issue: August 2005

188 Makran Coast, or Sistan-Baluchistan Province, Iran
Photographer: George Steinmetz
Issue: January 2010

190 Gozo, Malta
Photographer: Buss Wojtek
Issue: June 1999

192 Sarangkot, Nepal
Photographer: Josef Polleross/Anzenberger
Issue: January 2001

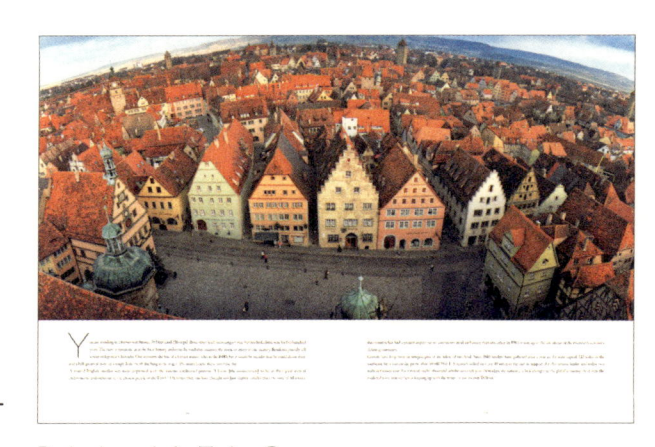

194 Rothenburg ob der Tauber, Germany
Photographer: Macduff Everton
Issue: October 1999

196 Babbacombe Model Village, England
Photographer: Geof Kern
Issue: February 2001

198 Badami, India
Photographer: Michel Séméniako
Issue: January 1999

200

Pentecost Island, Vanuatu
Photographer: Chris Sattlberger/Anzenberger
Issue: May 2001

202

Cousine Island, Seychelles
Photographer: Håkan Ludwigson
Issue: July 2005

204

Fontaine des Quatre Parties du Monde, Paris, France
Photographer: Patrick Tourneboeuf
Issue: September 2008

206

Treehotel, Harads, Sweden
Photographer: Håkan Ludwigson
Issue: October 2010

ABOUT CONDÉ NAST TRAVELER

Condé Nast Traveler is the most trusted name in travel journalism. Since its launch in 1987, the magazine has been committed to its unique philosophy of Truth in Travel. It is independent of the travel industry; this means its correspondents do not accept free or discounted trips or accommodations and, as far as possible, travel anonymously. By doing so, they experience the world as the magazine's readers do—good and bad—and their reports and recommendations are fair, impartial, and authoritative. *Condé Nast Traveler* has been nominated for 24 National Magazine Awards, 7 of which were in the General Excellence category, and has won 6 awards in various categories, including Special Interest, Design, Photography, and General Excellence.

ACKNOWLEDGMENTS

I would like to thank all of the photographers and staff writers who have contributed to *Condé Nast Traveler*'s "Where Are You?" during the past eighteen-plus years. Their work has helped us to create this most intriguing and popular of magazine features—one our readers never tire of.

My gratitude goes to Peter W. Kaplan, whose brainchild "Where Are You?" was way back in 1993, during his first stint at this magazine, and to my predecessor as editor in chief of *Condé Nast Traveler*, Thomas J. Wallace, who recognized a good thing and ran with it. Thanks as well to senior consulting editor Clive Irving, our invaluable sounding board and presiding sage for countless magazine endeavors, including this one. On behalf of all of us, I would like to thank S. I. Newhouse, Jr., chairman of Condé Nast, for so staunchly supporting *Condé Nast Traveler*, and for recognizing the value and imperative of our Truth in Travel philosophy.

I am immensely appreciative of the energy and attention to detail of features editor Alison Humes, the organizing force behind this volume, and of the vision and enterprise of photography director Kathleen Klech and picture editor Esin Göknar. My thanks, too, to the magazine's publisher, Chris Mitchell, and his associate Susan Harrington for helping to make this project a reality, and to managing editor Dee Aldrich for her assistance.

My thanks, too, to John Oseid not only for fact-checking and updating all of these entries but also for writing them during the last eight years. Other staff writers and editors have also contributed to "Where Are You?" and to this volume, and I thank them all: Sanjay Surana, who wrote the feature for five years, Rebecca Ciletti, Eric Crites, Matthew Fox, Lisa Gill, Lucy Gilmour, Maura Henninger, Anna Jefferys, Nathan Lump, Marisa Milanese, Ted Moncreiff, John Newton, and Irene Ricasio.

Last but by no means least, I am immensely grateful to Prosper Assouline and the members of his team—including editorial director Esther Kremer and designers Camille Dubois and Cécilia Maurin, as well as Nicole Lanctot, Naomi Leibowitz, and Gina Amorelli—for loving our "Where Are You?" pages and thinking they would make a fun and beautiful book. —K. G.